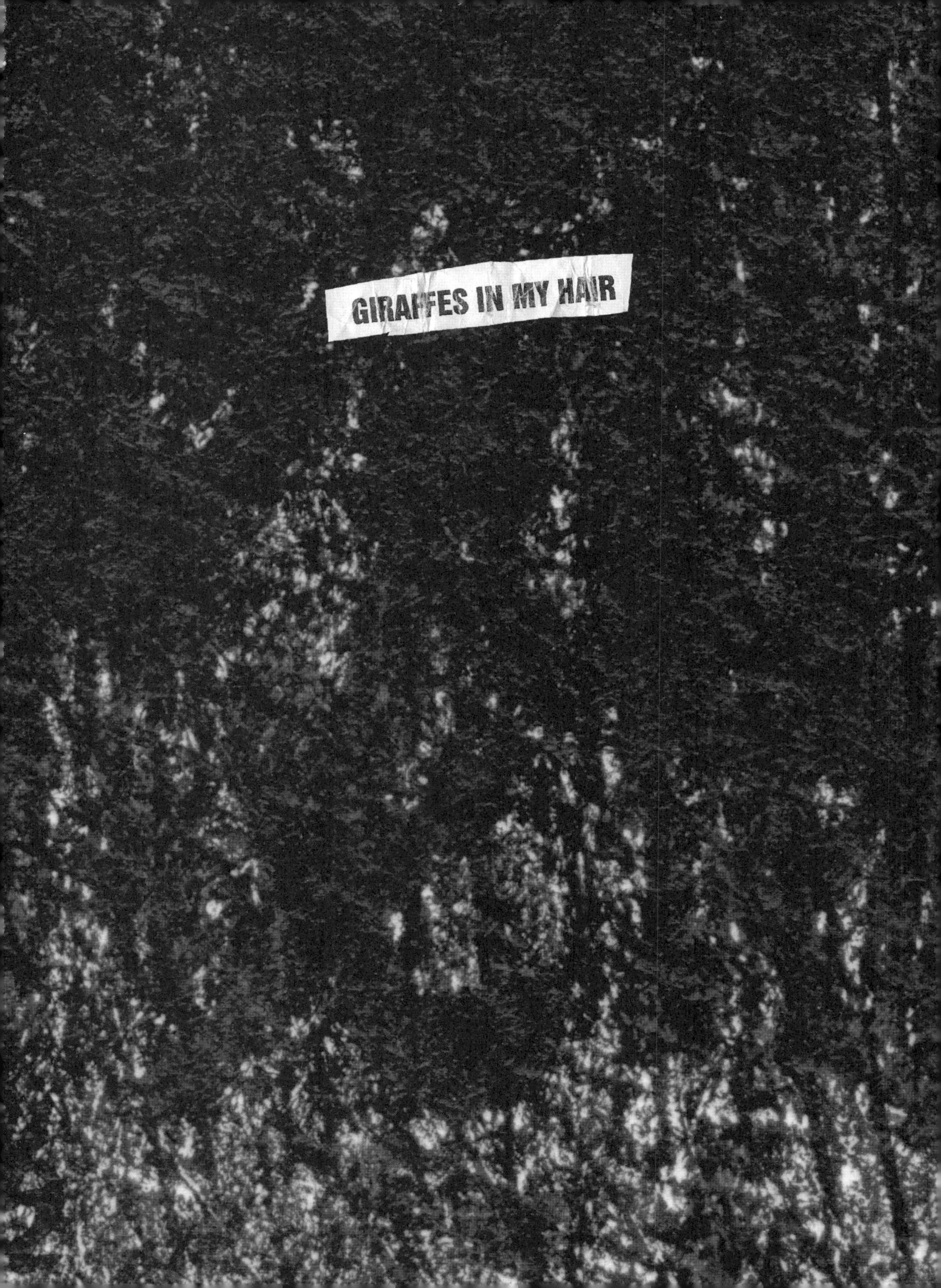
GIRAFFES IN MY HAIR

GIRAFFES IN MY HAIR: A ROCK 'N' ROLL LIFE

By Bruce Paley and Carol Swain

CONTENTS

FANTAGRAPHICS BOOKS

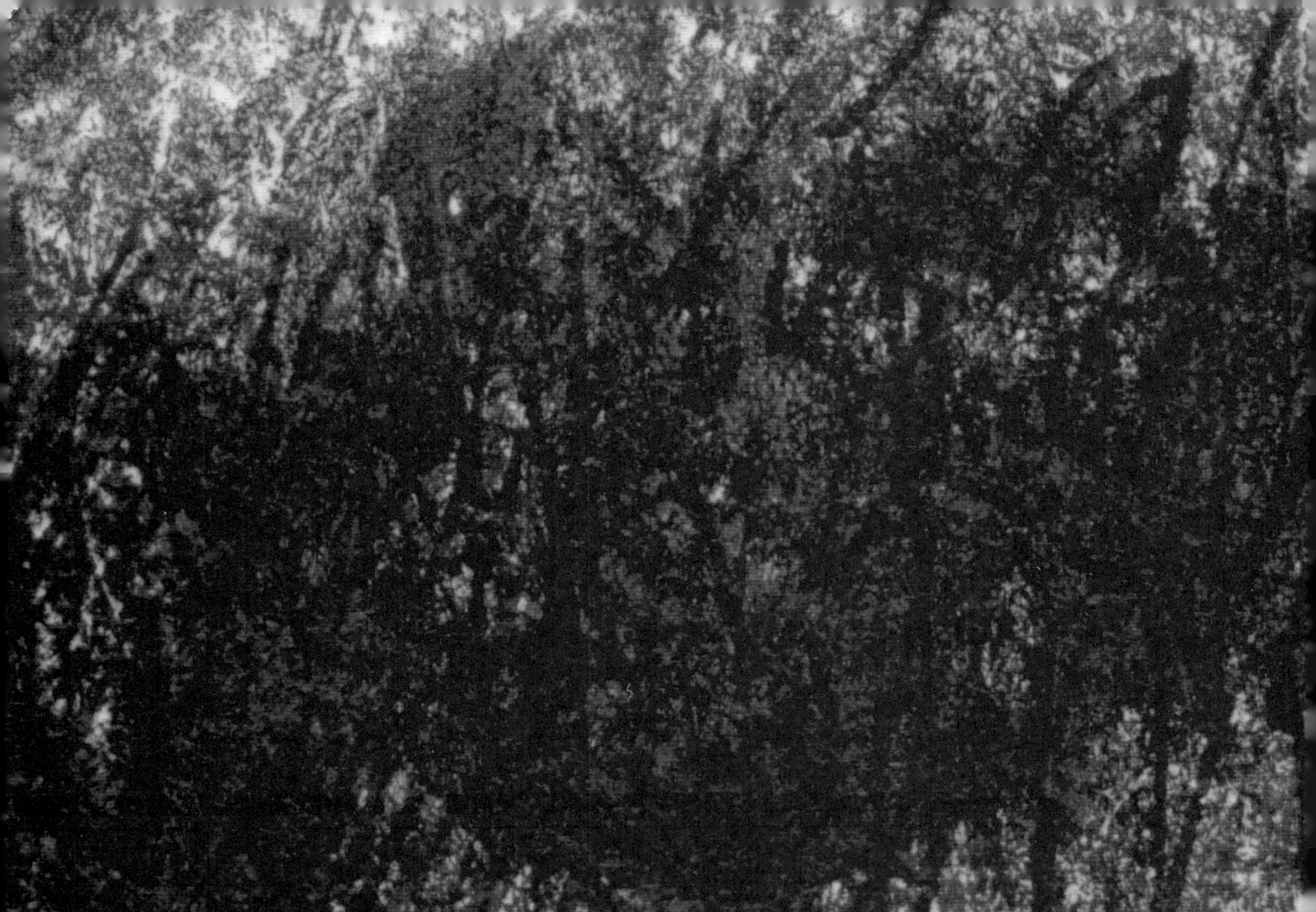

Editor: Gary Groth. Designer: Adam Grano. Publicist: Eric Reynolds.
Publishers: Gary Groth & Kim Thompson. *Giraffes in My Hair*
is copyright © 2009 Fantagraphics Books. Contents copyright ©
2009 Bruce Paley and Carol Swain. Cover photo by Gordon Hecht;
copyright © 2009 Gordon Hecht. All rights reserved. Permission
to quote or reproduce material for reviews must be obtained from
the authors or the publisher. Fantagraphics Books, Inc. 7563 Lake
City Way, Seattle, WA 98115. To receive a free catalogue of fine
comics and books, call 1-800-657-1100 or visit our website at
Fantagraphics.com. Distributed in the U.S. by W.W. Norton and
Company, Inc. (212-354-5500). Distributed in Canada by the
Canadian Manda Group (416-516-0911). Distributed in the UK by
Turnaround Distribution (208-829-3009). Distributed to comics
stores by Diamond Comics Distributors (800-452-6642). ISBN:
978-1-60699-162-6. Printed in Singapore.

Janet, a Summer Odyssey part 1

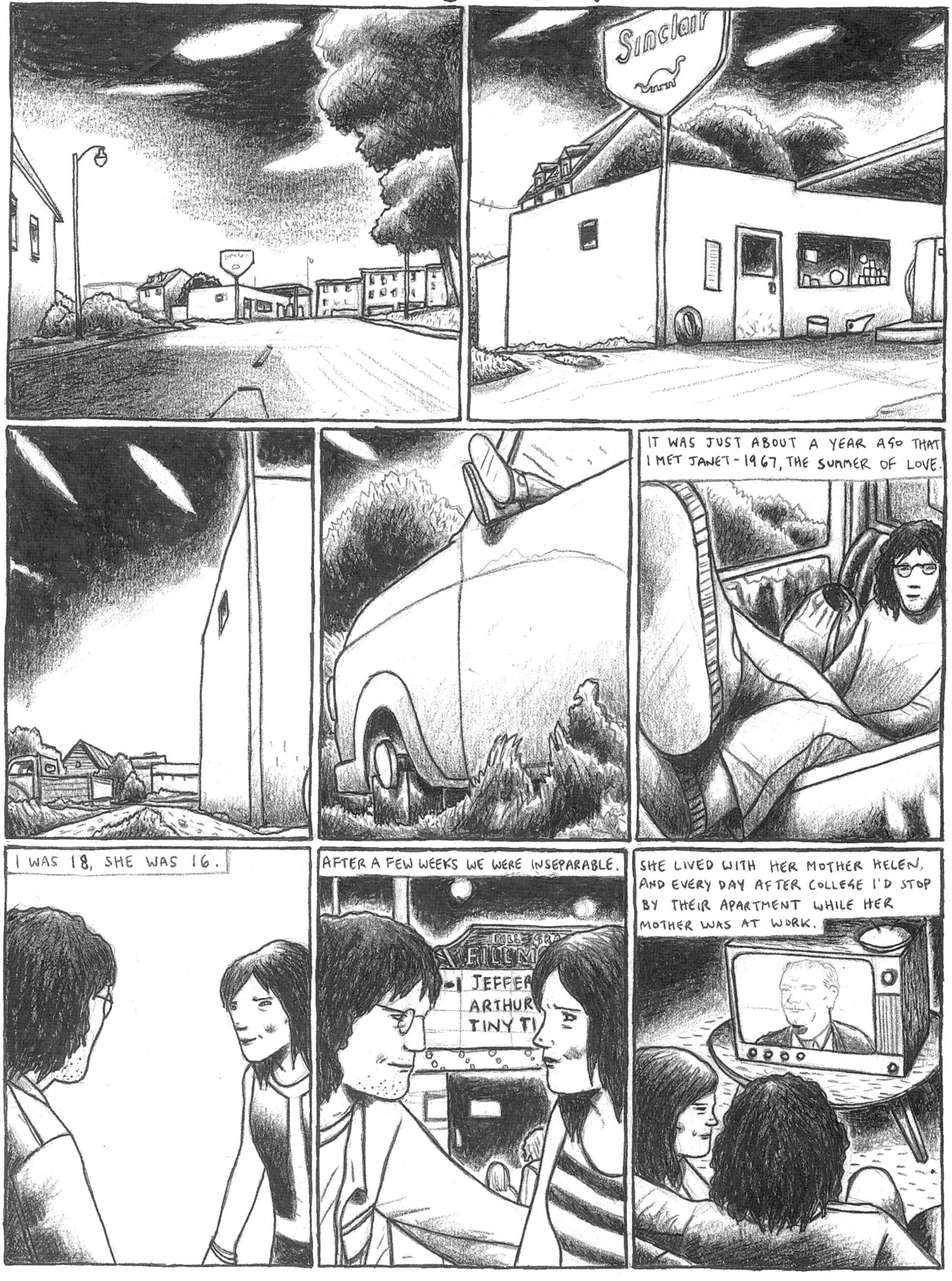
Sinclair
IT WAS JUST ABOUT A YEAR AGO THAT I MET JANET - 1967, THE SUMMER OF LOVE.
I WAS 18, SHE WAS 16.
AFTER A FEW WEEKS WE WERE INSEPARABLE.
JEFFER
ARTHUR
TINY TI
SHE LIVED WITH HER MOTHER HELEN, AND EVERY DAY AFTER COLLEGE I'D STOP BY THEIR APARTMENT WHILE HER MOTHER WAS AT WORK.

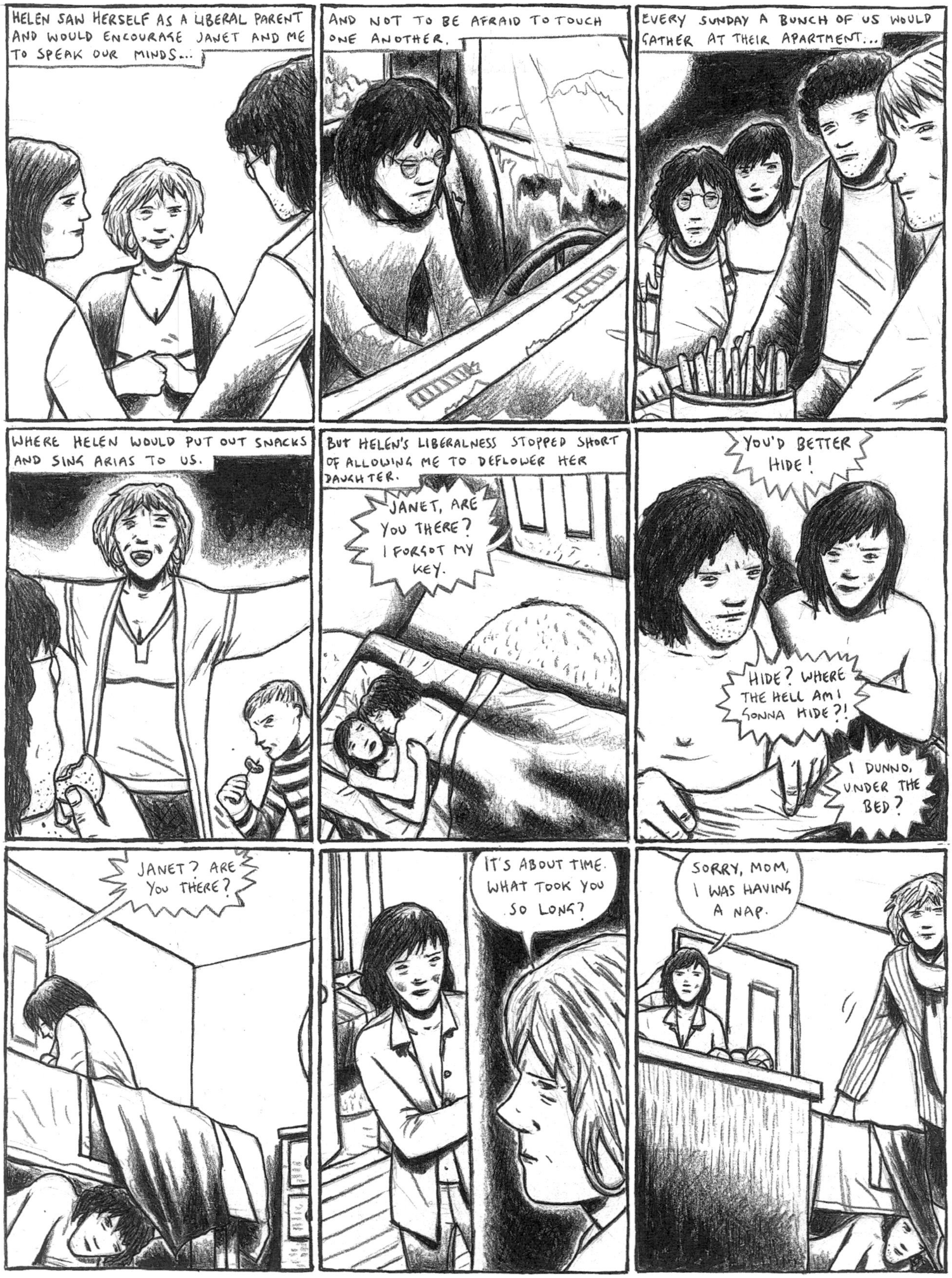
HELEN SAW HERSELF AS A LIBERAL PARENT AND WOULD ENCOURAGE JANET AND ME TO SPEAK OUR MINDS...
AND NOT TO BE AFRAID TO TOUCH ONE ANOTHER.
EVERY SUNDAY A BUNCH OF US WOULD GATHER AT THEIR APARTMENT...
WHERE HELEN WOULD PUT OUT SNACKS AND SING ARIAS TO US.
BUT HELEN'S LIBERALNESS STOPPED SHORT OF ALLOWING ME TO DEFLOWER HER DAUGHTER.
JANET, ARE YOU THERE? I FORGOT MY KEY.
YOU'D BETTER HIDE!
HIDE? WHERE THE HELL AM I GONNA HIDE?!
I DUNNO, UNDER THE BED?
JANET? ARE YOU THERE?
IT'S ABOUT TIME. WHAT TOOK YOU SO LONG?
SORRY, MOM, I WAS HAVING A NAP.

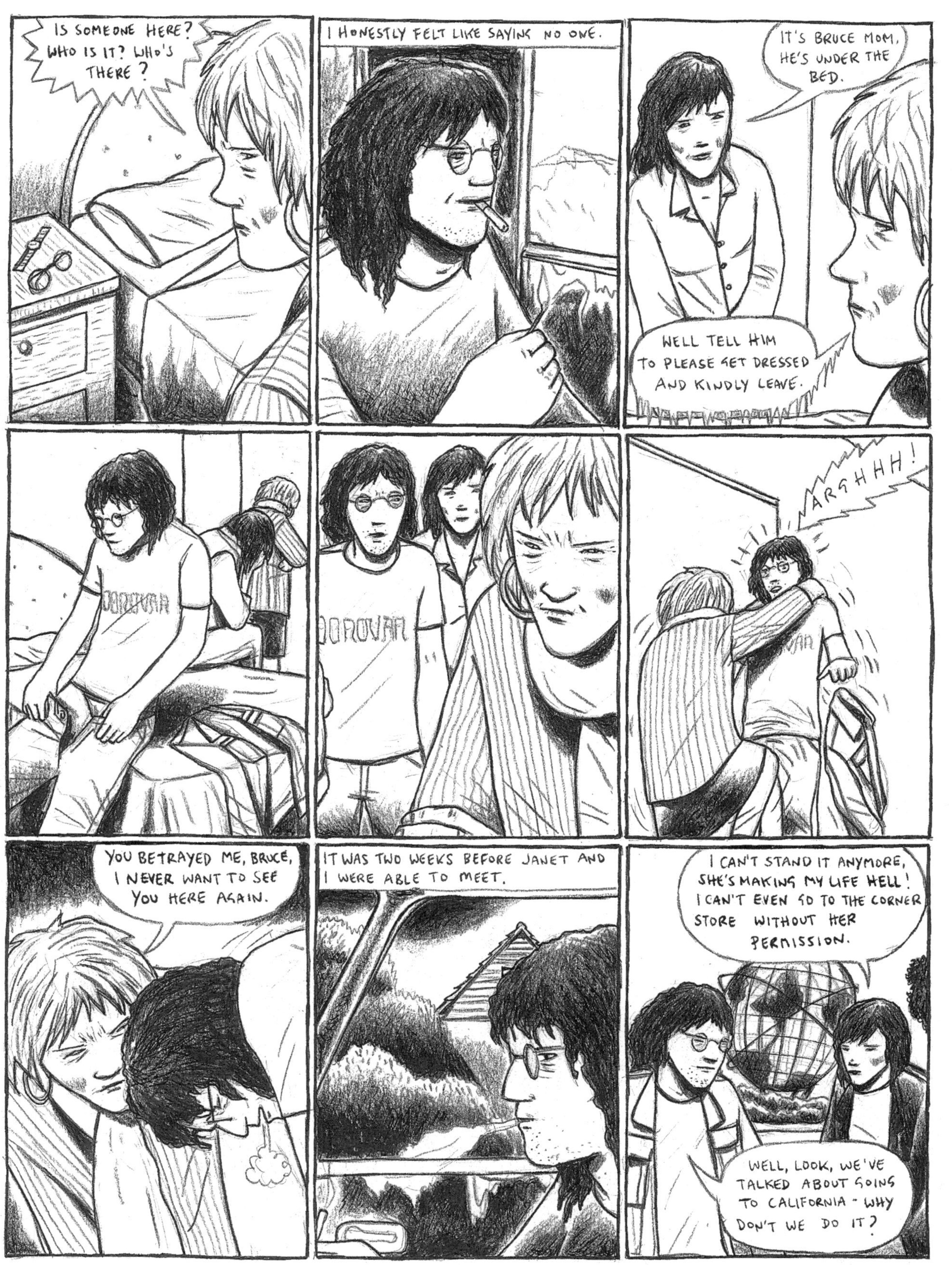
IS SOMEONE HERE? WHO IS IT? WHO'S THERE?
I HONESTLY FELT LIKE SAYING NO ONE.
IT'S BRUCE MOM, HE'S UNDER THE BED.
WELL TELL HIM TO PLEASE GET DRESSED AND KINDLY LEAVE.
DONOVAN
DONOVAN
ARGHHH!
YOU BETRAYED ME, BRUCE, I NEVER WANT TO SEE YOU HERE AGAIN.
IT WAS TWO WEEKS BEFORE JANET AND I WERE ABLE TO MEET.
I CAN'T STAND IT ANYMORE, SHE'S MAKING MY LIFE HELL! I CAN'T EVEN GO TO THE CORNER STORE WITHOUT HER PERMISSION.
WELL, LOOK, WE'VE TALKED ABOUT GOING TO CALIFORNIA - WHY DON'T WE DO IT?

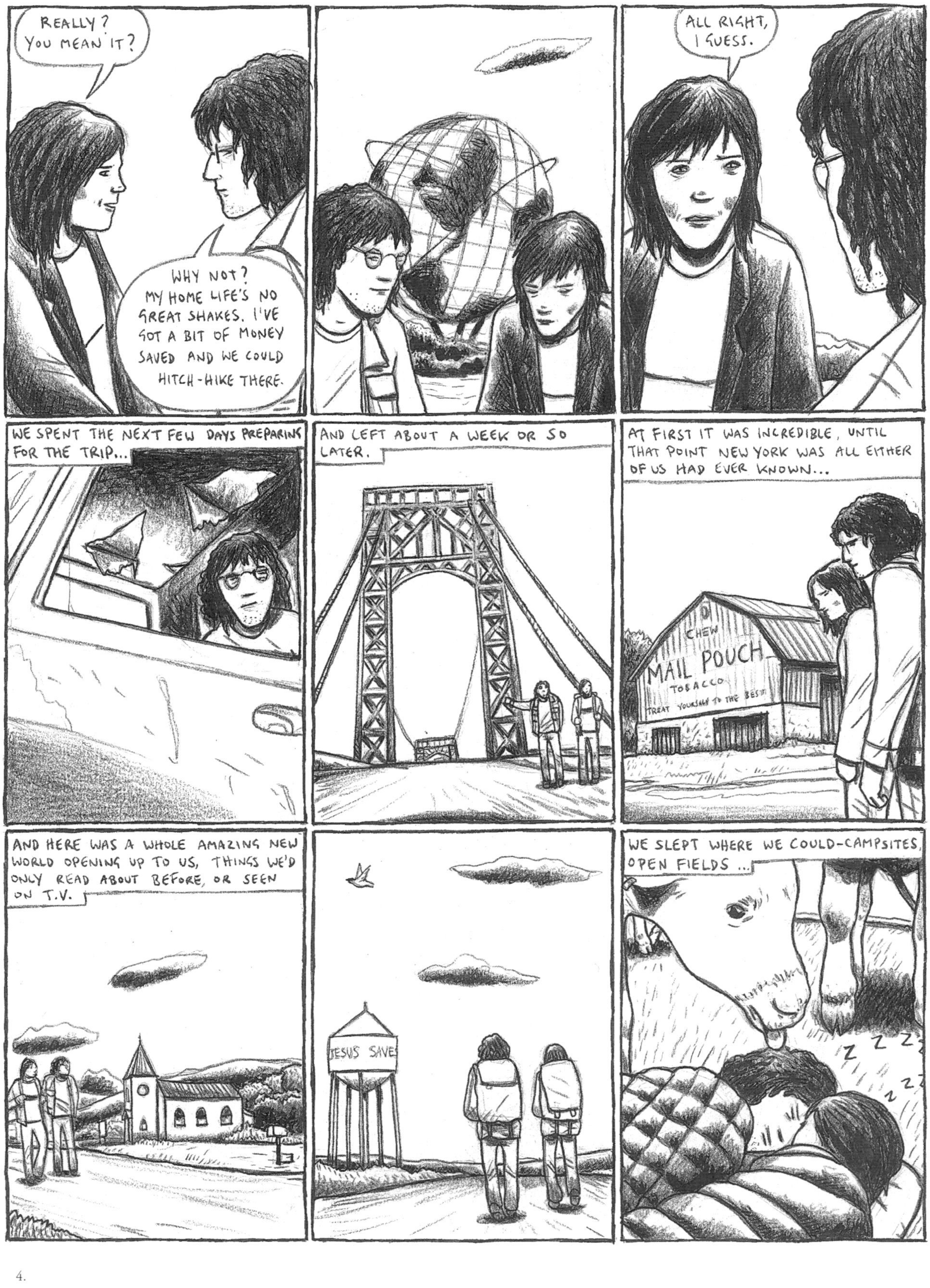
REALLY? YOU MEAN IT?
WHY NOT? MY HOME LIFE'S NO GREAT SHAKES. I'VE GOT A BIT OF MONEY SAVED AND WE COULD HITCH-HIKE THERE.
ALL RIGHT, I GUESS.
WE SPENT THE NEXT FEW DAYS PREPARING FOR THE TRIP...
AND LEFT ABOUT A WEEK OR SO LATER.
AT FIRST IT WAS INCREDIBLE, UNTIL THAT POINT NEW YORK WAS ALL EITHER OF US HAD EVER KNOWN...
CHEW
MAIL POUCH
TOBACCO
TREAT YOURSELF TO THE BEST
AND HERE WAS A WHOLE AMAZING NEW WORLD OPENING UP TO US, THINGS WE'D ONLY READ ABOUT BEFORE, OR SEEN ON T.V.
JESUS SAVE
WE SLEPT WHERE WE COULD-CAMPSITES, OPEN FIELDS...
Z Z Z
Z Z Z

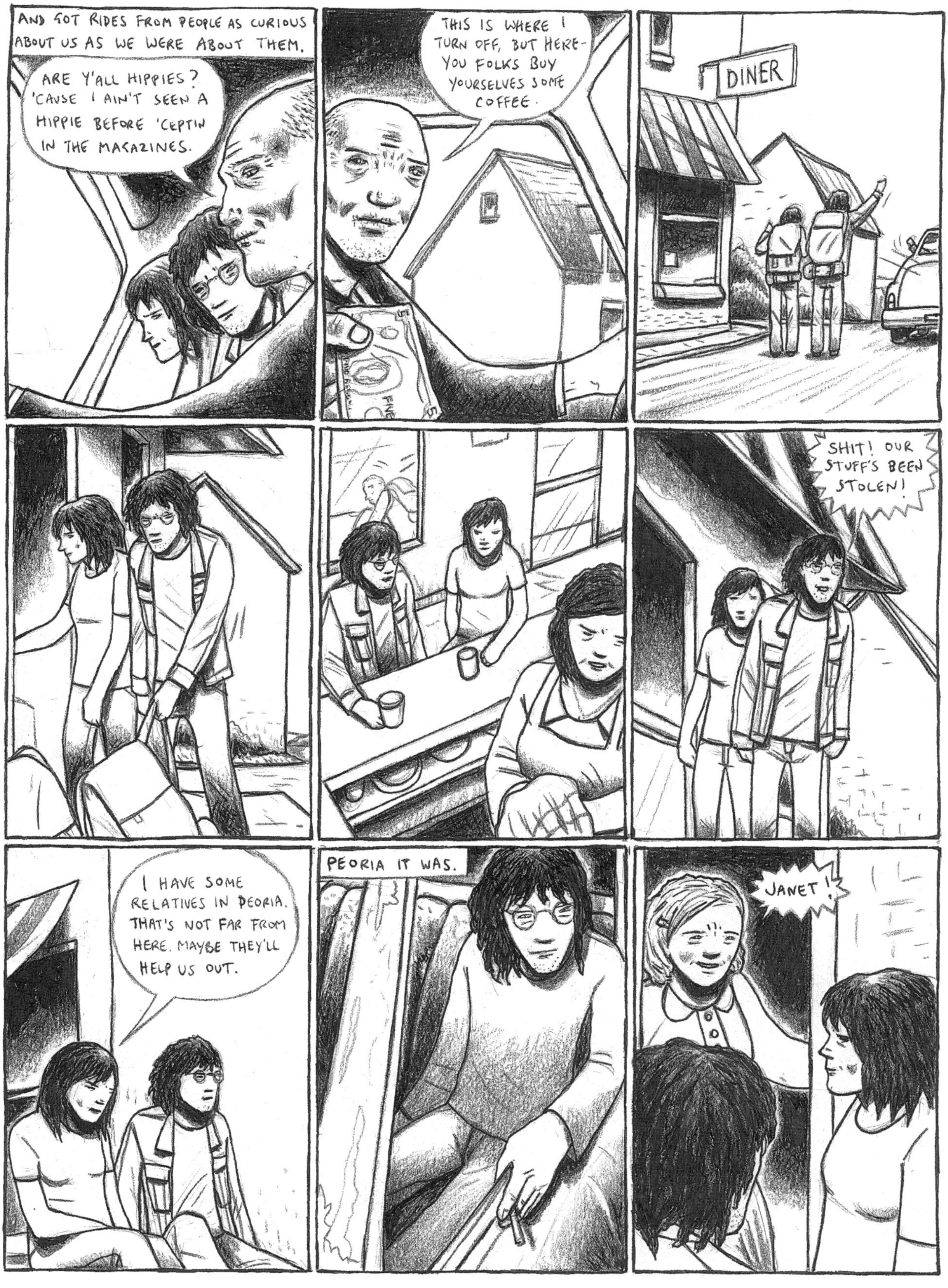
AND GOT RIDES FROM PEOPLE AS CURIOUS ABOUT US AS WE WERE ABOUT THEM.
ARE Y'ALL HIPPIES? 'CAUSE I AIN'T SEEN A HIPPIE BEFORE 'CEPTIN IN THE MAGAZINES.
THIS IS WHERE I TURN OFF, BUT HERE- YOU FOLKS BUY YOURSELVES SOME COFFEE.
DINER
SHIT! OUR STUFF'S BEEN STOLEN!
I HAVE SOME RELATIVES IN PEORIA. THAT'S NOT FAR FROM HERE. MAYBE THEY'LL HELP US OUT.
PEORIA IT WAS.
JANET!

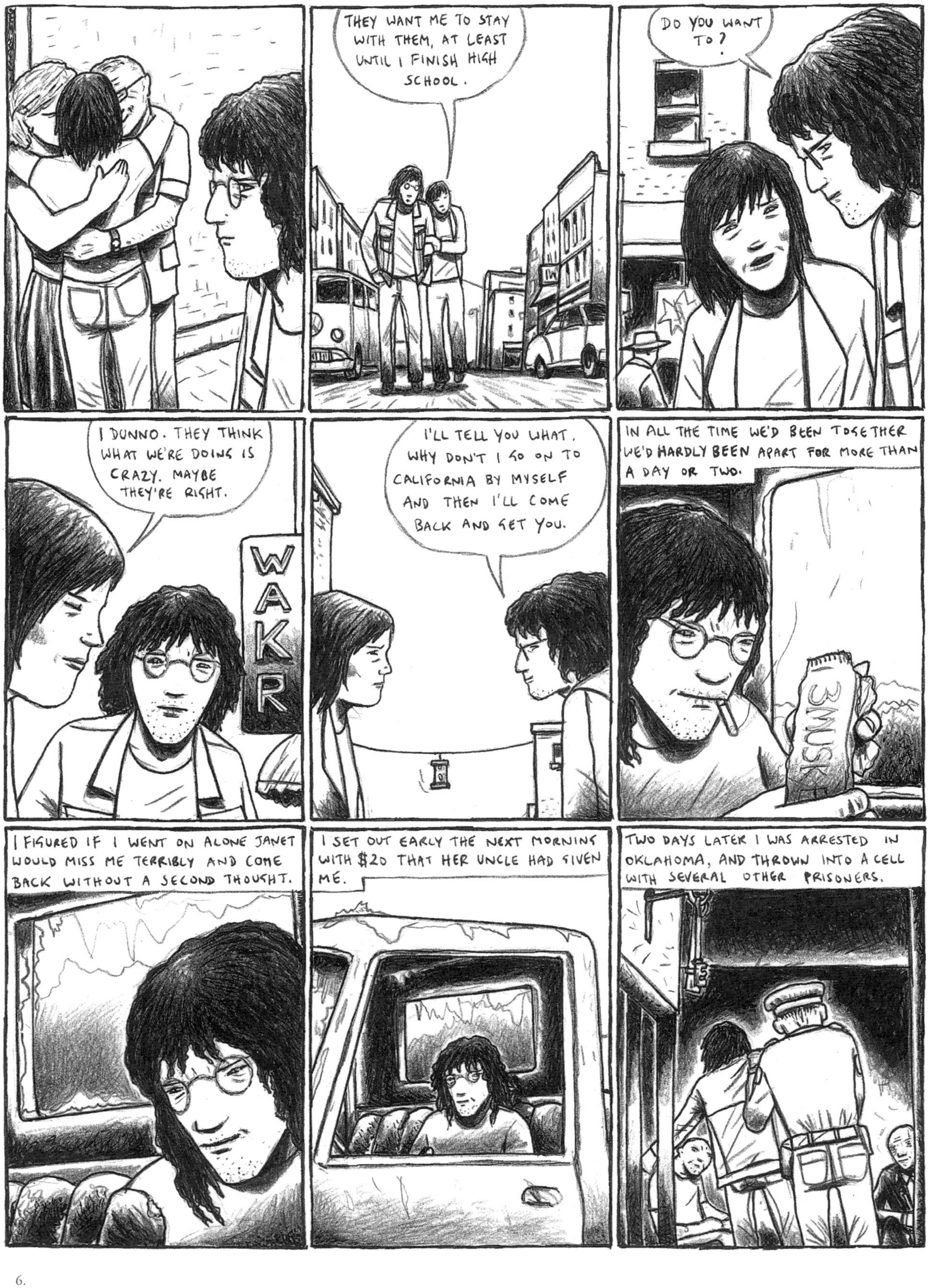
THEY WANT ME TO STAY WITH THEM, AT LEAST UNTIL I FINISH HIGH SCHOOL.
DO YOU WANT TO?
I DUNNO. THEY THINK WHAT WE'RE DOING IS CRAZY. MAYBE THEY'RE RIGHT.
WAKR
I'LL TELL YOU WHAT. WHY DON'T I GO ON TO CALIFORNIA BY MYSELF AND THEN I'LL COME BACK AND GET YOU.
IN ALL THE TIME WE'D BEEN TOGETHER WE'D HARDLY BEEN APART FOR MORE THAN A DAY OR TWO.
I FIGURED IF I WENT ON ALONE JANET WOULD MISS ME TERRIBLY AND COME BACK WITHOUT A SECOND THOUGHT.
I SET OUT EARLY THE NEXT MORNING WITH $20 THAT HER UNCLE HAD GIVEN ME.
TWO DAYS LATER I WAS ARRESTED IN OKLAHOMA, AND THROWN INTO A CELL WITH SEVERAL OTHER PRISONERS.

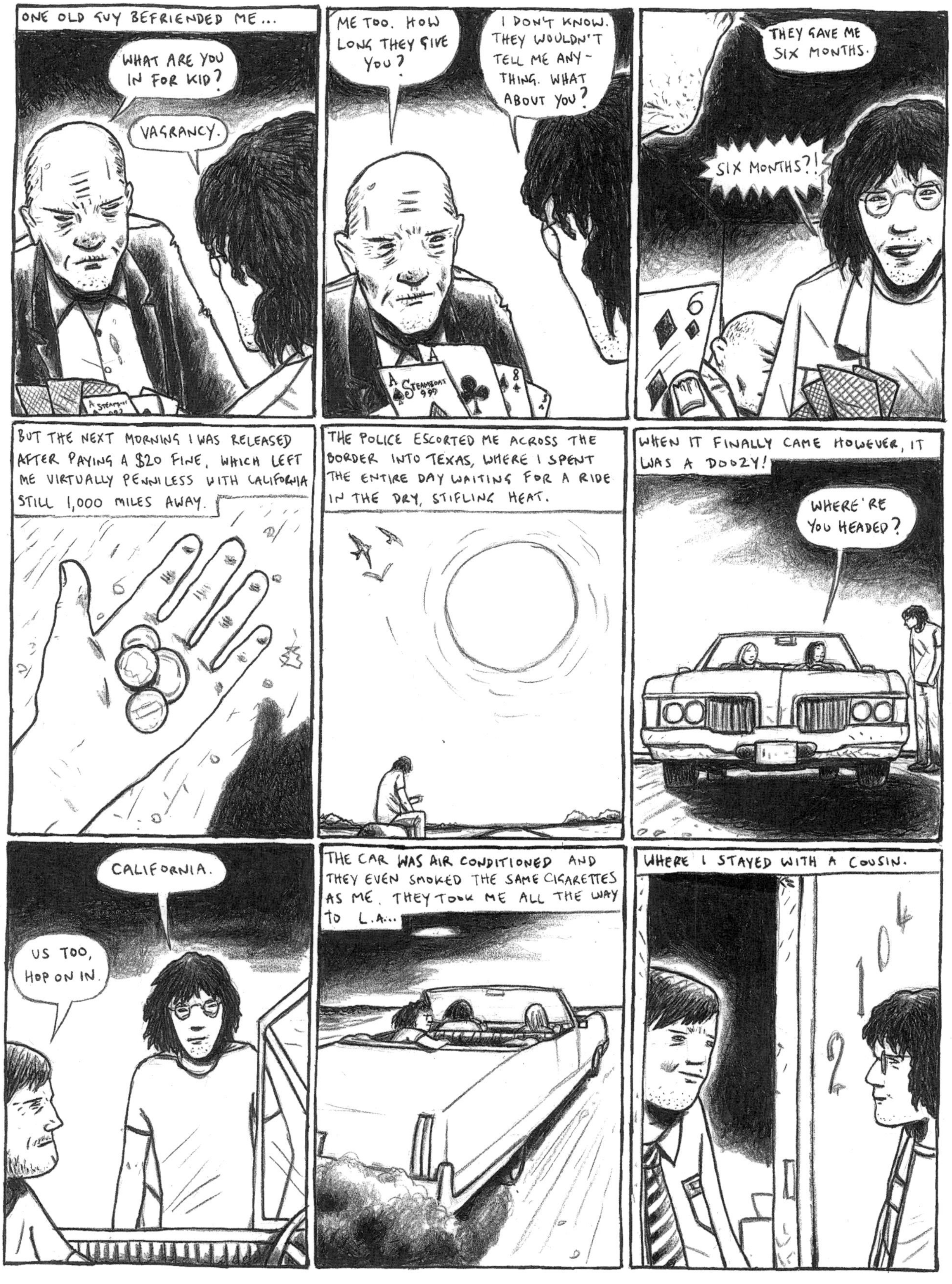
ONE OLD GUY BEFRIENDED ME...
WHAT ARE YOU IN FOR KID?
VAGRANCY.
ME TOO. HOW LONG THEY GIVE YOU?
I DON'T KNOW. THEY WOULDN'T TELL ME ANY-THING. WHAT ABOUT YOU?
THEY GAVE ME SIX MONTHS.
SIX MONTHS?!
BUT THE NEXT MORNING I WAS RELEASED AFTER PAYING A $20 FINE, WHICH LEFT ME VIRTUALLY PENNILESS WITH CALIFORNIA STILL 1,000 MILES AWAY.
THE POLICE ESCORTED ME ACROSS THE BORDER INTO TEXAS, WHERE I SPENT THE ENTIRE DAY WAITING FOR A RIDE IN THE DRY, STIFLING HEAT.
WHEN IT FINALLY CAME HOWEVER, IT WAS A DOOZY!
WHERE'RE YOU HEADED?
CALIFORNIA.
US TOO, HOP ON IN.
THE CAR WAS AIR CONDITIONED AND THEY EVEN SMOKED THE SAME CIGARETTES AS ME. THEY TOOK ME ALL THE WAY TO L.A...
WHERE I STAYED WITH A COUSIN.

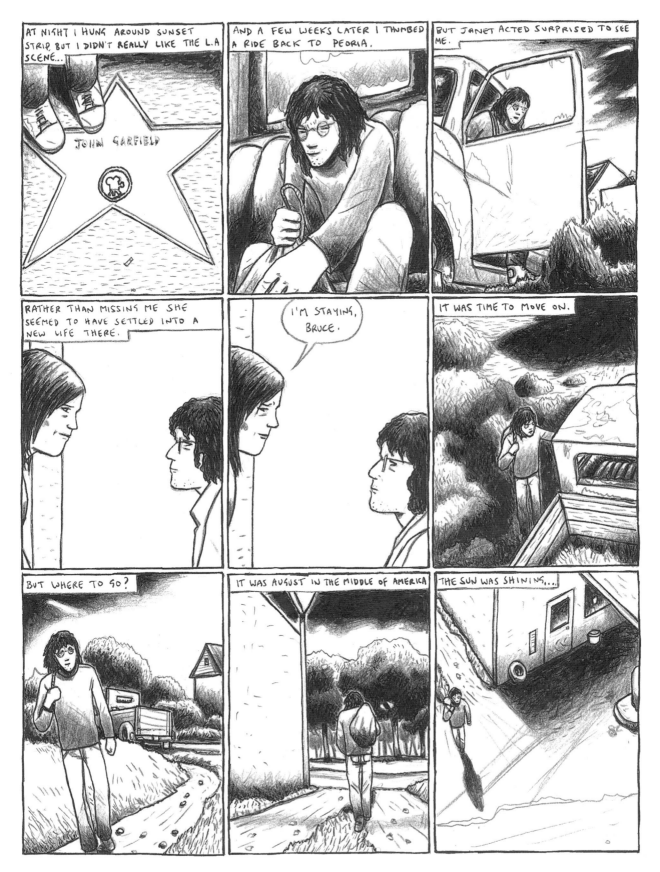

AT NIGHT I HUNG AROUND SUNSET STRIP BUT I DIDN'T REALLY LIKE THE L.A SCENE...

JOHN GARFIELD

AND A FEW WEEKS LATER I THUMBED A RIDE BACK TO PEORIA.

BUT JANET ACTED SURPRISED TO SEE ME.

RATHER THAN MISSING ME SHE SEEMED TO HAVE SETTLED INTO A NEW LIFE THERE.

I'M STAYING, BRUCE.

IT WAS TIME TO MOVE ON.

BUT WHERE TO GO?

IT WAS AUGUST IN THE MIDDLE OF AMERICA

THE SUN WAS SHINING,...

8.

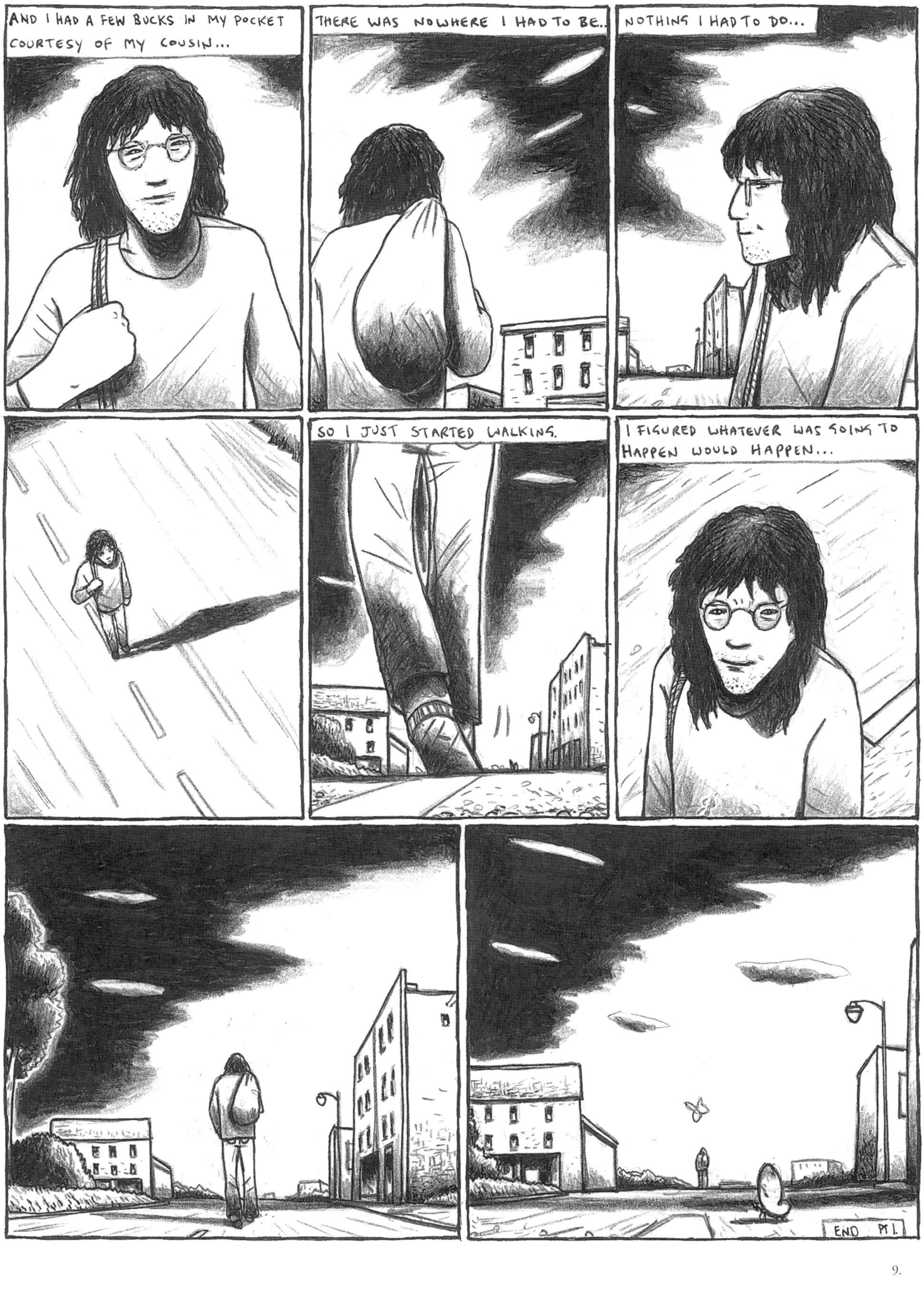
AND I HAD A FEW BUCKS IN MY POCKET COURTESY OF MY COUSIN...
THERE WAS NOWHERE I HAD TO BE...
NOTHING I HAD TO DO...
SO I JUST STARTED WALKING.
I FIGURED WHATEVER WAS GOING TO HAPPEN WOULD HAPPEN...
END PT 1.

On the road again, a summer odyssey part 2

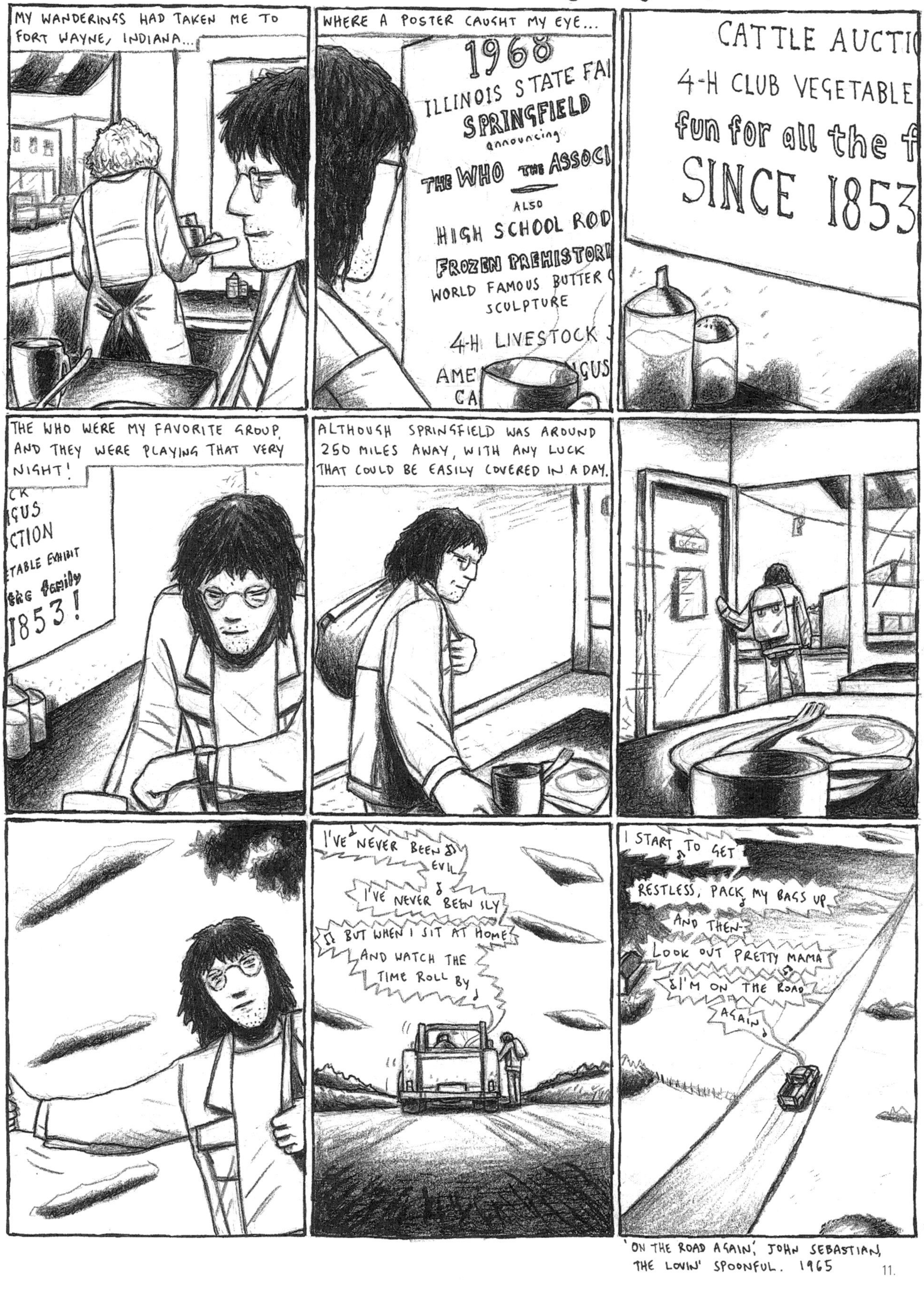

MY WANDERINGS HAD TAKEN ME TO FORT WAYNE, INDIANA...
WHERE A POSTER CAUGHT MY EYE...
1968
ILLINOIS STATE FAI
SPRINGFIELD
announcing
THE WHO THE ASSOCI
ALSO
HIGH SCHOOL ROD
FROZEN PREHISTORI
WORLD FAMOUS BUTTER
SCULPTURE
4-H LIVESTOCK
CATTLE AUCTI
4-H CLUB VEGETABLE
fun for all the f
SINCE 1853
THE WHO WERE MY FAVORITE GROUP, AND THEY WERE PLAYING THAT VERY NIGHT!
CTION
ETABLE EXHIBIT
the family
1853!
ALTHOUGH SPRINGFIELD WAS AROUND 250 MILES AWAY, WITH ANY LUCK THAT COULD BE EASILY COVERED IN A DAY.
I'VE NEVER BEEN EVIL
I'VE NEVER BEEN SLY
BUT WHEN I SIT AT HOME
AND WATCH THE TIME ROLL BY
I START TO GET
RESTLESS, PACK MY BAGS UP
AND THEN-
LOOK OUT PRETTY MAMA
&I'M ON THE ROAD
AGAIN

'ON THE ROAD AGAIN', JOHN SEBASTIAN, THE LOVIN' SPOONFUL. 1965

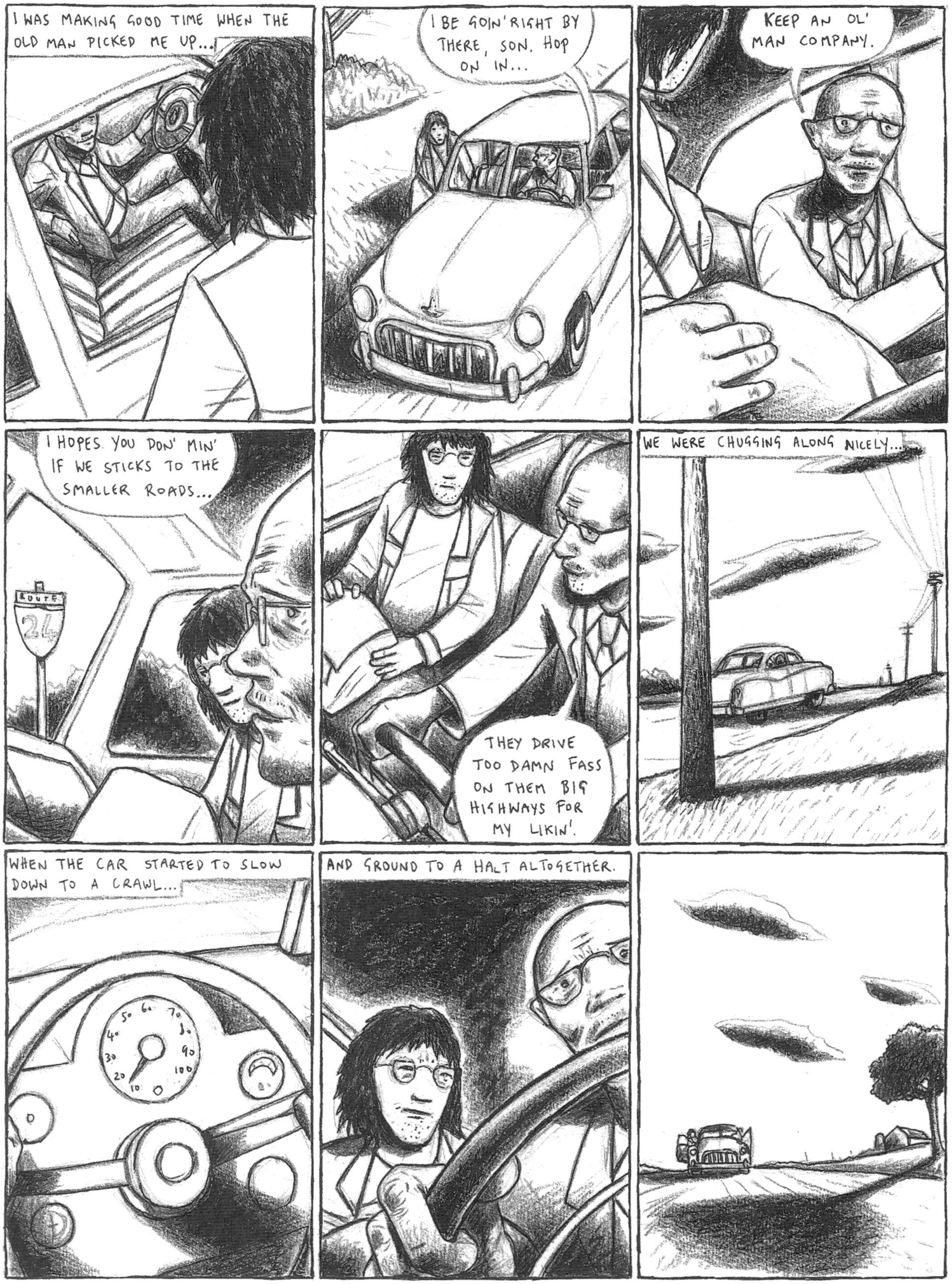
I WAS MAKING GOOD TIME WHEN THE OLD MAN PICKED ME UP...
I BE GOIN' RIGHT BY THERE, SON. HOP ON IN...
KEEP AN OL' MAN COMPANY.
I HOPES YOU DON' MIN' IF WE STICKS TO THE SMALLER ROADS...
ROUTE 24
THEY DRIVE TOO DAMN FASS ON THEM BIG HIGHWAYS FOR MY LIKIN'.
WE WERE CHUGGING ALONG NICELY...
WHEN THE CAR STARTED TO SLOW DOWN TO A CRAWL...
AND GROUND TO A HALT ALTOGETHER.

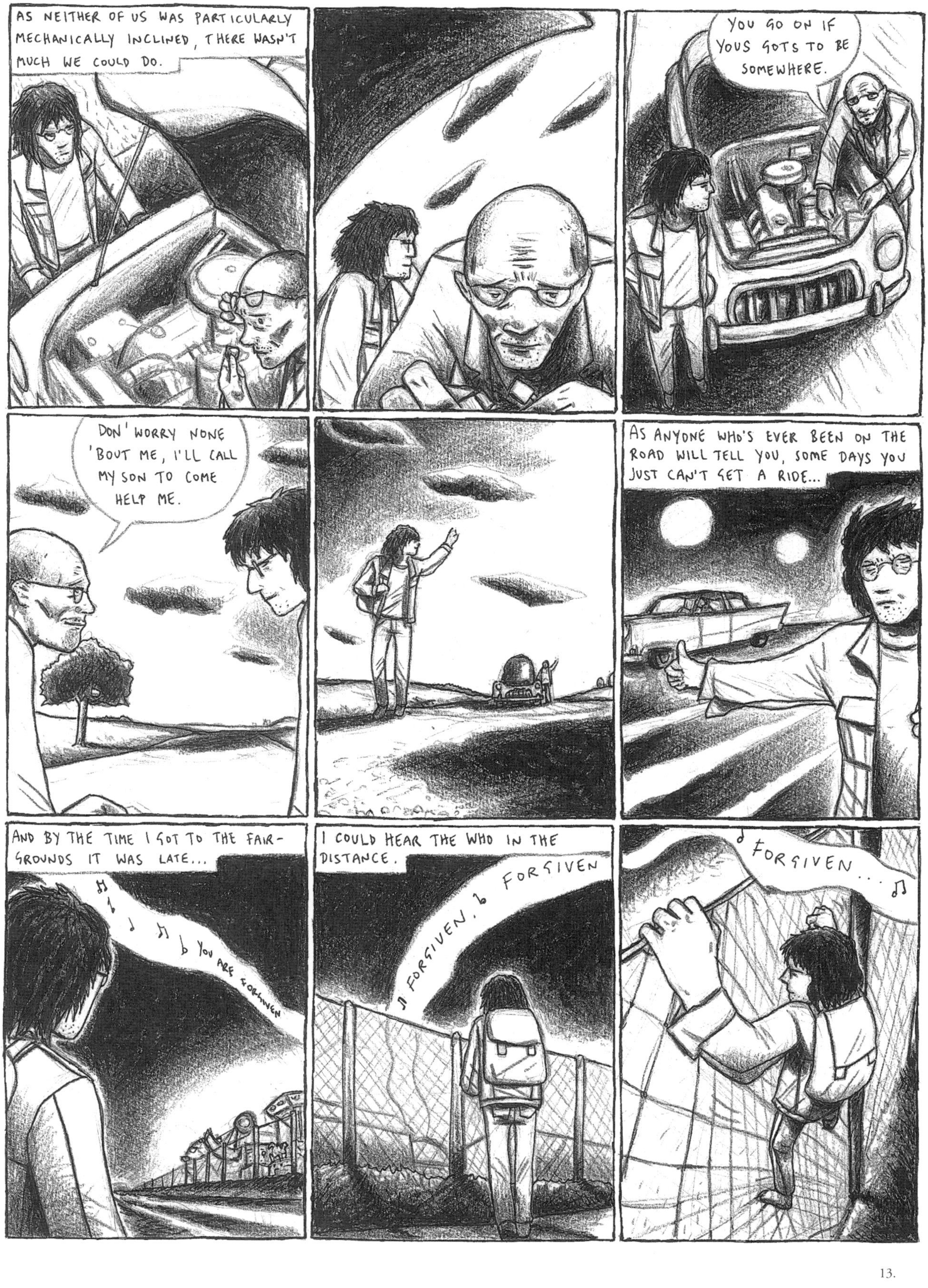
AS NEITHER OF US WAS PARTICULARLY MECHANICALLY INCLINED, THERE WASN'T MUCH WE COULD DO.
YOU GO ON IF YOUS GOTS TO BE SOMEWHERE.
DON' WORRY NONE 'BOUT ME, I'LL CALL MY SON TO COME HELP ME.
AS ANYONE WHO'S EVER BEEN ON THE ROAD WILL TELL YOU, SOME DAYS YOU JUST CAN'T GET A RIDE...
AND BY THE TIME I GOT TO THE FAIR-GROUNDS IT WAS LATE...
YOU ARE FORGIVEN
I COULD HEAR THE WHO IN THE DISTANCE.
FORGIVEN, FORGIVEN
FORGIVEN...

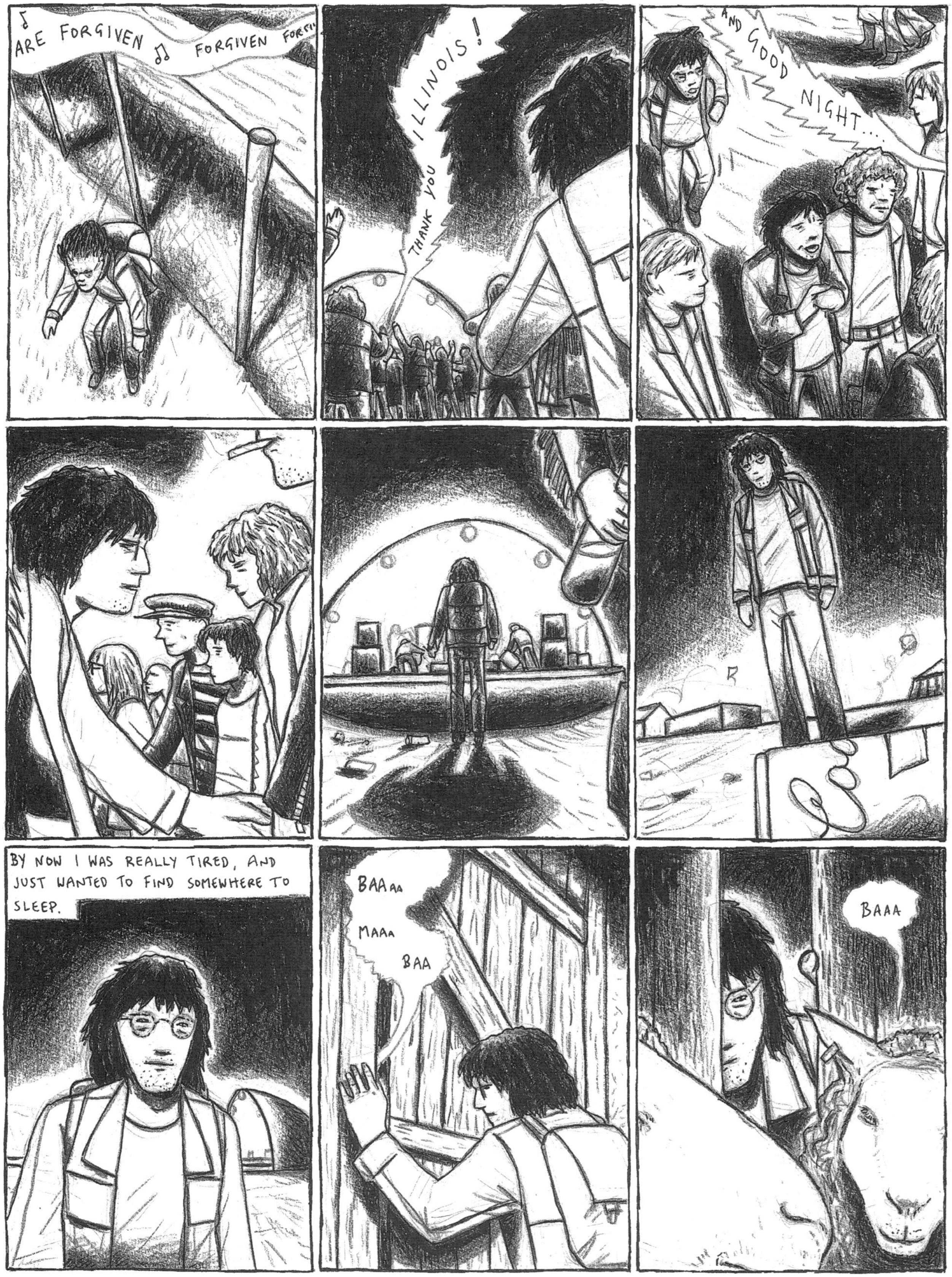
ARE FORGIVEN FORGIVEN FORGI
THANK YOU ILLINOIS!
AND GOOD NIGHT....
BY NOW I WAS REALLY TIRED, AND JUST WANTED TO FIND SOMEWHERE TO SLEEP.
BAAaa
MAAa
BAA
BAAA

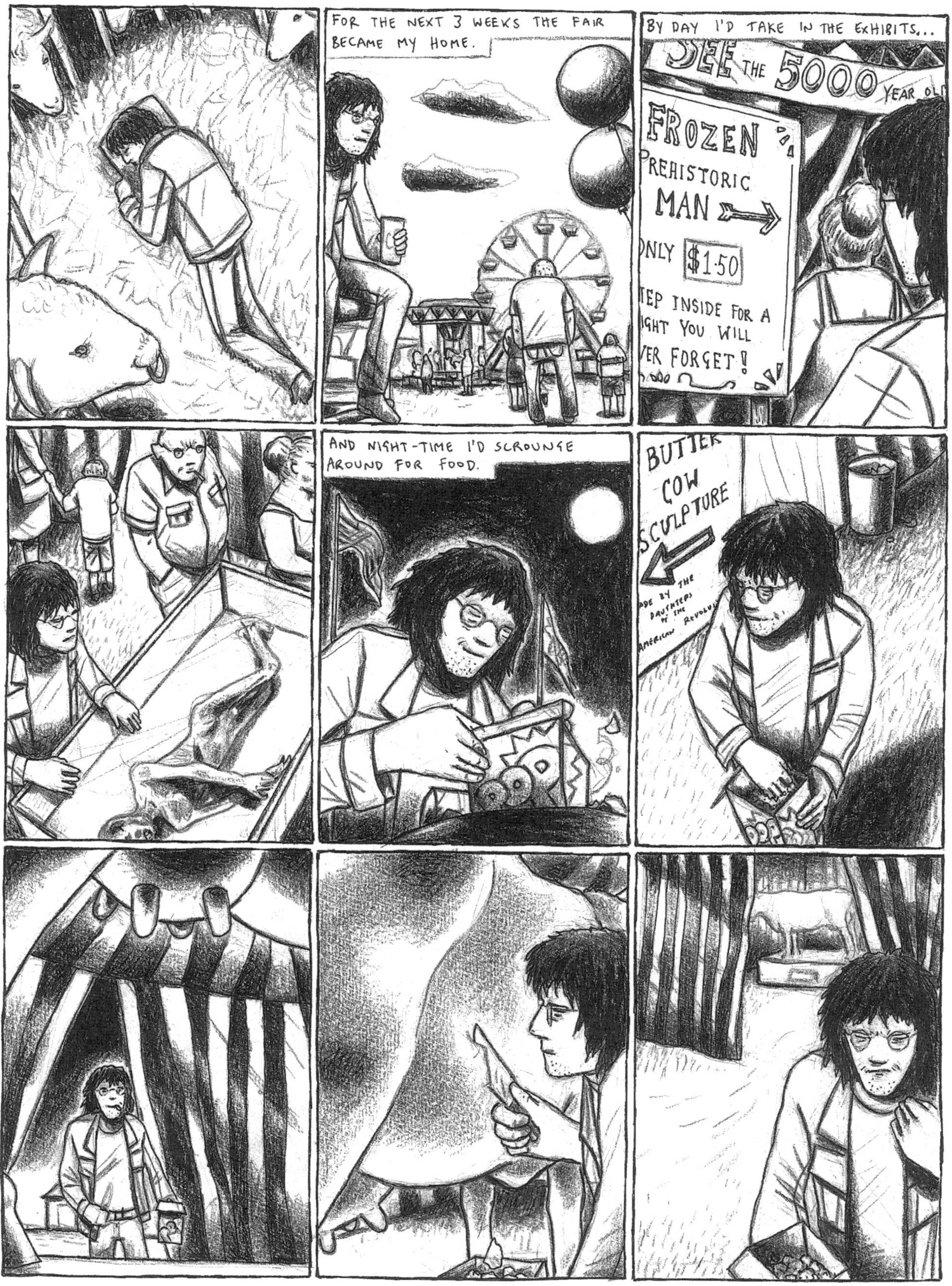
FOR THE NEXT 3 WEEKS THE FAIR BECAME MY HOME.
BY DAY I'D TAKE IN THE EXHIBITS...
SEE THE 5000 YEAR OL
FROZEN PREHISTORIC MAN
NLY $1.50
TEP INSIDE FOR A IGHT YOU WILL VER FORGET!
AND NIGHT-TIME I'D SCROUNGE AROUND FOR FOOD.
BUTTER COW SCULPTURE
DE BY THE DAUGHTERS OF THE AMERICAN REVOLU

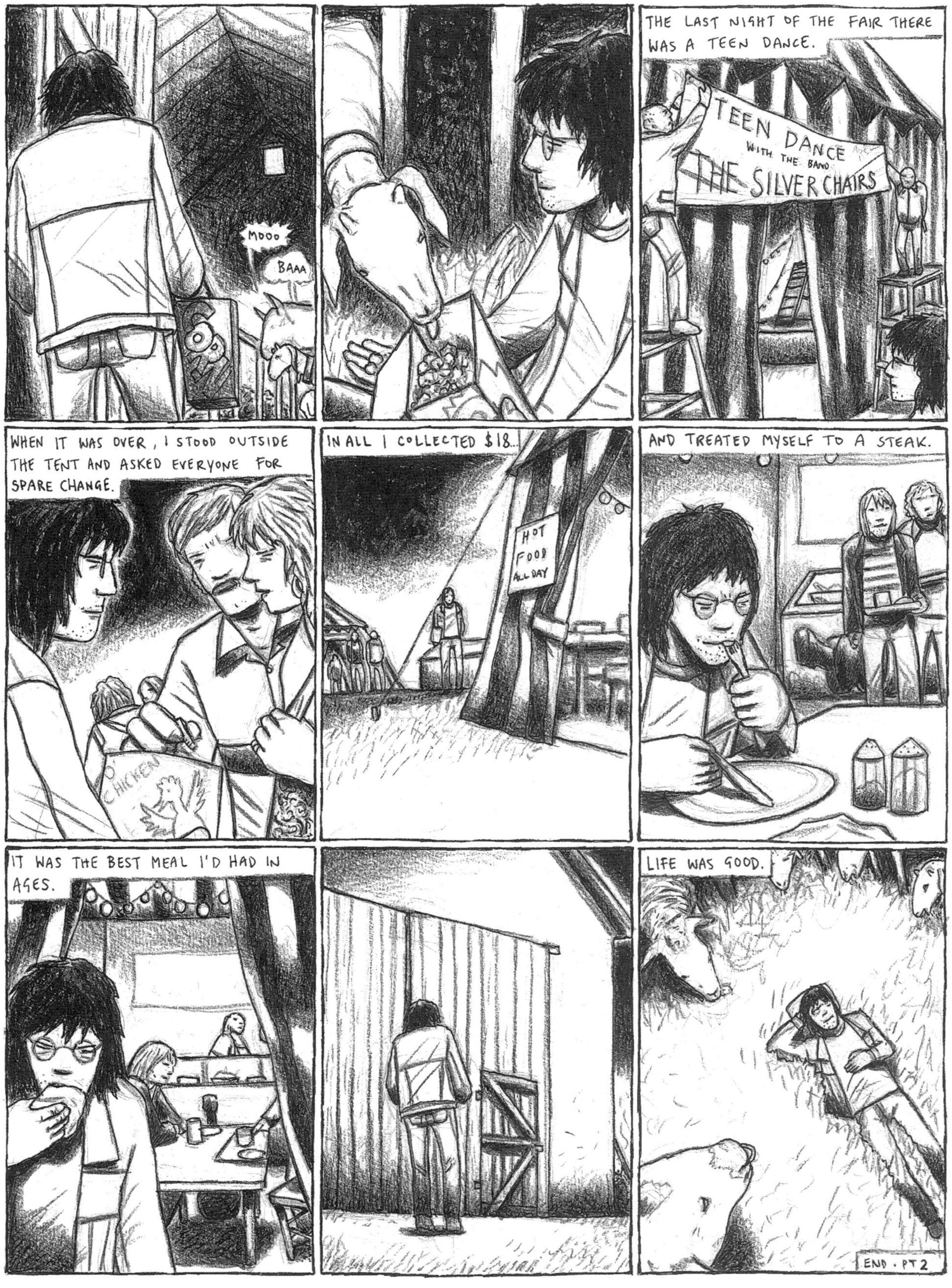

MOOO
BAAA
THE LAST NIGHT OF THE FAIR THERE WAS A TEEN DANCE.
TEEN DANCE WITH THE BAND THE SILVER CHAIRS
WHEN IT WAS OVER, I STOOD OUTSIDE THE TENT AND ASKED EVERYONE FOR SPARE CHANGE.
CHICKEN
IN ALL I COLLECTED $18...
HOT FOOD ALL DAY
AND TREATED MYSELF TO A STEAK.
IT WAS THE BEST MEAL I'D HAD IN AGES.
LIFE WAS GOOD.
END. PT 2

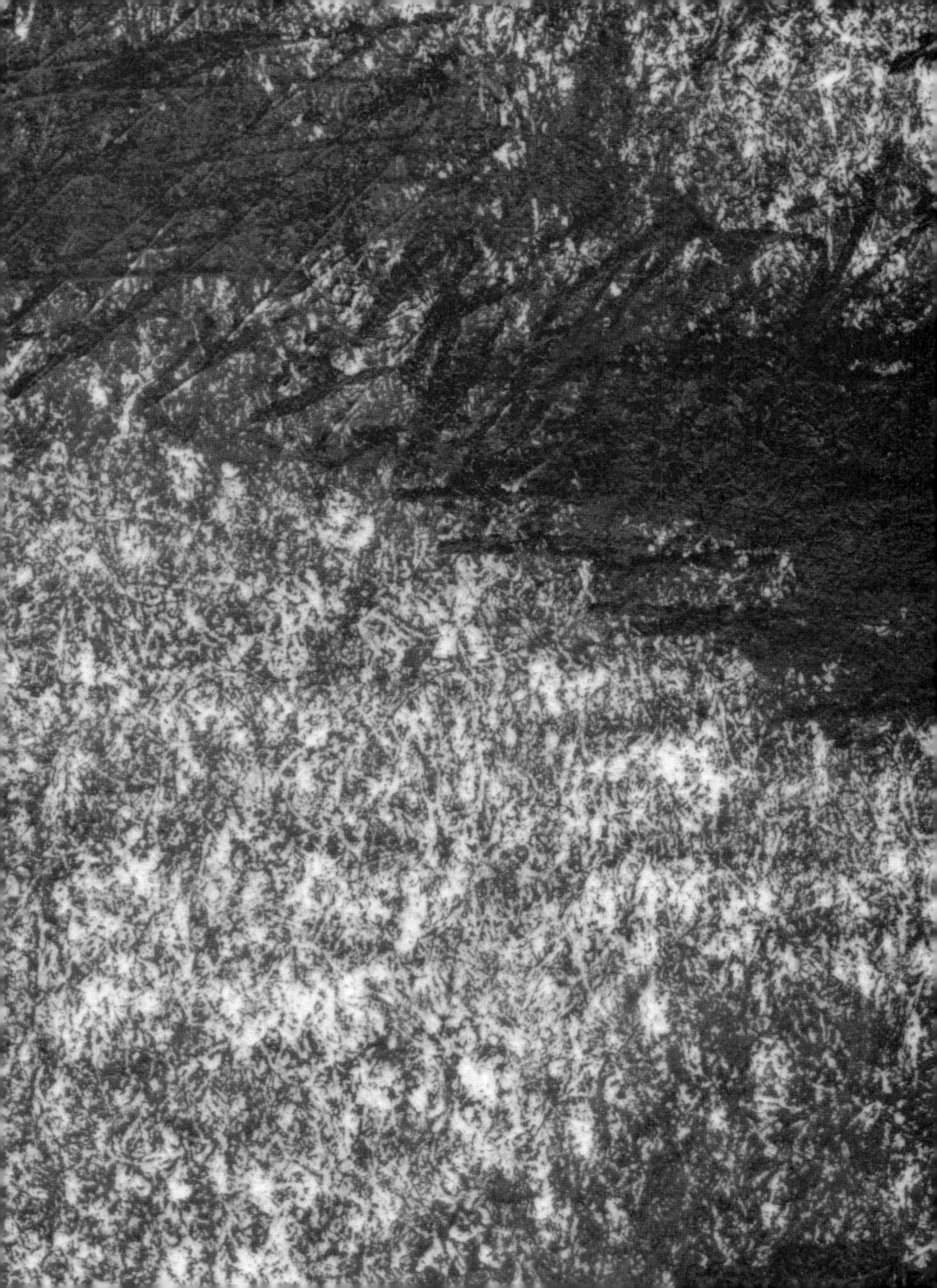

Chicago, a Summer Odyssey part 3

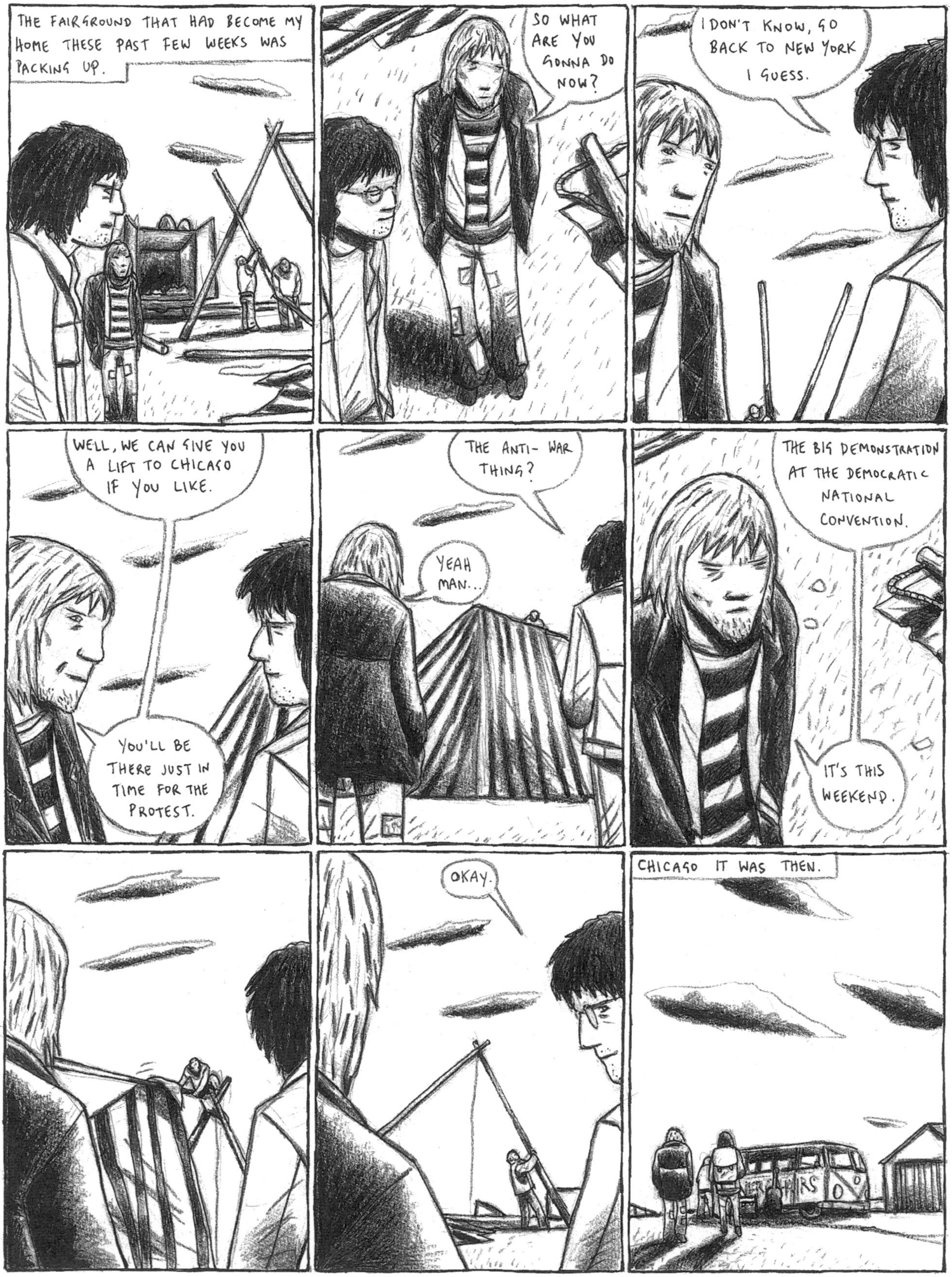

THE FAIRGROUND THAT HAD BECOME MY HOME THESE PAST FEW WEEKS WAS PACKING UP.
SO WHAT ARE YOU GONNA DO NOW?
I DON'T KNOW, GO BACK TO NEW YORK I GUESS.
WELL, WE CAN GIVE YOU A LIFT TO CHICAGO IF YOU LIKE.
YOU'LL BE THERE JUST IN TIME FOR THE PROTEST.
THE ANTI- WAR THING?
YEAH MAN...
THE BIG DEMONSTRATION AT THE DEMOCRATIC NATIONAL CONVENTION.
IT'S THIS WEEKEND.
OKAY.
CHICAGO IT WAS THEN.

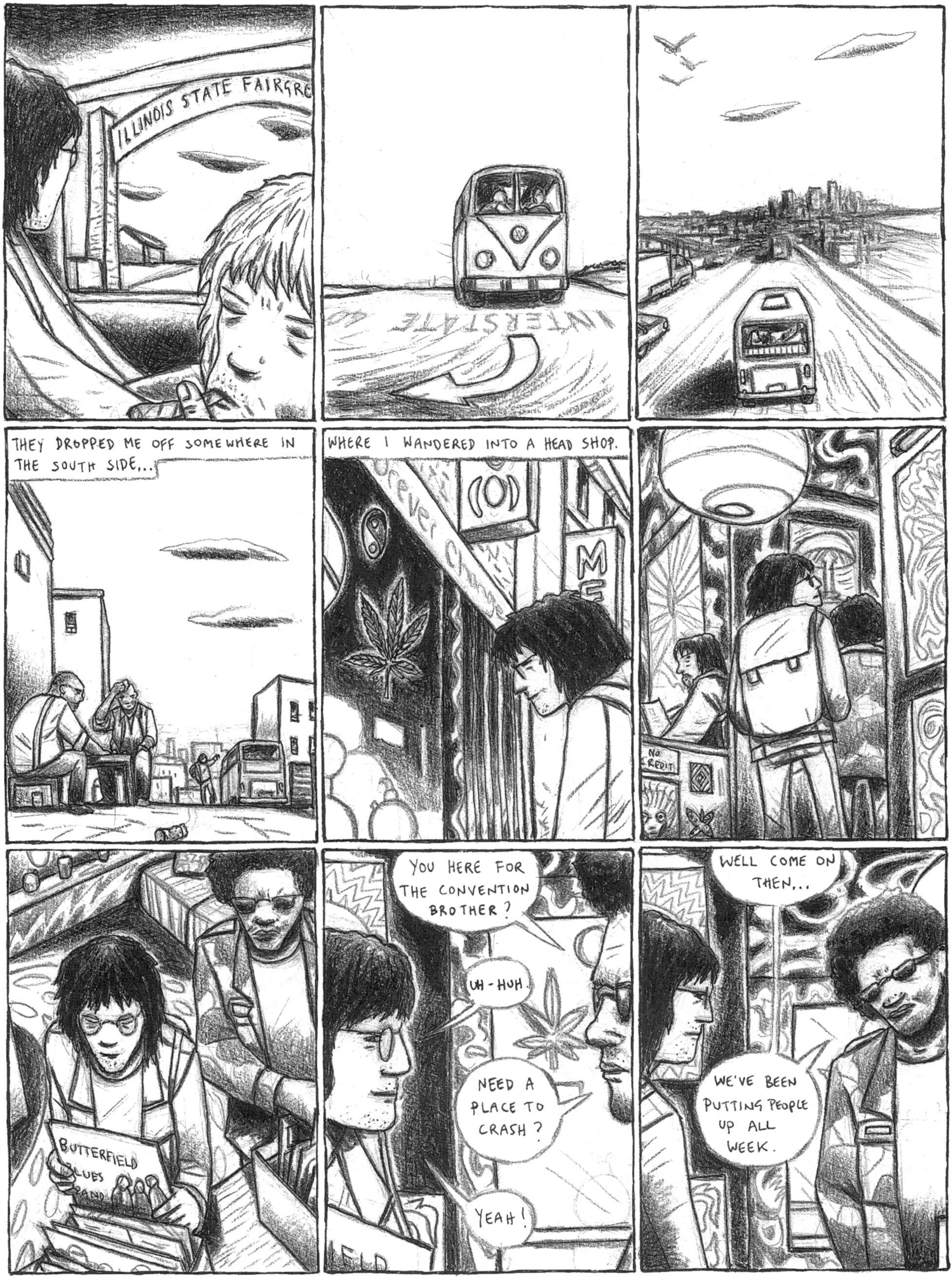

ILLINOIS STATE FAIRGR
INTERSTATE
THEY DROPPED ME OFF SOMEWHERE IN THE SOUTH SIDE...
WHERE I WANDERED INTO A HEAD SHOP.
NO CREDIT
BUTTERFIELD BLUES BAND
YOU HERE FOR THE CONVENTION BROTHER?
UH-HUH.
NEED A PLACE TO CRASH?
YEAH!
WELL COME ON THEN...
WE'VE BEEN PUTTING PEOPLE UP ALL WEEK.

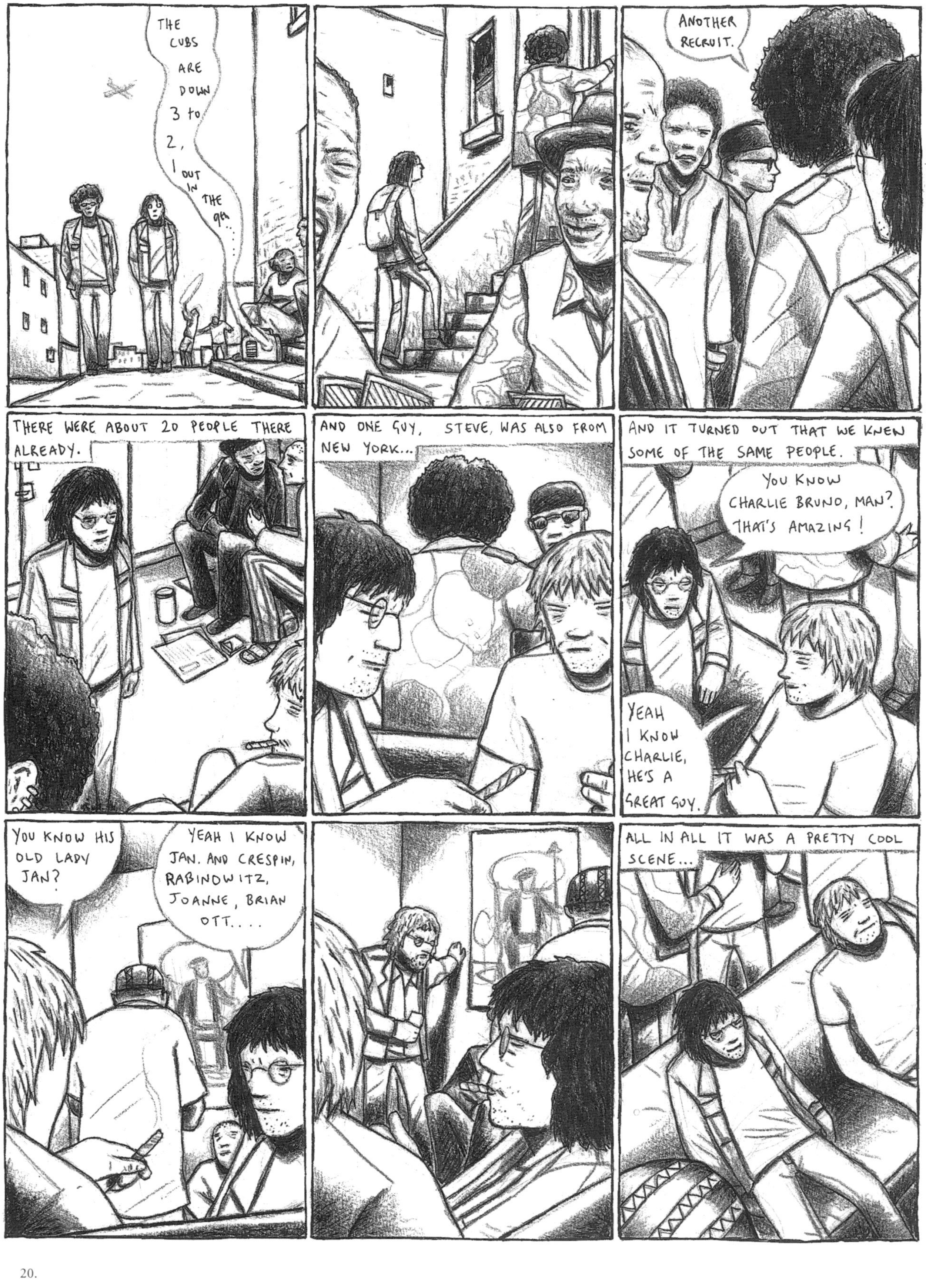
THE CUBS ARE DOWN 3 to 2, 1 OUT IN THE 9th...
ANOTHER RECRUIT.
THERE WERE ABOUT 20 PEOPLE THERE ALREADY.
AND ONE GUY, STEVE, WAS ALSO FROM NEW YORK...
AND IT TURNED OUT THAT WE KNEW SOME OF THE SAME PEOPLE.
YOU KNOW CHARLIE BRUNO, MAN? THAT'S AMAZING!
YEAH I KNOW CHARLIE, HE'S A GREAT GUY.
YOU KNOW HIS OLD LADY JAN?
YEAH I KNOW JAN. AND CRESPIN, RABINOWITZ, JOANNE, BRIAN OTT....
ALL IN ALL IT WAS A PRETTY COOL SCENE...

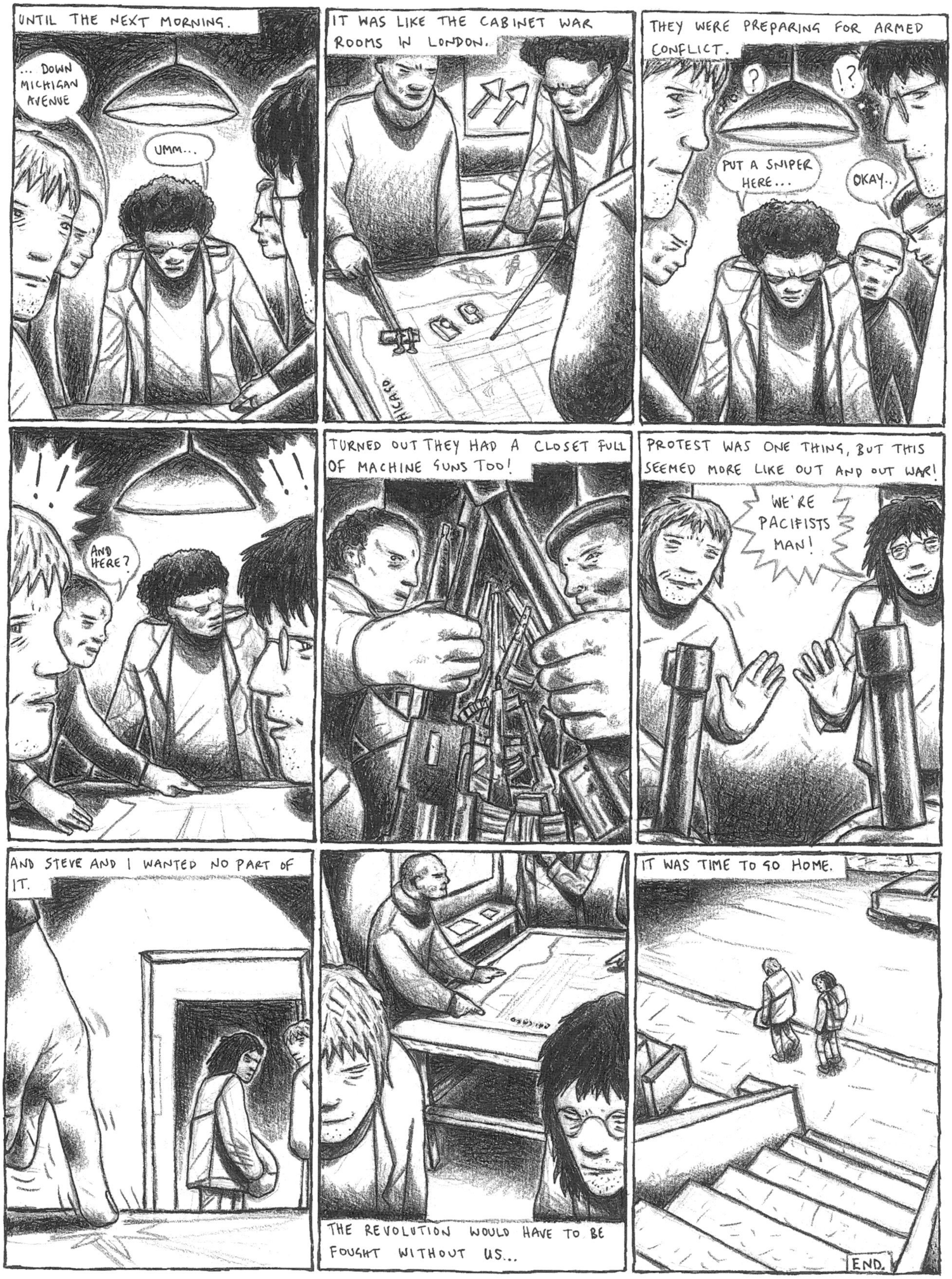
UNTIL THE NEXT MORNING.
... DOWN MICHIGAN AVENUE
UMM...
IT WAS LIKE THE CABINET WAR ROOMS IN LONDON.
CHICAGO
THEY WERE PREPARING FOR ARMED CONFLICT.
?
!?
PUT A SNIPER HERE...
OKAY..
!!
!!
AND HERE?
TURNED OUT THEY HAD A CLOSET FULL OF MACHINE GUNS TOO!
PROTEST WAS ONE THING, BUT THIS SEEMED MORE LIKE OUT AND OUT WAR!
WE'RE PACIFISTS MAN!
AND STEVE AND I WANTED NO PART OF IT.
THE REVOLUTION WOULD HAVE TO BE FOUGHT WITHOUT US...
IT WAS TIME TO GO HOME.
END.

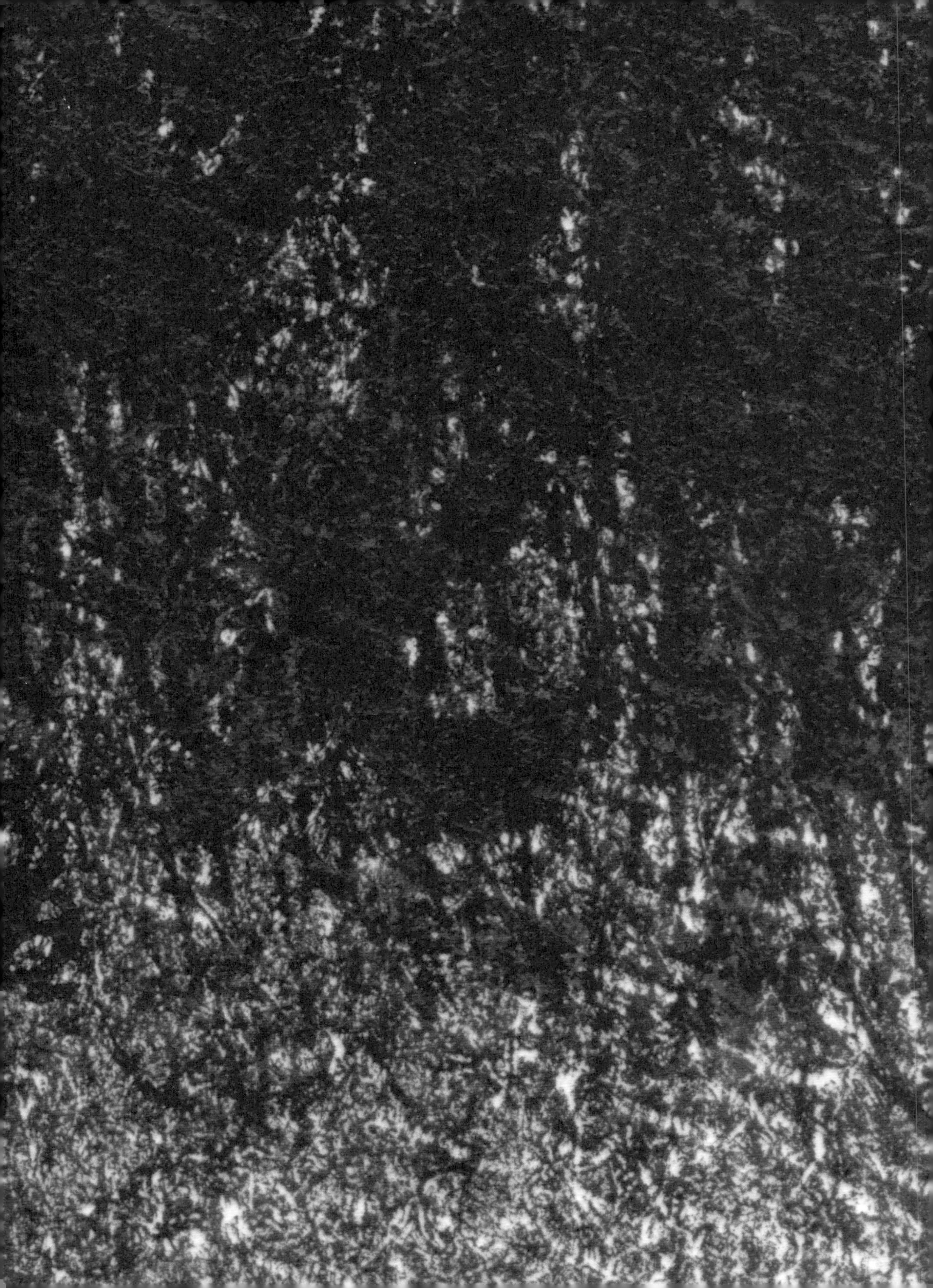

rambler man

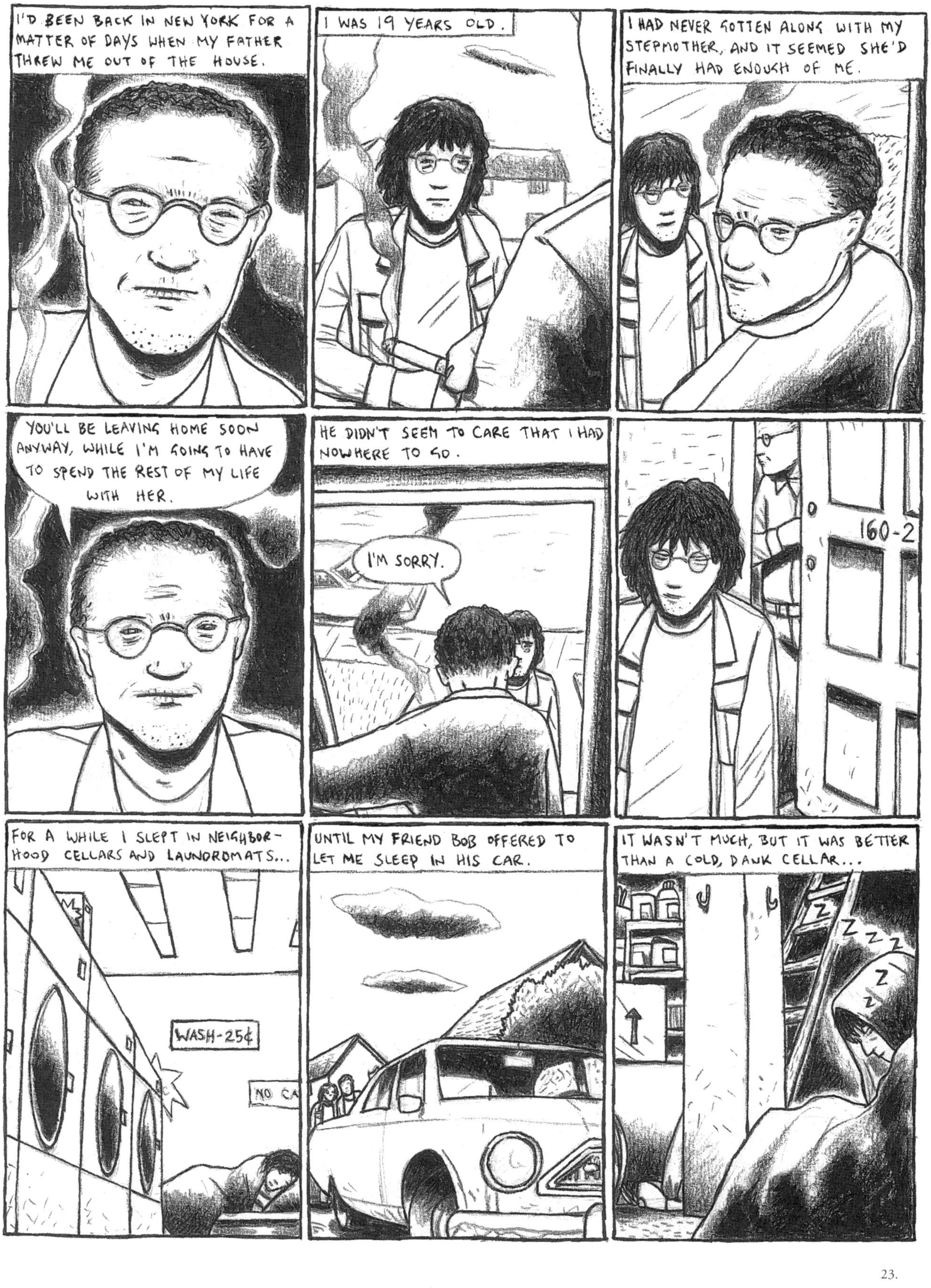
I'D BEEN BACK IN NEW YORK FOR A MATTER OF DAYS WHEN MY FATHER THREW ME OUT OF THE HOUSE.
I WAS 19 YEARS OLD.
I HAD NEVER GOTTEN ALONG WITH MY STEPMOTHER, AND IT SEEMED SHE'D FINALLY HAD ENOUGH OF ME.
YOU'LL BE LEAVING HOME SOON ANYWAY, WHILE I'M GOING TO HAVE TO SPEND THE REST OF MY LIFE WITH HER.
HE DIDN'T SEEM TO CARE THAT I HAD NOWHERE TO GO.
I'M SORRY.
160-2
FOR A WHILE I SLEPT IN NEIGHBOR-HOOD CELLARS AND LAUNDROMATS...
WASH-25¢
NO CA
UNTIL MY FRIEND BOB OFFERED TO LET ME SLEEP IN HIS CAR.
IT WASN'T MUCH, BUT IT WAS BETTER THAN A COLD, DANK CELLAR...
Z Z Z Z Z Z

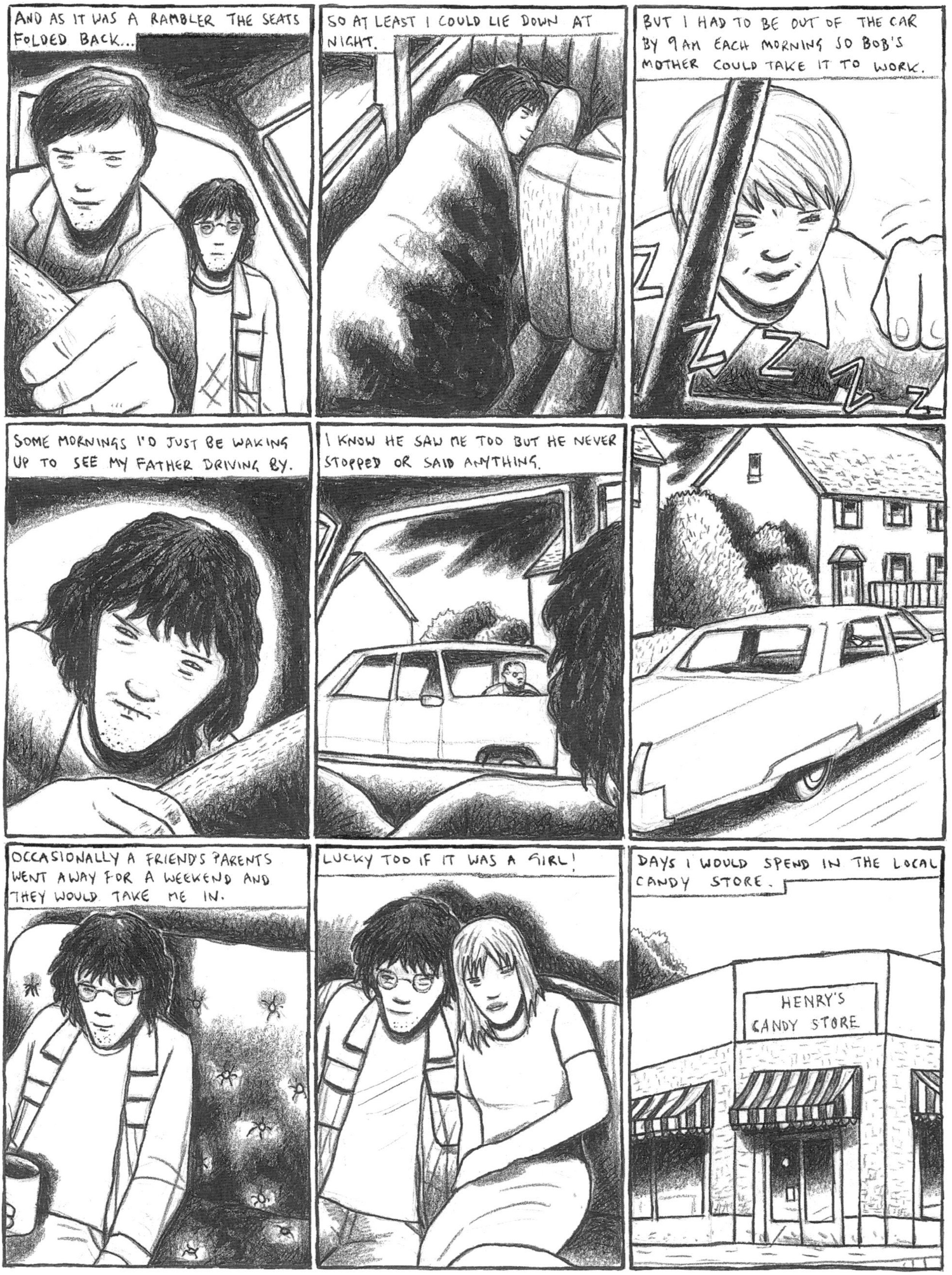
AND AS IT WAS A RAMBLER THE SEATS FOLDED BACK...
SO AT LEAST I COULD LIE DOWN AT NIGHT.
BUT I HAD TO BE OUT OF THE CAR BY 9AM EACH MORNING SO BOB'S MOTHER COULD TAKE IT TO WORK.
Z Z Z Z Z Z
SOME MORNINGS I'D JUST BE WAKING UP TO SEE MY FATHER DRIVING BY.
I KNOW HE SAW ME TOO BUT HE NEVER STOPPED OR SAID ANYTHING.
OCCASIONALLY A FRIEND'S PARENTS WENT AWAY FOR A WEEKEND AND THEY WOULD TAKE ME IN.
LUCKY TOO IF IT WAS A GIRL!
DAYS I WOULD SPEND IN THE LOCAL CANDY STORE.
HENRY'S CANDY STORE

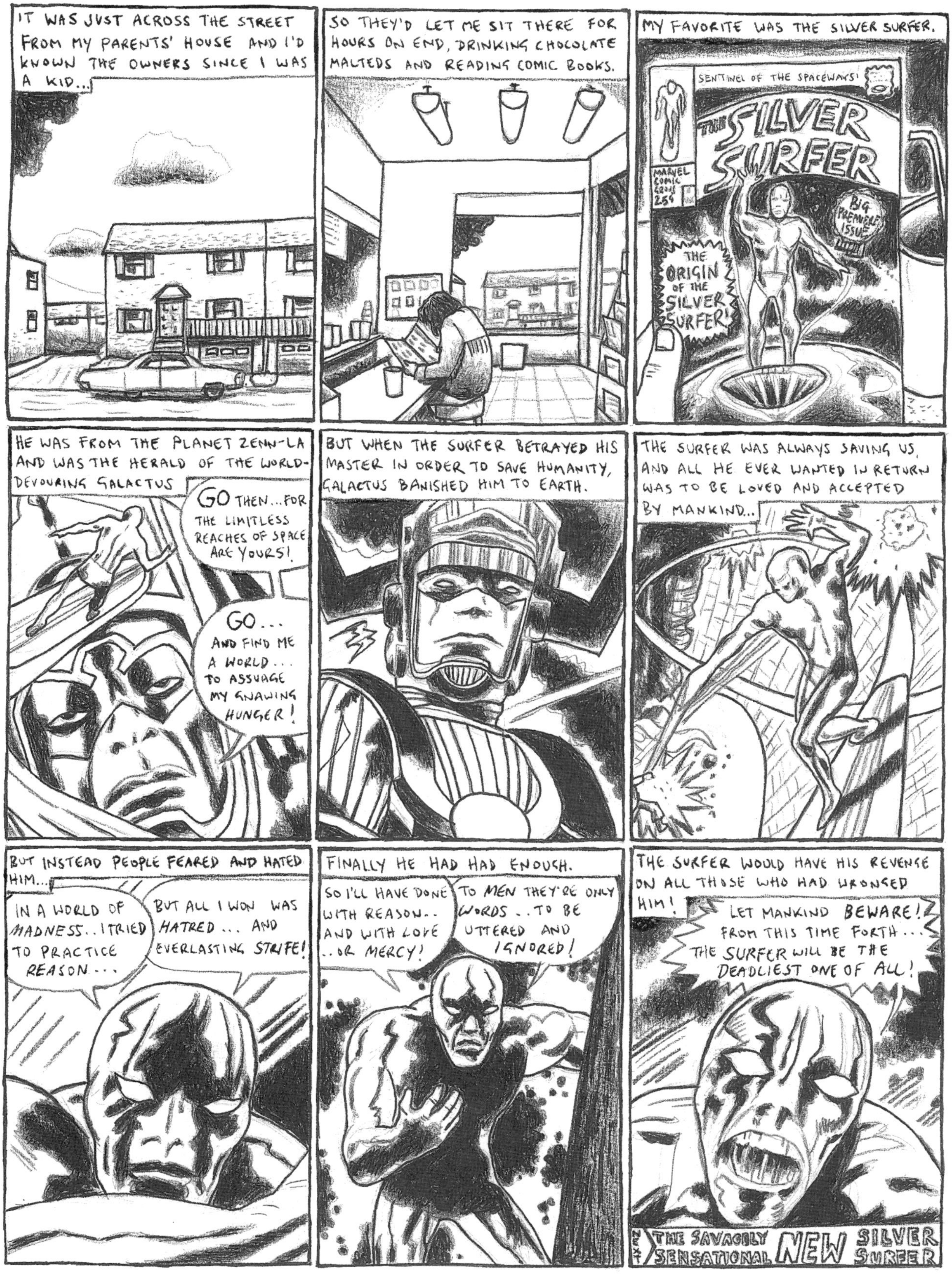
IT WAS JUST ACROSS THE STREET FROM MY PARENTS' HOUSE AND I'D KNOWN THE OWNERS SINCE I WAS A KID...
SO THEY'D LET ME SIT THERE FOR HOURS ON END, DRINKING CHOCOLATE MALTEDS AND READING COMIC BOOKS.
MY FAVORITE WAS THE SILVER SURFER.
SENTINEL OF THE SPACEWAYS!
THE SILVER SURFER
MARVEL COMIC GROUP 25¢
BIG PREMIERE ISSUE
THE ORIGIN OF THE SILVER SURFER!
HE WAS FROM THE PLANET ZENN-LA AND WAS THE HERALD OF THE WORLD-DEVOURING GALACTUS
GO THEN...FOR THE LIMITLESS REACHES OF SPACE ARE YOURS!
GO... AND FIND ME A WORLD... TO ASSUAGE MY GNAWING HUNGER!
BUT WHEN THE SURFER BETRAYED HIS MASTER IN ORDER TO SAVE HUMANITY, GALACTUS BANISHED HIM TO EARTH.
THE SURFER WAS ALWAYS SAVING US, AND ALL HE EVER WANTED IN RETURN WAS TO BE LOVED AND ACCEPTED BY MANKIND...
BUT INSTEAD PEOPLE FEARED AND HATED HIM...
IN A WORLD OF MADNESS.. I TRIED TO PRACTICE REASON...
BUT ALL I WON WAS HATRED ... AND EVERLASTING STRIFE!
FINALLY HE HAD HAD ENOUGH.
SO I'LL HAVE DONE WITH REASON.. AND WITH LOVE ..OR MERCY!
TO MEN THEY'RE ONLY WORDS ..TO BE UTTERED AND IGNORED!
THE SURFER WOULD HAVE HIS REVENGE ON ALL THOSE WHO HAD WRONGED HIM!
LET MANKIND BEWARE! FROM THIS TIME FORTH... THE SURFER WILL BE THE DEADLIEST ONE OF ALL!
NEXT
THE SAVAGELY SENSATIONAL NEW SILVER SURFER

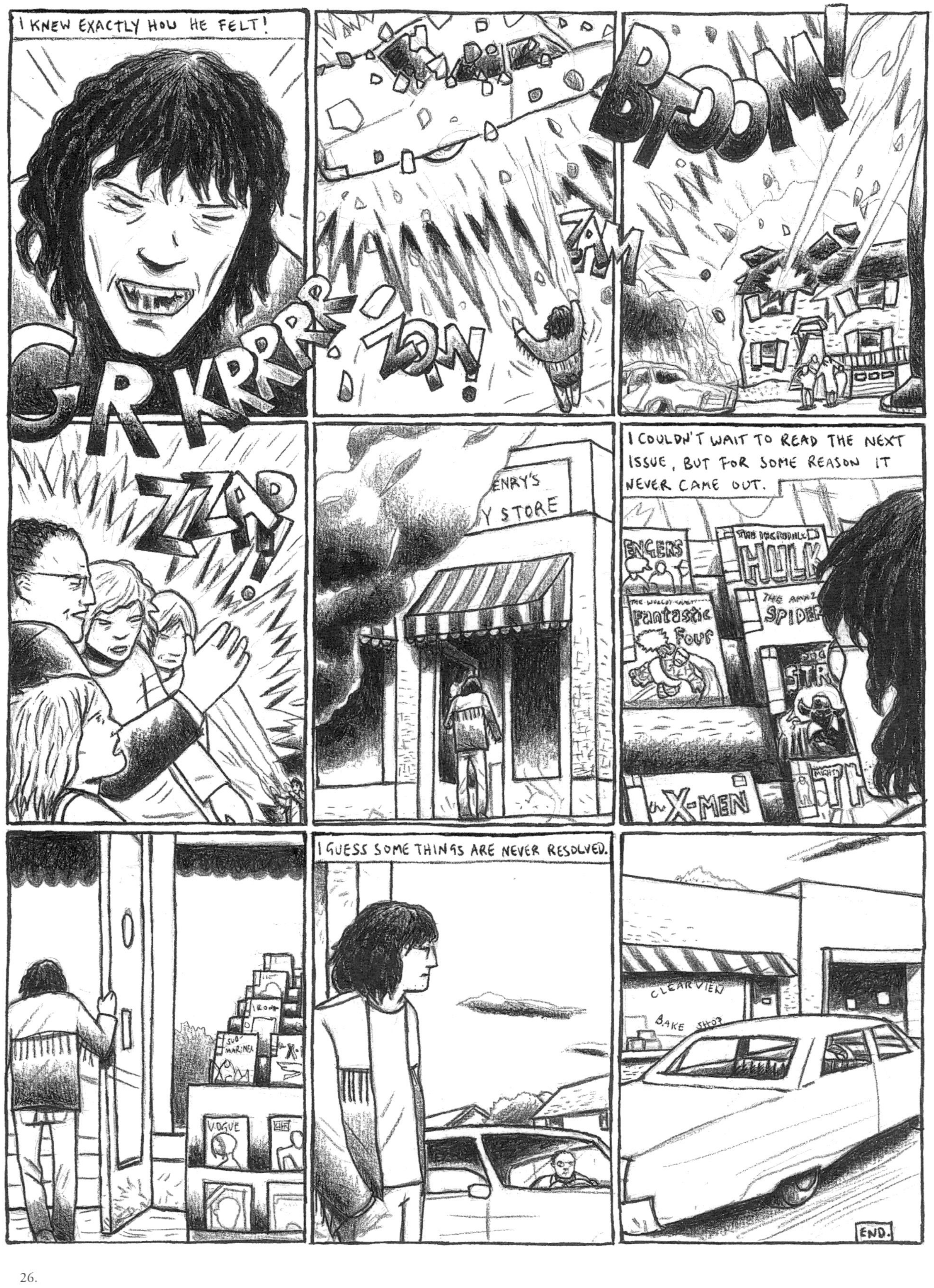

I KNEW EXACTLY HOW HE FELT!
GRKRRR
ZON!
ZAM
BTOOM!
ZZAP!
ENRY'S
Y STORE
I COULDN'T WAIT TO READ THE NEXT ISSUE, BUT FOR SOME REASON IT NEVER CAME OUT.
ENGERS
THE INCREDIBLE HULK
THE AMAZ
SPIDER
Fantastic Four
X-MEN
SUB-MARINER
VOGUE
I GUESS SOME THINGS ARE NEVER RESOLVED.
CLEARVIEW
BAKE SHOP
END.

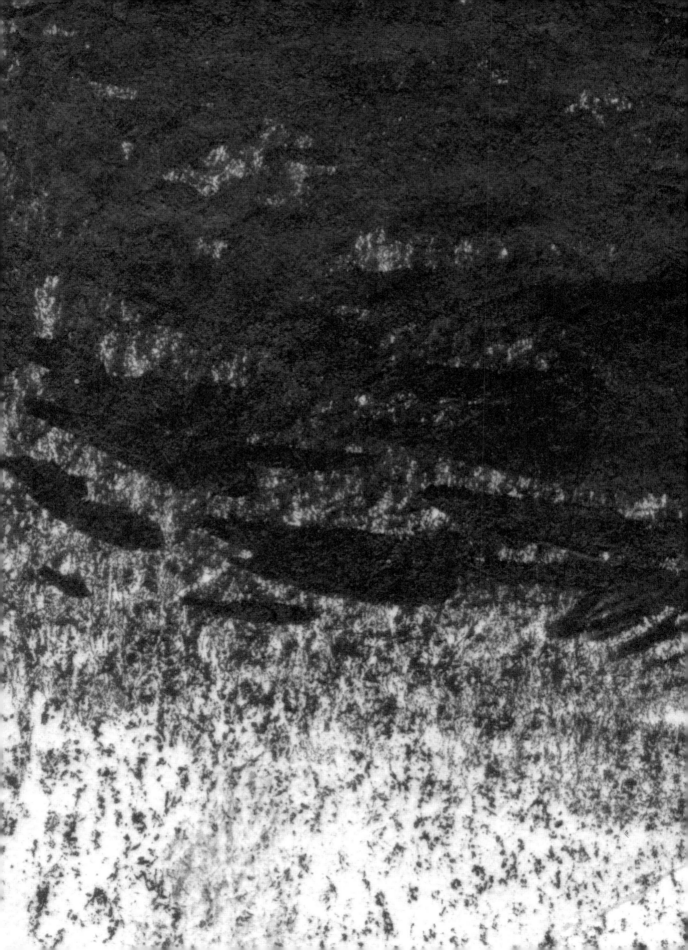

Safe in heaven dead (for Jack Kerouac)

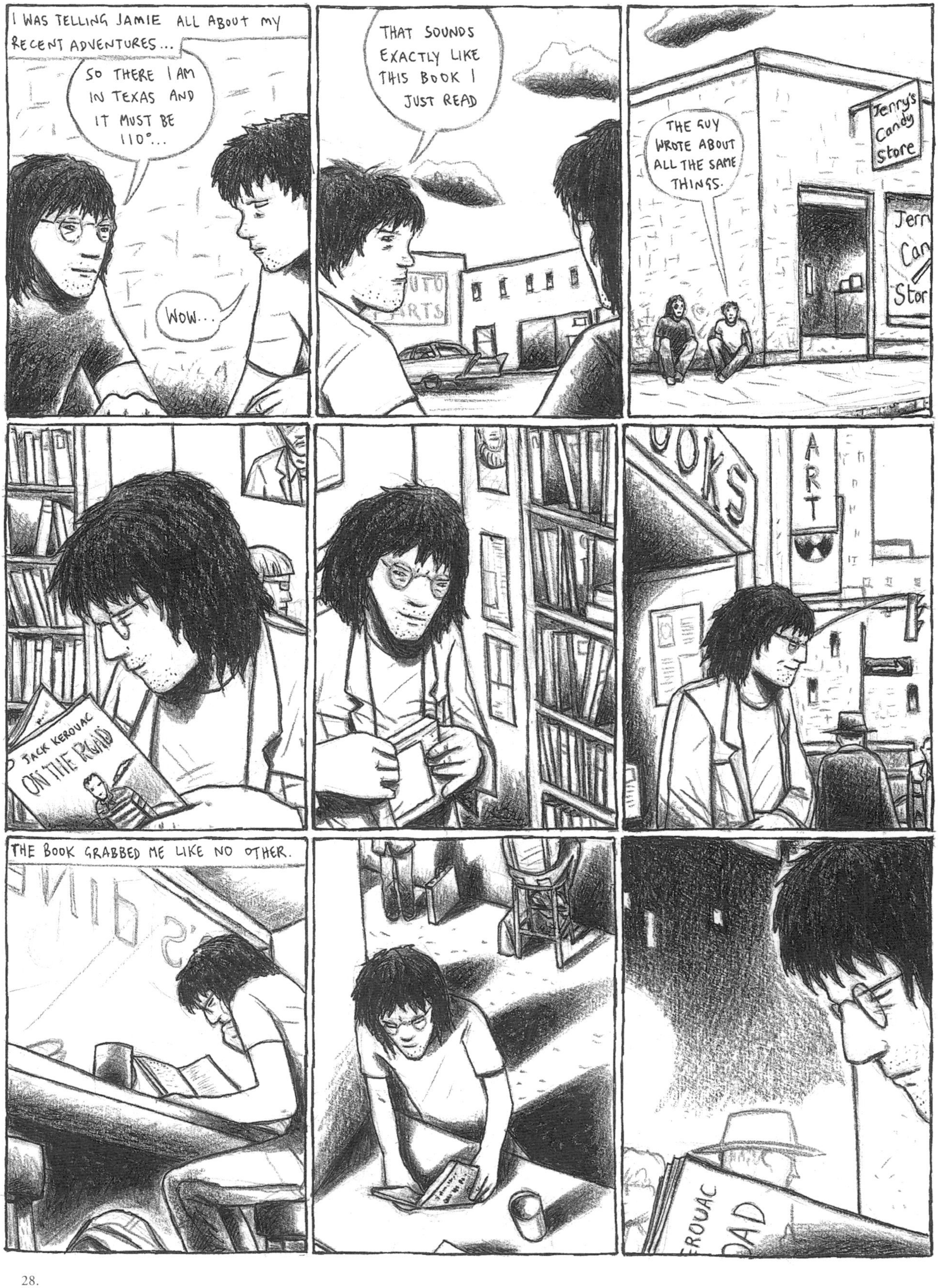
I WAS TELLING JAMIE ALL ABOUT MY RECENT ADVENTURES...
SO THERE I AM IN TEXAS AND IT MUST BE 110°...
WOW...
THAT SOUNDS EXACTLY LIKE THIS BOOK I JUST READ
Jerry's Candy Store
THE GUY WROTE ABOUT ALL THE SAME THINGS.
JACK KEROUAC
ON THE ROAD
ART
THE BOOK GRABBED ME LIKE NO OTHER.

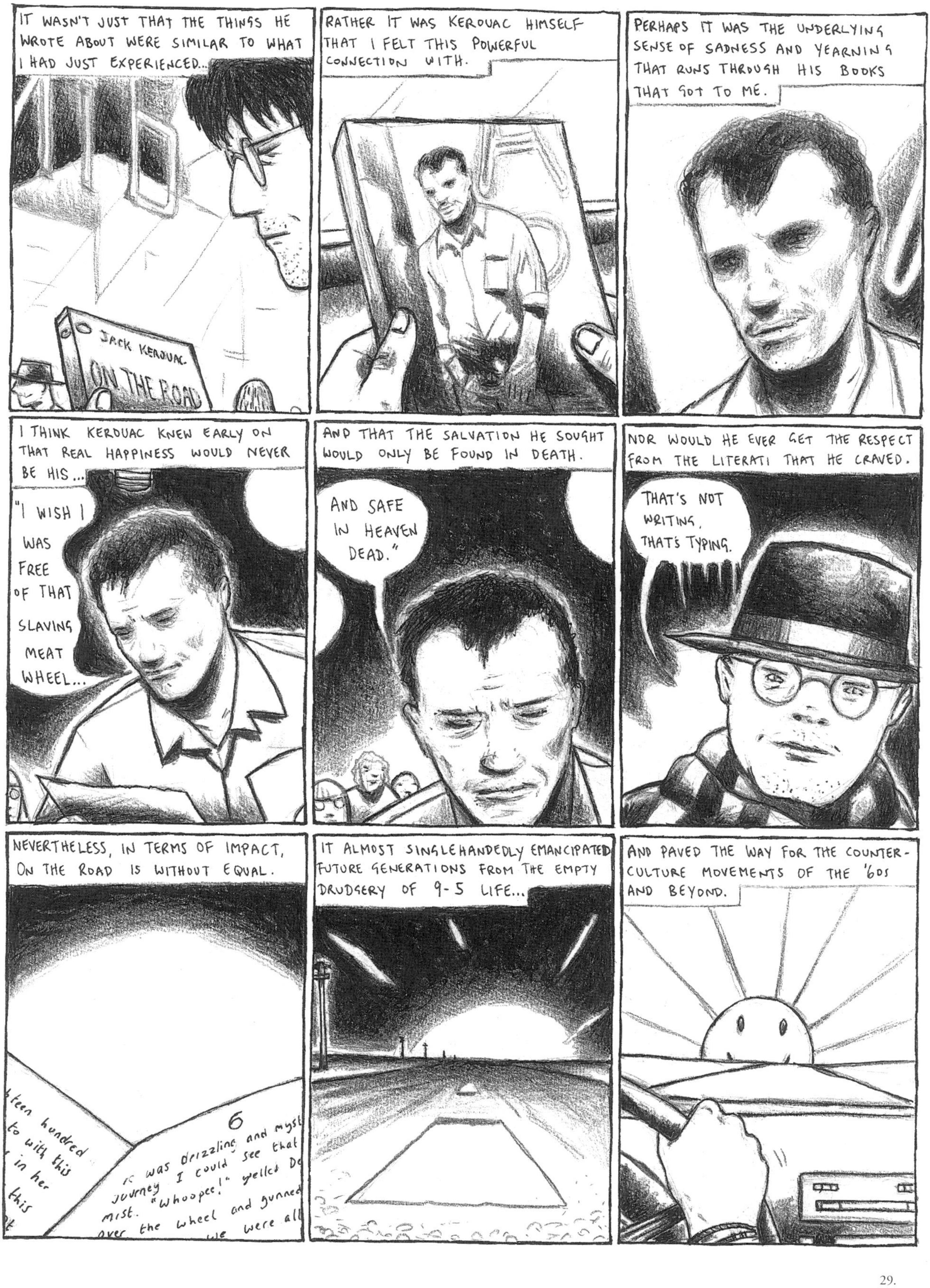

IT WASN'T JUST THAT THE THINGS HE WROTE ABOUT WERE SIMILAR TO WHAT I HAD JUST EXPERIENCED...
JACK KEROUAC
ON THE ROAD
RATHER IT WAS KEROUAC HIMSELF THAT I FELT THIS POWERFUL CONNECTION WITH.
PERHAPS IT WAS THE UNDERLYING SENSE OF SADNESS AND YEARNING THAT RUNS THROUGH HIS BOOKS THAT GOT TO ME.
I THINK KEROUAC KNEW EARLY ON THAT REAL HAPPINESS WOULD NEVER BE HIS...
"I WISH I WAS FREE OF THAT SLAVING MEAT WHEEL...
AND THAT THE SALVATION HE SOUGHT WOULD ONLY BE FOUND IN DEATH.
AND SAFE IN HEAVEN DEAD."
NOR WOULD HE EVER GET THE RESPECT FROM THE LITERATI THAT HE CRAVED.
THAT'S NOT WRITING, THAT'S TYPING.
NEVERTHELESS, IN TERMS OF IMPACT, ON THE ROAD IS WITHOUT EQUAL.
IT ALMOST SINGLEHANDEDLY EMANCIPATED FUTURE GENERATIONS FROM THE EMPTY DRUDGERY OF 9-5 LIFE...
AND PAVED THE WAY FOR THE COUNTER-CULTURE MOVEMENTS OF THE '60S AND BEYOND.

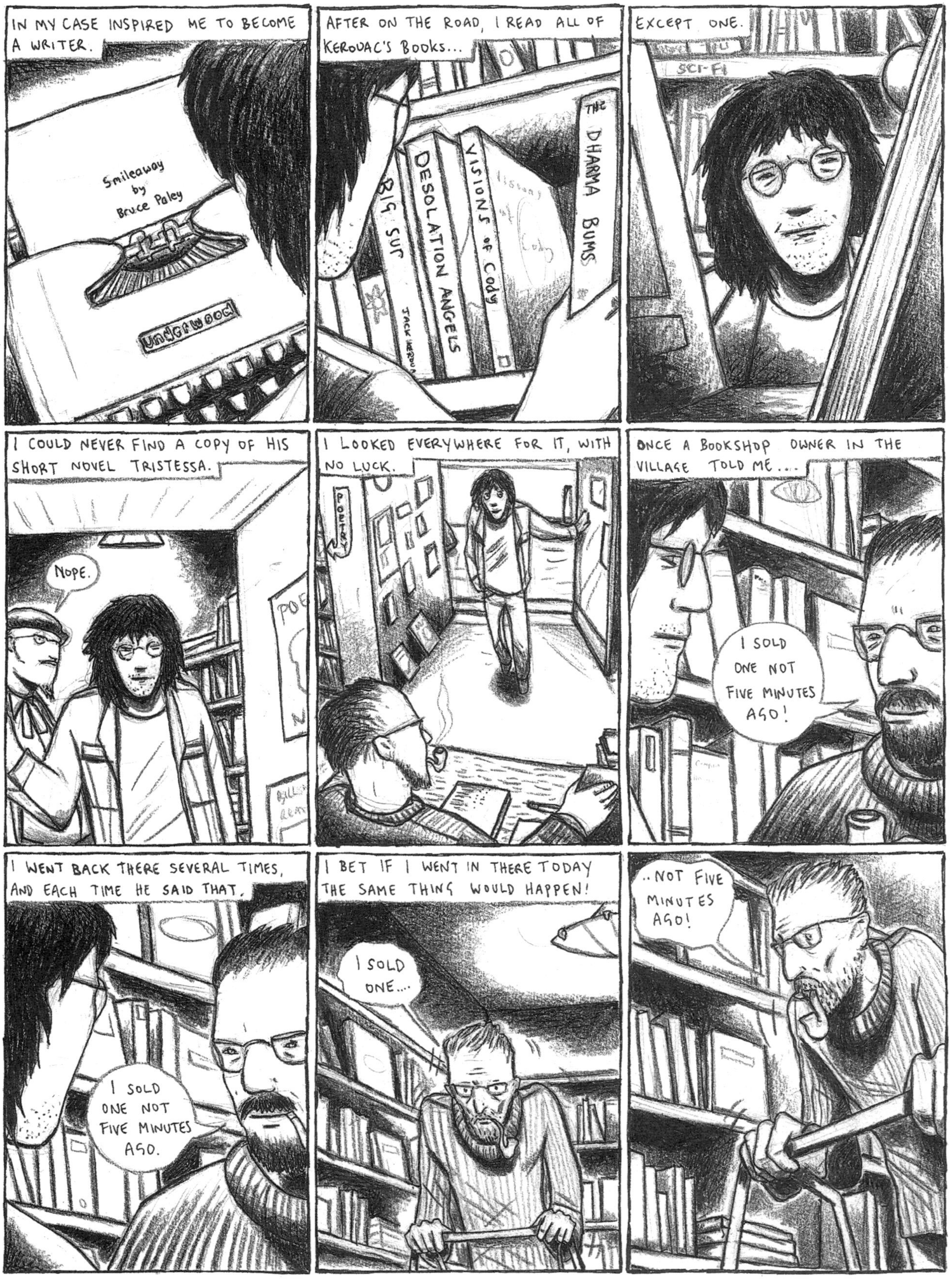
IN MY CASE INSPIRED ME TO BECOME A WRITER.
Smileaway by Bruce Paley
Underwood
AFTER ON THE ROAD, I READ ALL OF KEROUAC'S BOOKS...
THE DHARMA BUMS
VISIONS OF CODY
DESOLATION ANGELS
BIG SUR
JACK KEROUAC
EXCEPT ONE.
SCI-FI
I COULD NEVER FIND A COPY OF HIS SHORT NOVEL TRISTESSA.
NOPE.
I LOOKED EVERYWHERE FOR IT, WITH NO LUCK.
POETRY
ONCE A BOOKSHOP OWNER IN THE VILLAGE TOLD ME....
I SOLD ONE NOT FIVE MINUTES AGO!
I WENT BACK THERE SEVERAL TIMES, AND EACH TIME HE SAID THAT.
I SOLD ONE NOT FIVE MINUTES AGO.
I BET IF I WENT IN THERE TODAY THE SAME THING WOULD HAPPEN!
I SOLD ONE....
..NOT FIVE MINUTES AGO!

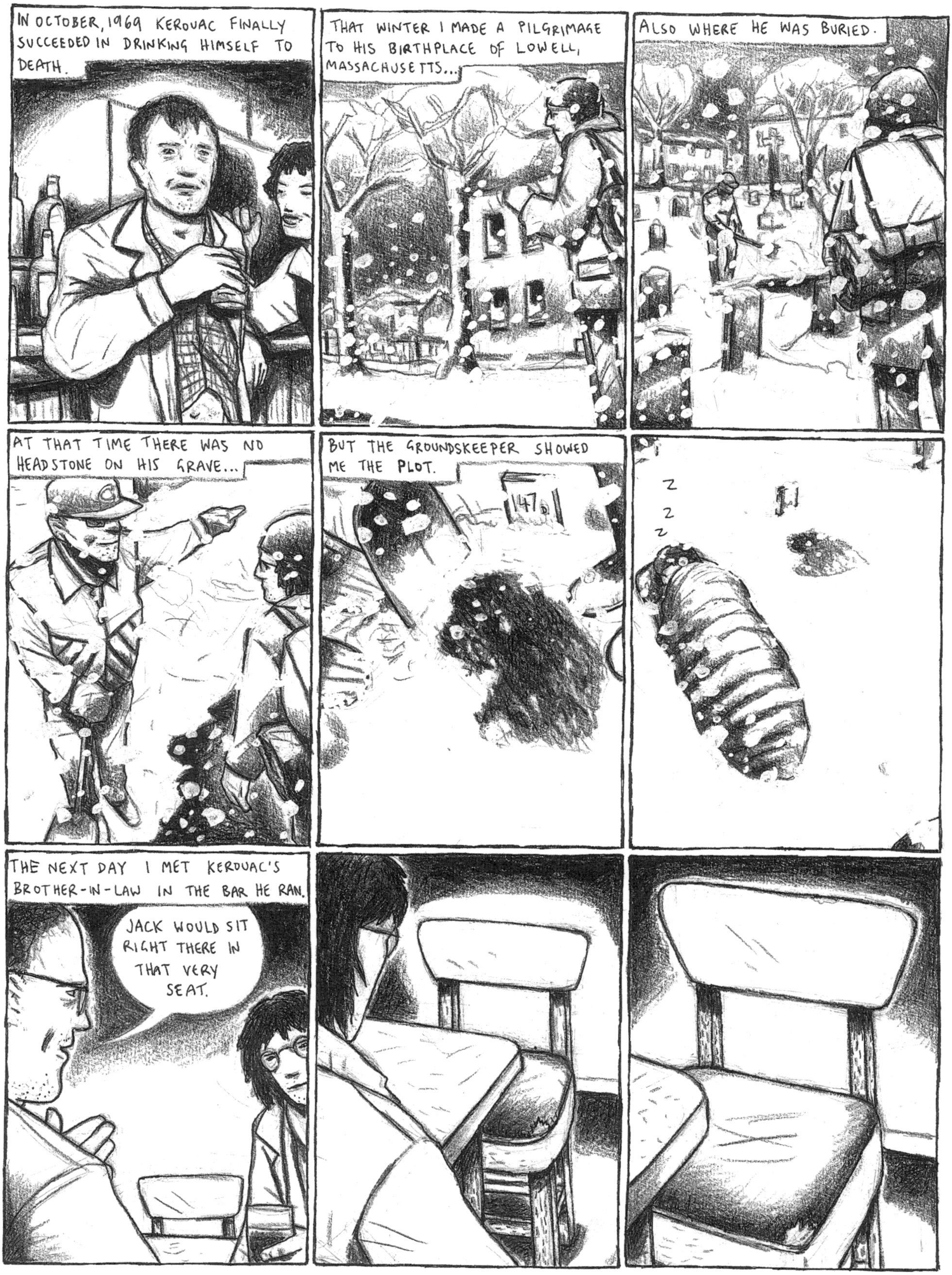
IN OCTOBER, 1969 KEROUAC FINALLY SUCCEEDED IN DRINKING HIMSELF TO DEATH.
THAT WINTER I MADE A PILGRIMAGE TO HIS BIRTHPLACE OF LOWELL, MASSACHUSETTS...
ALSO WHERE HE WAS BURIED.
AT THAT TIME THERE WAS NO HEADSTONE ON HIS GRAVE...
BUT THE GROUNDSKEEPER SHOWED ME THE PLOT.
147 D
Z Z Z
THE NEXT DAY I MET KEROUAC'S BROTHER-IN-LAW IN THE BAR HE RAN.
JACK WOULD SIT RIGHT THERE IN THAT VERY SEAT.

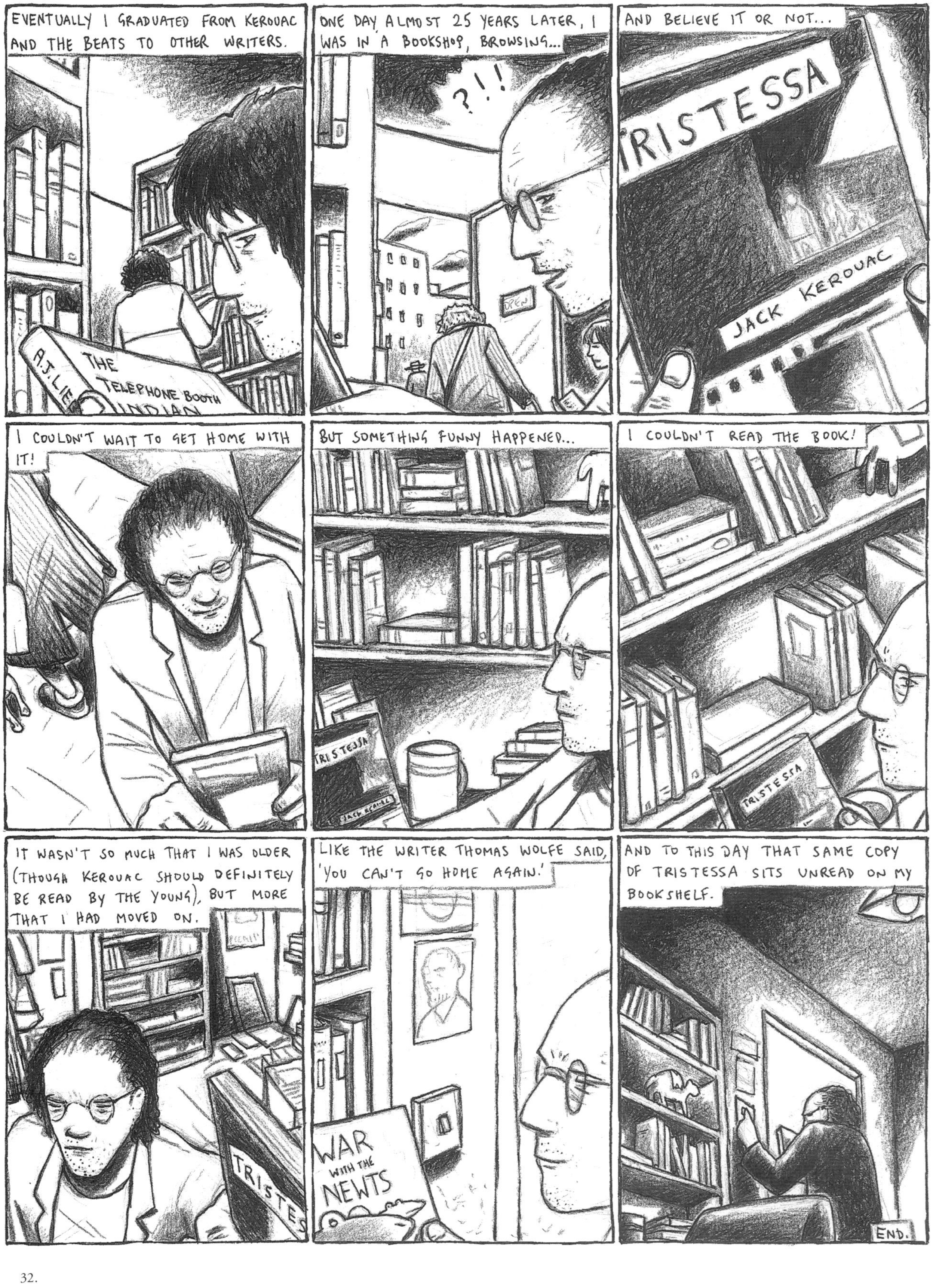

EVENTUALLY I GRADUATED FROM KEROUAC AND THE BEATS TO OTHER WRITERS.
A.J. LIE
THE TELEPHONE BOOTH
ONE DAY ALMOST 25 YEARS LATER, I WAS IN A BOOKSHOP, BROWSING...
?!!
OPEN
AND BELIEVE IT OR NOT...
TRISTESSA
JACK KEROUAC
I COULDN'T WAIT TO GET HOME WITH IT!
BUT SOMETHING FUNNY HAPPENED...
TRISTESSA
I COULDN'T READ THE BOOK!
TRISTESSA
IT WASN'T SO MUCH THAT I WAS OLDER (THOUGH KEROUAC SHOULD DEFINITELY BE READ BY THE YOUNG), BUT MORE THAT I HAD MOVED ON.
TRISTES
LIKE THE WRITER THOMAS WOLFE SAID, 'YOU CAN'T GO HOME AGAIN.'
WAR WITH THE NEWTS
AND TO THIS DAY THAT SAME COPY OF TRISTESSA SITS UNREAD ON MY BOOKSHELF.
END.

the draft

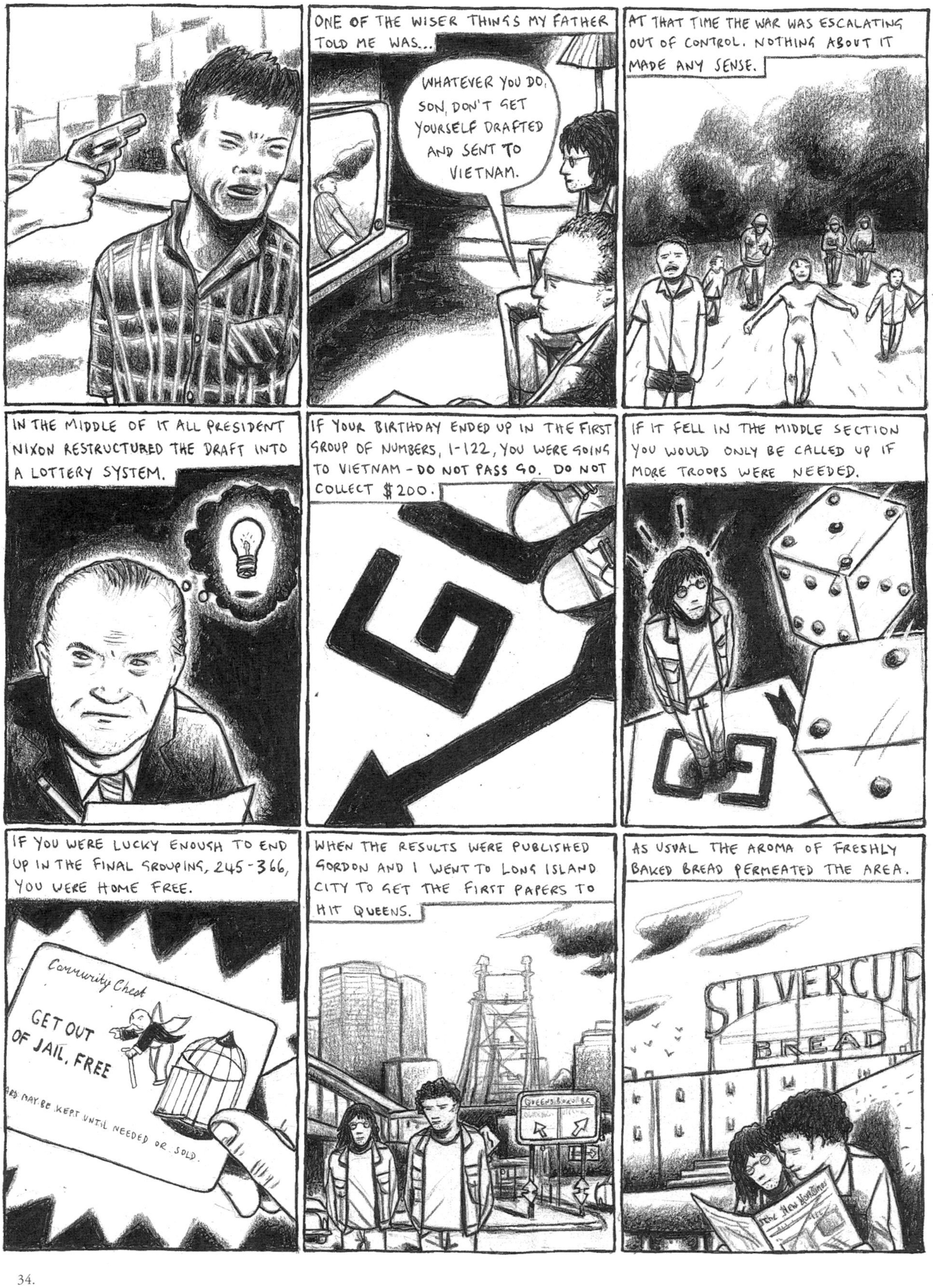
ONE OF THE WISER THINGS MY FATHER TOLD ME WAS...
WHATEVER YOU DO, SON, DON'T GET YOURSELF DRAFTED AND SENT TO VIETNAM.
AT THAT TIME THE WAR WAS ESCALATING OUT OF CONTROL. NOTHING ABOUT IT MADE ANY SENSE.
IN THE MIDDLE OF IT ALL PRESIDENT NIXON RESTRUCTURED THE DRAFT INTO A LOTTERY SYSTEM.
IF YOUR BIRTHDAY ENDED UP IN THE FIRST GROUP OF NUMBERS, 1-122, YOU WERE GOING TO VIETNAM - DO NOT PASS GO. DO NOT COLLECT $200.
GO
IF IT FELL IN THE MIDDLE SECTION YOU WOULD ONLY BE CALLED UP IF MORE TROOPS WERE NEEDED.
GO
IF YOU WERE LUCKY ENOUGH TO END UP IN THE FINAL GROUPING, 245-366, YOU WERE HOME FREE.
Community Chest
GET OUT OF JAIL, FREE
MAY BE KEPT UNTIL NEEDED OR SOLD.
WHEN THE RESULTS WERE PUBLISHED GORDON AND I WENT TO LONG ISLAND CITY TO GET THE FIRST PAPERS TO HIT QUEENS.
QUEENS BORO BR
AS USUAL THE AROMA OF FRESHLY BAKED BREAD PERMEATED THE AREA.
SILVERCUP
BREAD
The New York Times

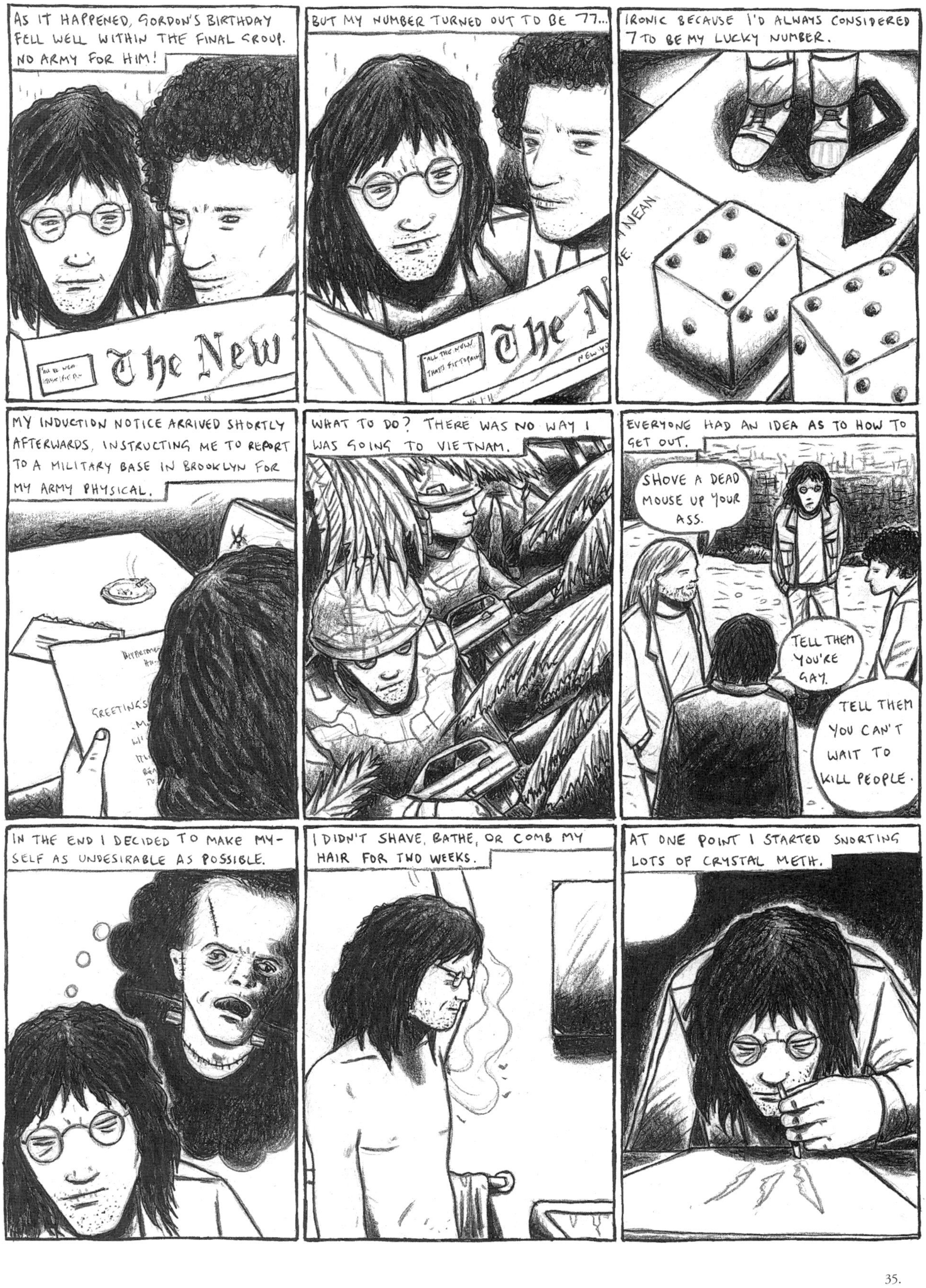

AS IT HAPPENED, GORDON'S BIRTHDAY FELL WELL WITHIN THE FINAL GROUP. NO ARMY FOR HIM!
The New
BUT MY NUMBER TURNED OUT TO BE 77...
The N
"ALL THE NEWS THAT'S FIT TO PRINT"
IRONIC BECAUSE I'D ALWAYS CONSIDERED 7 TO BE MY LUCKY NUMBER.
MY INDUCTION NOTICE ARRIVED SHORTLY AFTERWARDS, INSTRUCTING ME TO REPORT TO A MILITARY BASE IN BROOKLYN FOR MY ARMY PHYSICAL.
GREETINGS
WHAT TO DO? THERE WAS NO WAY I WAS GOING TO VIETNAM.
EVERYONE HAD AN IDEA AS TO HOW TO GET OUT.
SHOVE A DEAD MOUSE UP YOUR ASS.
TELL THEM YOU'RE GAY.
TELL THEM YOU CAN'T WAIT TO KILL PEOPLE.
IN THE END I DECIDED TO MAKE MYSELF AS UNDESIRABLE AS POSSIBLE.
I DIDN'T SHAVE, BATHE, OR COMB MY HAIR FOR TWO WEEKS.
AT ONE POINT I STARTED SNORTING LOTS OF CRYSTAL METH.

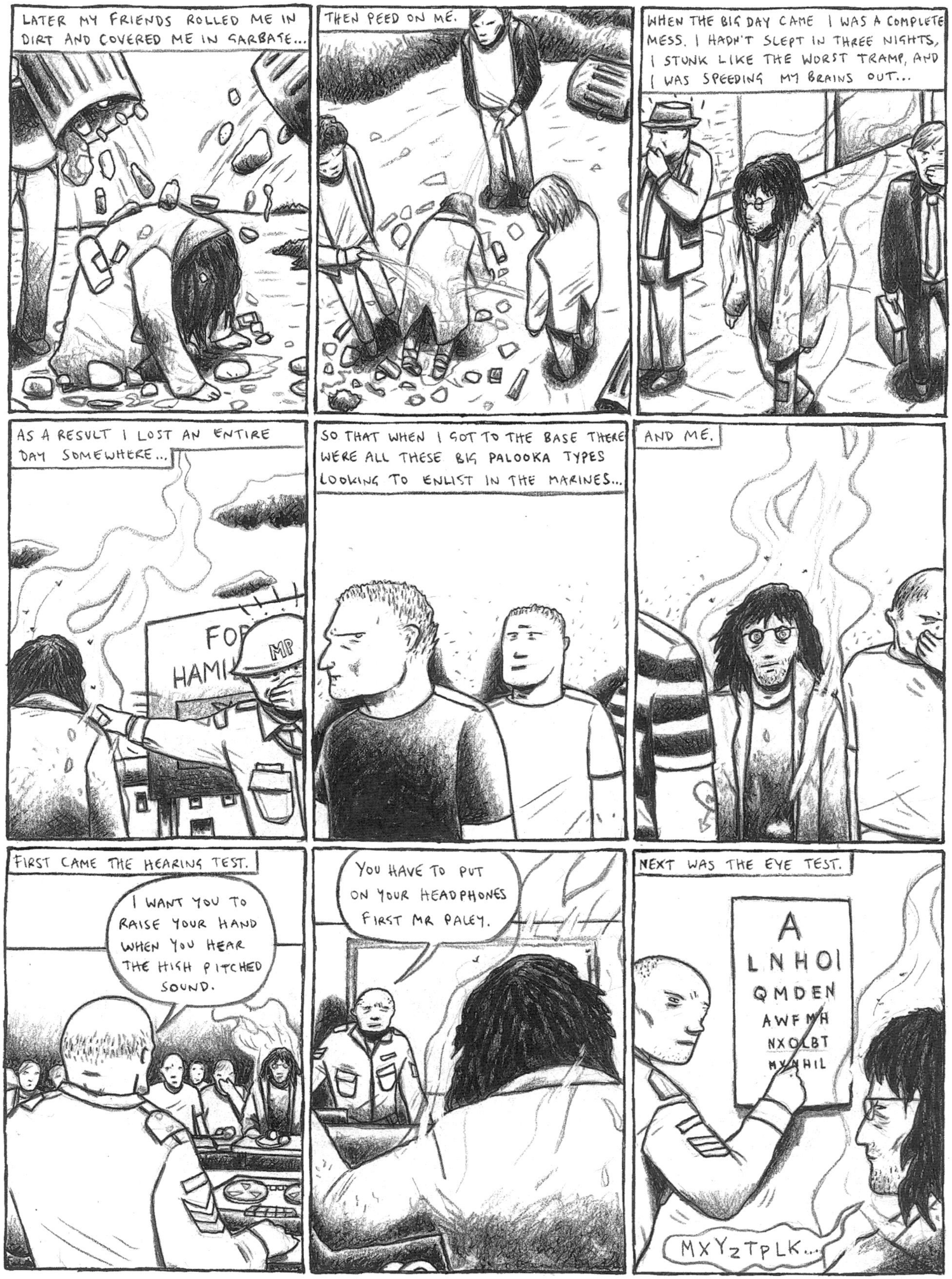
LATER MY FRIENDS ROLLED ME IN DIRT AND COVERED ME IN GARBAGE...
THEN PEED ON ME.
WHEN THE BIG DAY CAME I WAS A COMPLETE MESS. I HADN'T SLEPT IN THREE NIGHTS, I STUNK LIKE THE WORST TRAMP, AND I WAS SPEEDING MY BRAINS OUT...
AS A RESULT I LOST AN ENTIRE DAY SOMEWHERE...
MP
SO THAT WHEN I GOT TO THE BASE THERE WERE ALL THESE BIG PALOOKA TYPES LOOKING TO ENLIST IN THE MARINES...
AND ME.
FIRST CAME THE HEARING TEST.
I WANT YOU TO RAISE YOUR HAND WHEN YOU HEAR THE HIGH PITCHED SOUND.
YOU HAVE TO PUT ON YOUR HEADPHONES FIRST MR PALEY.
NEXT WAS THE EYE TEST.
A
LNHOI
QMDEN
NXOLBT
MXYZTPLK...

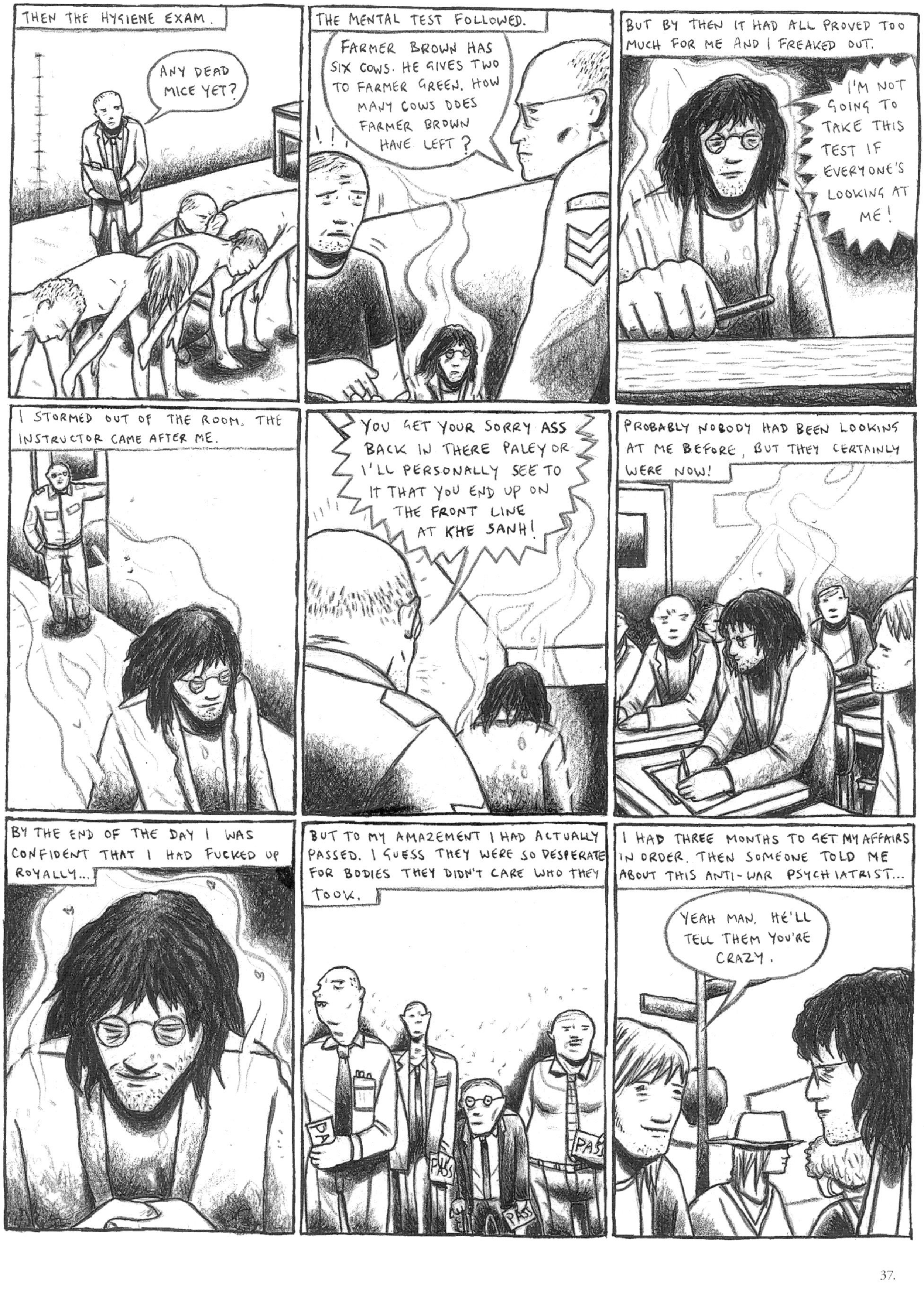
THEN THE HYGIENE EXAM.
ANY DEAD MICE YET?
THE MENTAL TEST FOLLOWED.
FARMER BROWN HAS SIX COWS. HE GIVES TWO TO FARMER GREEN. HOW MANY COWS DOES FARMER BROWN HAVE LEFT?
!!!
BUT BY THEN IT HAD ALL PROVED TOO MUCH FOR ME AND I FREAKED OUT.
I'M NOT GOING TO TAKE THIS TEST IF EVERYONE'S LOOKING AT ME!
I STORMED OUT OF THE ROOM. THE INSTRUCTOR CAME AFTER ME.
YOU GET YOUR SORRY ASS BACK IN THERE PALEY OR I'LL PERSONALLY SEE TO IT THAT YOU END UP ON THE FRONT LINE AT KHE SANH!
PROBABLY NOBODY HAD BEEN LOOKING AT ME BEFORE, BUT THEY CERTAINLY WERE NOW!
BY THE END OF THE DAY I WAS CONFIDENT THAT I HAD FUCKED UP ROYALLY...
BUT TO MY AMAZEMENT I HAD ACTUALLY PASSED. I GUESS THEY WERE SO DESPERATE FOR BODIES THEY DIDN'T CARE WHO THEY TOOK.
PASS
I HAD THREE MONTHS TO GET MY AFFAIRS IN ORDER. THEN SOMEONE TOLD ME ABOUT THIS ANTI-WAR PSYCHIATRIST...
YEAH MAN, HE'LL TELL THEM YOU'RE CRAZY.

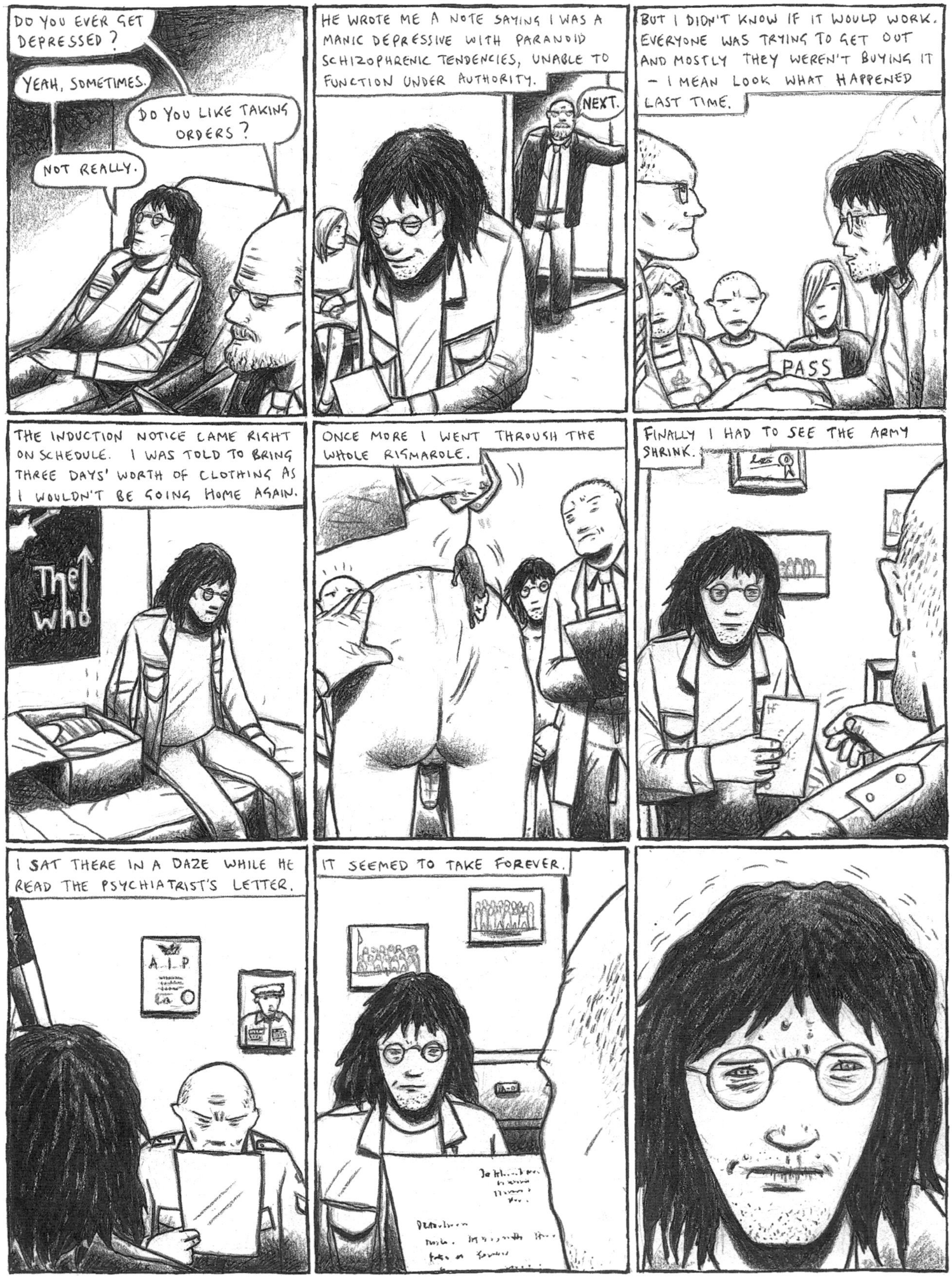
DO YOU EVER GET DEPRESSED?
YEAH, SOMETIMES.
DO YOU LIKE TAKING ORDERS?
NOT REALLY.
HE WROTE ME A NOTE SAYING I WAS A MANIC DEPRESSIVE WITH PARANOID SCHIZOPHRENIC TENDENCIES, UNABLE TO FUNCTION UNDER AUTHORITY.
NEXT.
BUT I DIDN'T KNOW IF IT WOULD WORK. EVERYONE WAS TRYING TO GET OUT AND MOSTLY THEY WEREN'T BUYING IT – I MEAN LOOK WHAT HAPPENED LAST TIME.
PASS
THE INDUCTION NOTICE CAME RIGHT ON SCHEDULE. I WAS TOLD TO BRING THREE DAYS' WORTH OF CLOTHING AS I WOULDN'T BE GOING HOME AGAIN.
The who
ONCE MORE I WENT THROUGH THE WHOLE RIGMAROLE.
FINALLY I HAD TO SEE THE ARMY SHRINK.
I SAT THERE IN A DAZE WHILE HE READ THE PSYCHIATRIST'S LETTER.
A.I.P.
IT SEEMED TO TAKE FOREVER.

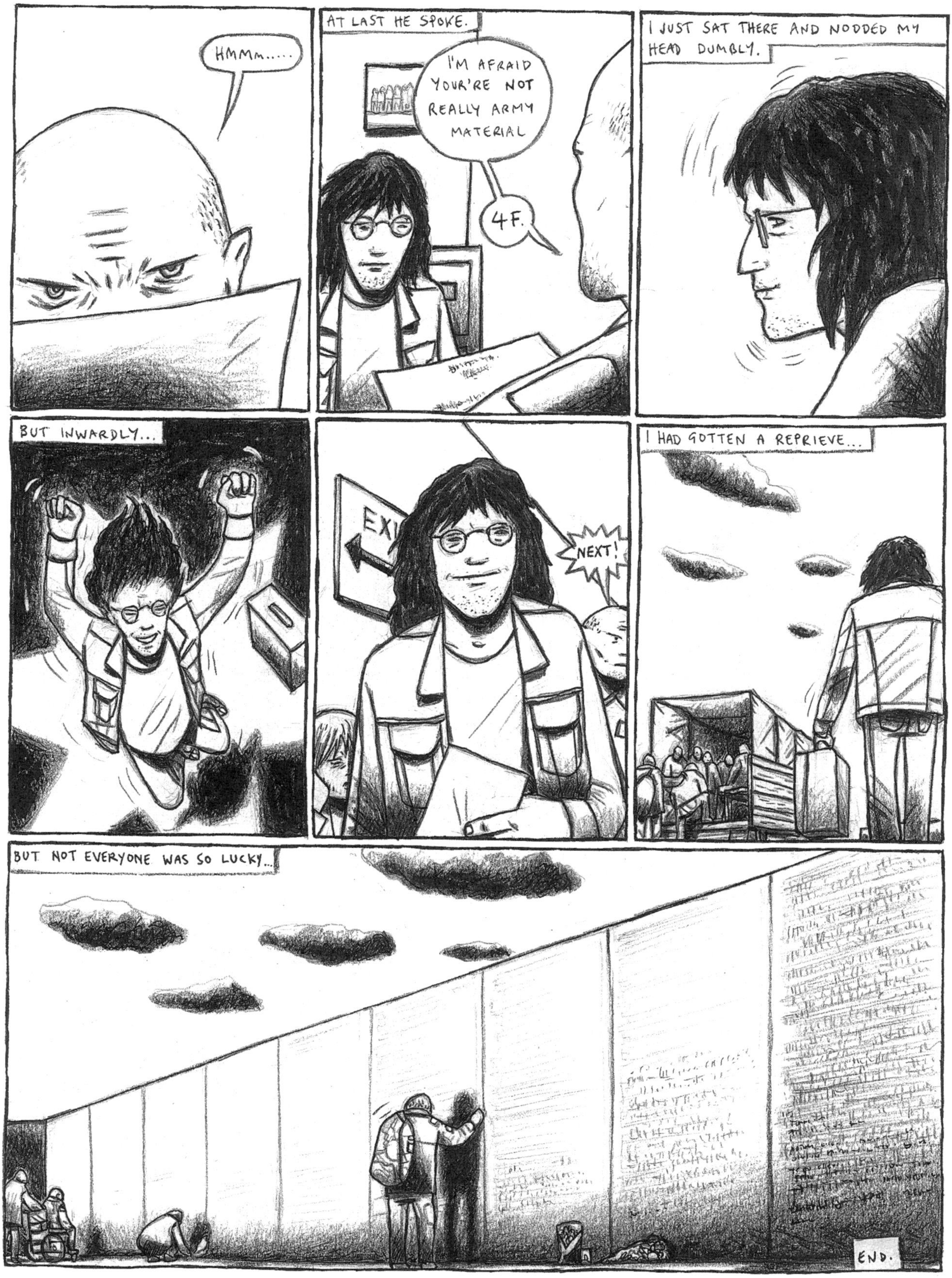
HMMM.....
AT LAST HE SPOKE.
I'M AFRAID YOUR'RE NOT REALLY ARMY MATERIAL
4F.
I JUST SAT THERE AND NODDED MY HEAD DUMBLY.
BUT INWARDLY...
EXI
NEXT!
I HAD GOTTEN A REPRIEVE...
BUT NOT EVERYONE WAS SO LUCKY...
END.

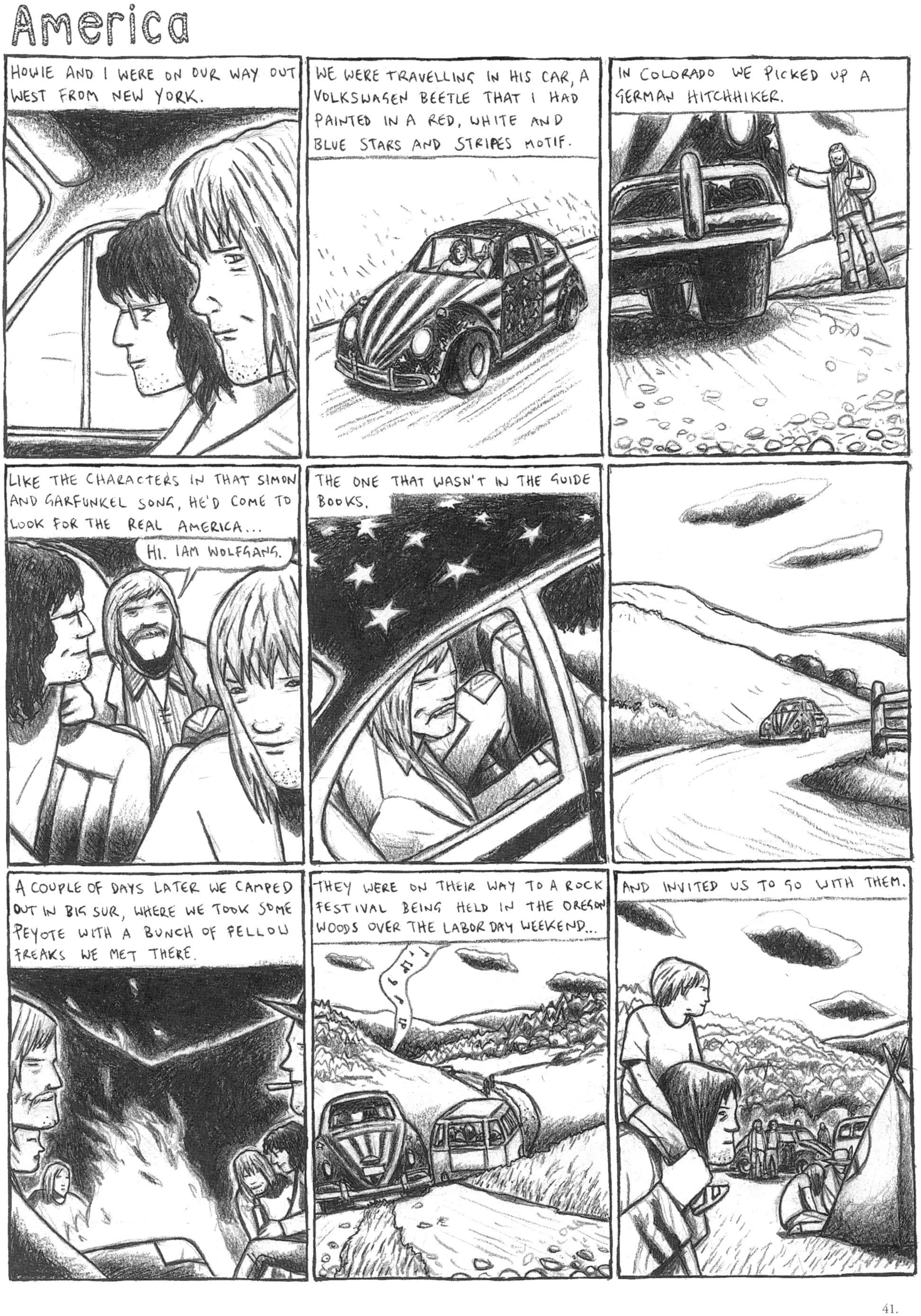
America
HOWIE AND I WERE ON OUR WAY OUT WEST FROM NEW YORK.
WE WERE TRAVELLING IN HIS CAR, A VOLKSWAGEN BEETLE THAT I HAD PAINTED IN A RED, WHITE AND BLUE STARS AND STRIPES MOTIF.
IN COLORADO WE PICKED UP A GERMAN HITCHHIKER.
LIKE THE CHARACTERS IN THAT SIMON AND GARFUNKEL SONG, HE'D COME TO LOOK FOR THE REAL AMERICA...
HI. I AM WOLFGANG.
THE ONE THAT WASN'T IN THE GUIDE BOOKS.
A COUPLE OF DAYS LATER WE CAMPED OUT IN BIG SUR, WHERE WE TOOK SOME PEYOTE WITH A BUNCH OF FELLOW FREAKS WE MET THERE.
THEY WERE ON THEIR WAY TO A ROCK FESTIVAL BEING HELD IN THE OREGON WOODS OVER THE LABOR DAY WEEKEND...
AND INVITED US TO GO WITH THEM.

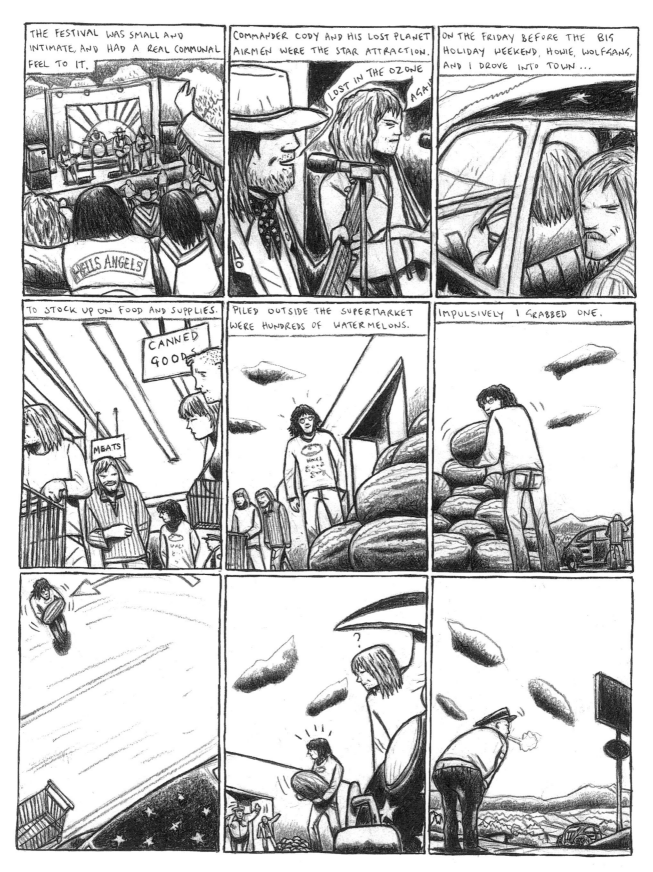

THE FESTIVAL WAS SMALL AND INTIMATE, AND HAD A REAL COMMUNAL FEEL TO IT.

COMMANDER CODY AND HIS LOST PLANET AIRMEN WERE THE STAR ATTRACTION.

LOST IN THE OZONE AGAIN

ON THE FRIDAY BEFORE THE BIG HOLIDAY WEEKEND, HOWIE, WOLFGANG, AND I DROVE INTO TOWN...

TO STOCK UP ON FOOD AND SUPPLIES.

CANNED GOODS

MEATS

PILED OUTSIDE THE SUPERMARKET WERE HUNDREDS OF WATERMELONS.

IMPULSIVELY I GRABBED ONE.

?

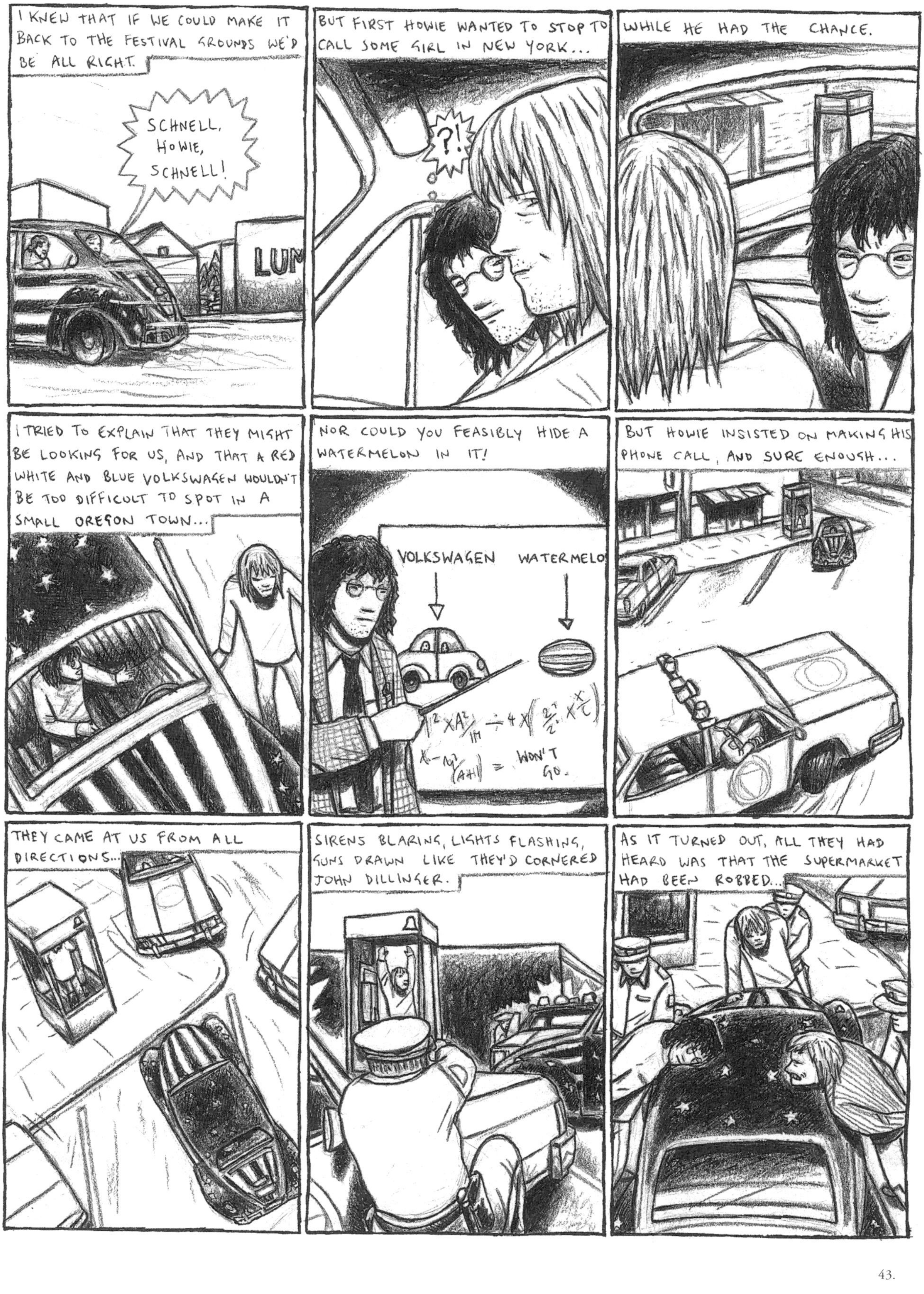
I KNEW THAT IF WE COULD MAKE IT BACK TO THE FESTIVAL GROUNDS WE'D BE ALL RIGHT.
SCHNELL, HOWIE, SCHNELL!
LUM
BUT FIRST HOWIE WANTED TO STOP TO CALL SOME GIRL IN NEW YORK...
?!
WHILE HE HAD THE CHANCE.
I TRIED TO EXPLAIN THAT THEY MIGHT BE LOOKING FOR US, AND THAT A RED WHITE AND BLUE VOLKSWAGEN WOULDN'T BE TOO DIFFICULT TO SPOT IN A SMALL OREGON TOWN...
NOR COULD YOU FEASIBLY HIDE A WATERMELON IN IT!
VOLKSWAGEN
WATERMELO
WON'T GO.
BUT HOWIE INSISTED ON MAKING HIS PHONE CALL, AND SURE ENOUGH...
THEY CAME AT US FROM ALL DIRECTIONS...
SIRENS BLARING, LIGHTS FLASHING, GUNS DRAWN LIKE THEY'D CORNERED JOHN DILLINGER.
AS IT TURNED OUT, ALL THEY HAD HEARD WAS THAT THE SUPERMARKET HAD BEEN ROBBED...

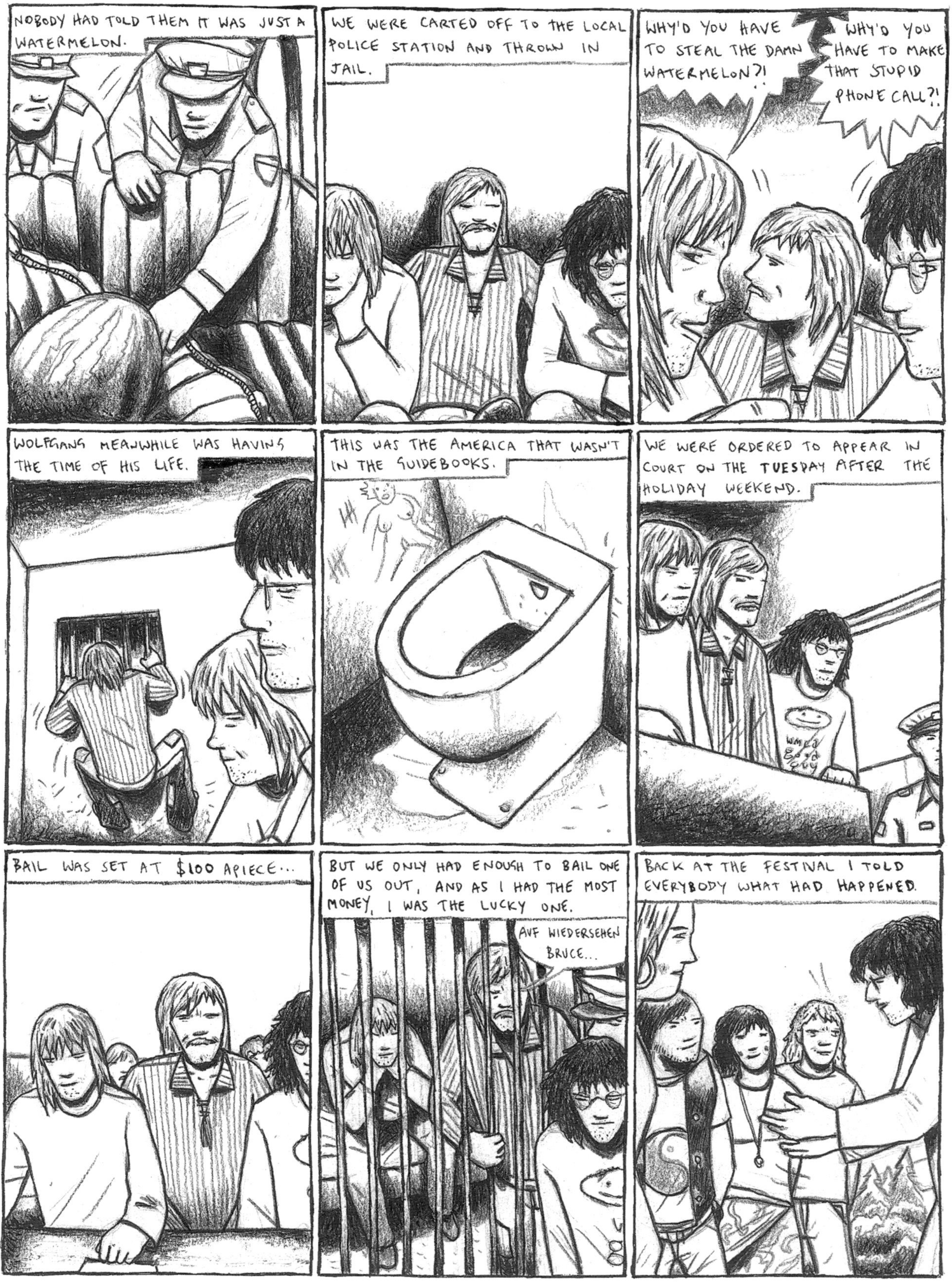
NOBODY HAD TOLD THEM IT WAS JUST A WATERMELON.
WE WERE CARTED OFF TO THE LOCAL POLICE STATION AND THROWN IN JAIL.
WHY'D YOU HAVE TO STEAL THE DAMN WATERMELON?!
WHY'D YOU HAVE TO MAKE THAT STUPID PHONE CALL?!
WOLFGANG MEANWHILE WAS HAVING THE TIME OF HIS LIFE.
THIS WAS THE AMERICA THAT WASN'T IN THE GUIDEBOOKS.
WE WERE ORDERED TO APPEAR IN COURT ON THE TUESDAY AFTER THE HOLIDAY WEEKEND.
BAIL WAS SET AT $100 APIECE...
BUT WE ONLY HAD ENOUGH TO BAIL ONE OF US OUT, AND AS I HAD THE MOST MONEY, I WAS THE LUCKY ONE.
AUF WIEDERSEHEN BRUCE...
BACK AT THE FESTIVAL I TOLD EVERYBODY WHAT HAD HAPPENED.

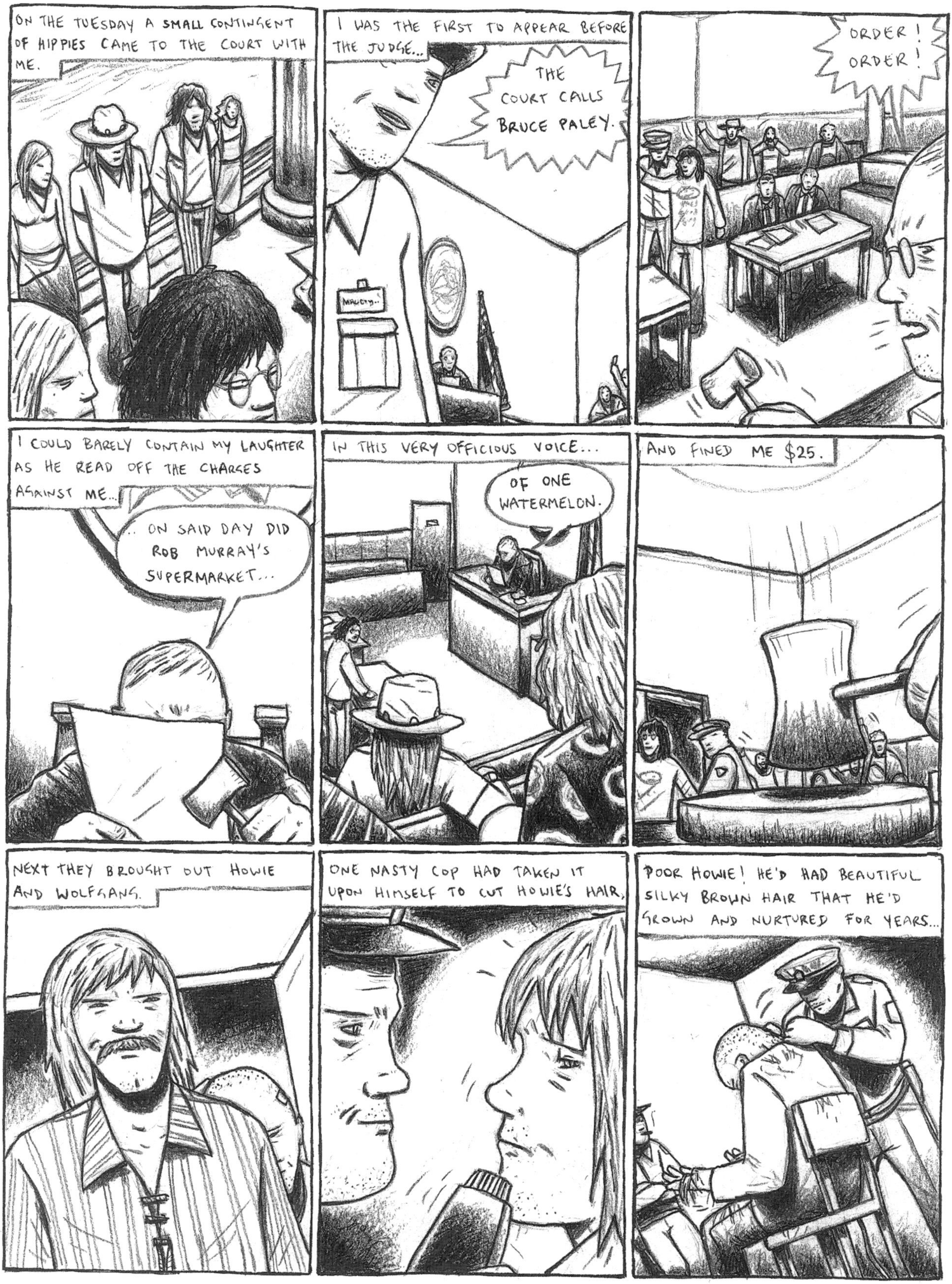
ON THE TUESDAY A SMALL CONTINGENT OF HIPPIES CAME TO THE COURT WITH ME.
I WAS THE FIRST TO APPEAR BEFORE THE JUDGE...
THE COURT CALLS BRUCE PALEY.
ORDER! ORDER!
I COULD BARELY CONTAIN MY LAUGHTER AS HE READ OFF THE CHARGES AGAINST ME...
...ON SAID DAY DID ROB MURRAY'S SUPERMARKET...
IN THIS VERY OFFICIOUS VOICE...
OF ONE WATERMELON.
AND FINED ME $25.
NEXT THEY BROUGHT OUT HOWIE AND WOLFGANG.
ONE NASTY COP HAD TAKEN IT UPON HIMSELF TO CUT HOWIE'S HAIR,
POOR HOWIE! HE'D HAD BEAUTIFUL SILKY BROWN HAIR THAT HE'D GROWN AND NURTURED FOR YEARS...

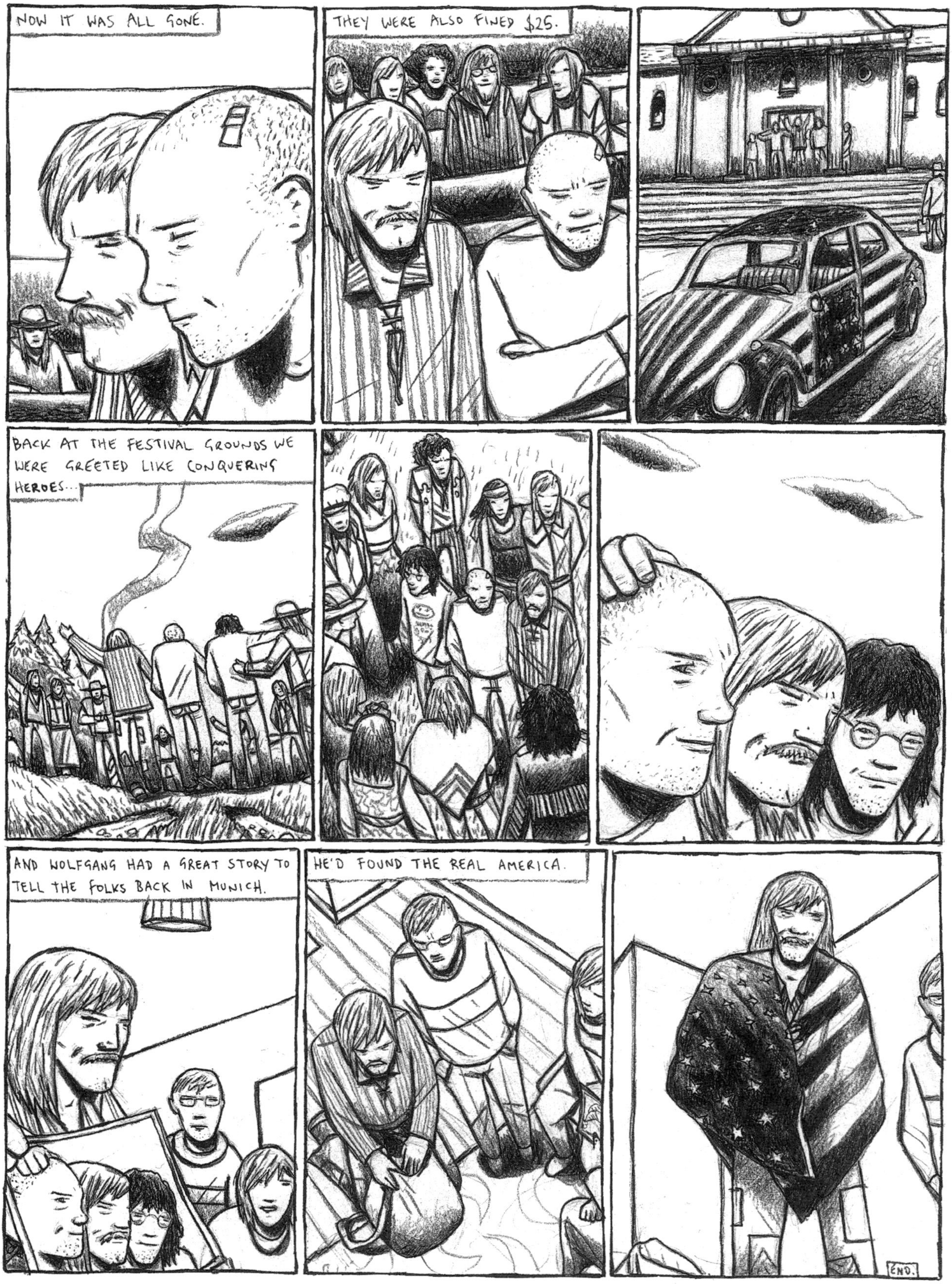
NOW IT WAS ALL GONE.
THEY WERE ALSO FINED $25.
BACK AT THE FESTIVAL GROUNDS WE WERE GREETED LIKE CONQUERING HEROES...
AND WOLFGANG HAD A GREAT STORY TO TELL THE FOLKS BACK IN MUNICH.
HE'D FOUND THE REAL AMERICA.
END.

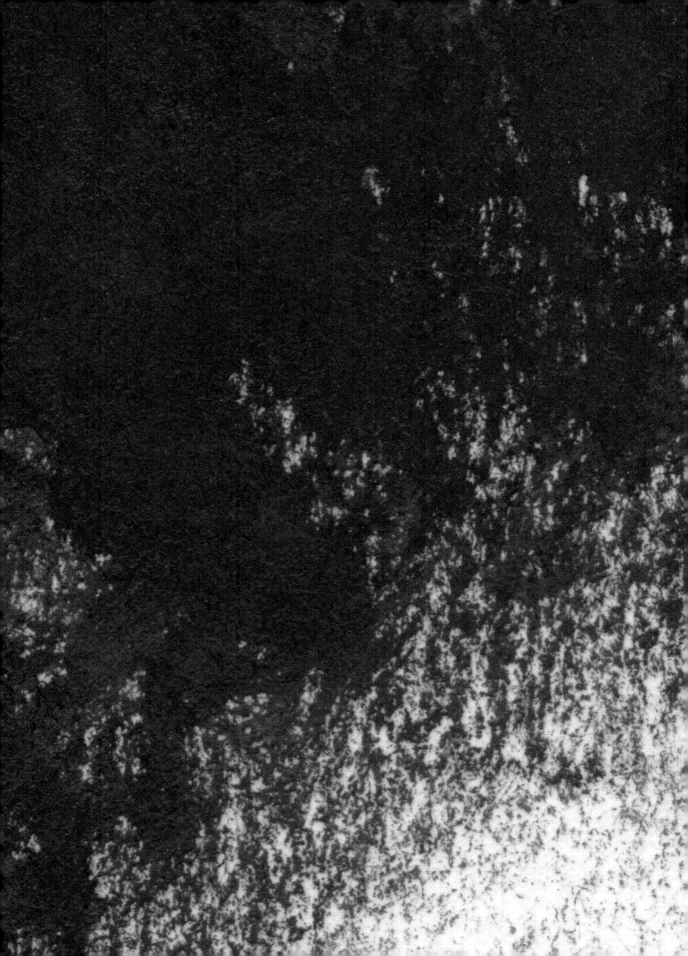

Camp Lejeune

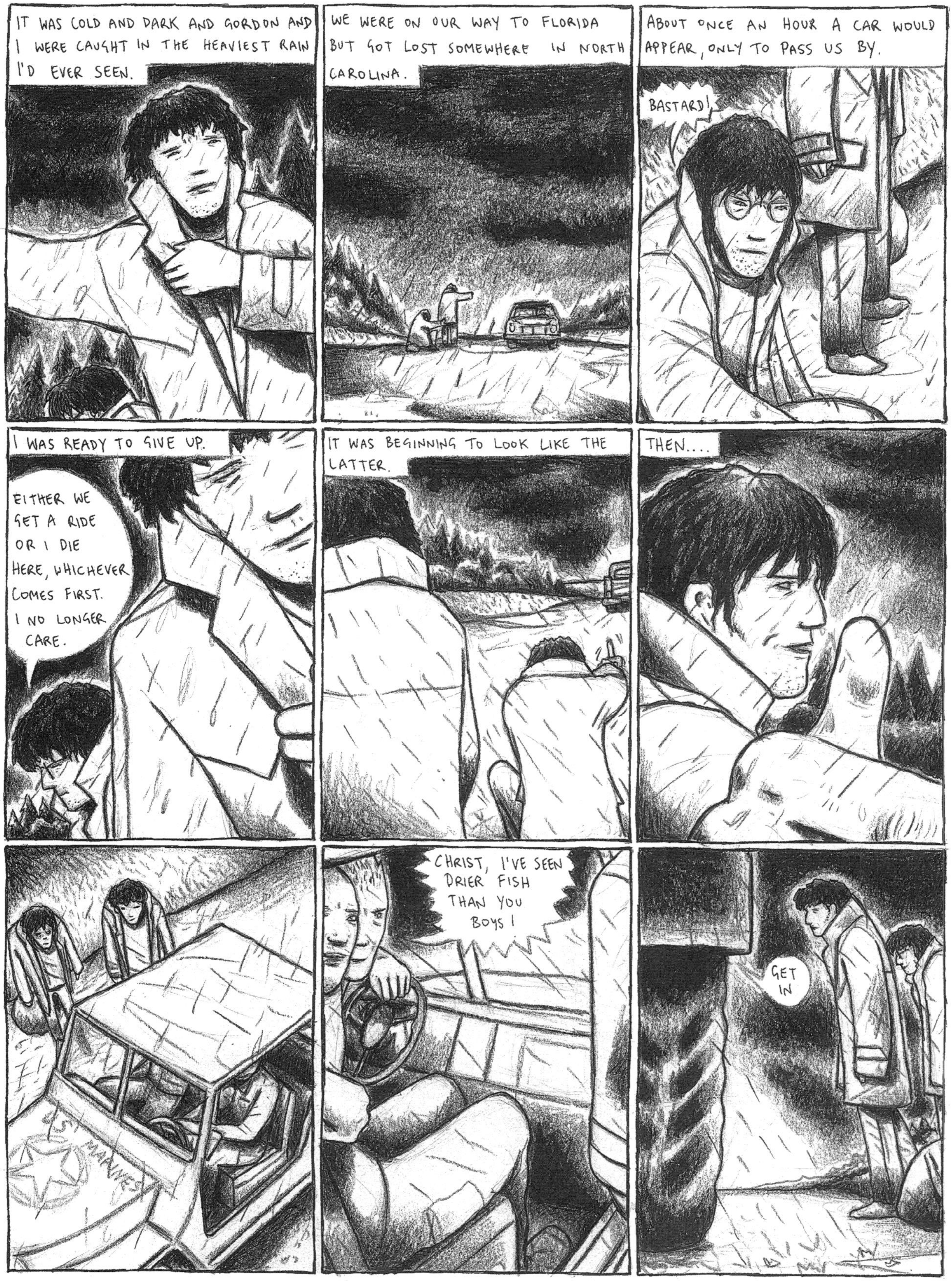

IT WAS COLD AND DARK AND GORDON AND I WERE CAUGHT IN THE HEAVIEST RAIN I'D EVER SEEN.
WE WERE ON OUR WAY TO FLORIDA BUT GOT LOST SOMEWHERE IN NORTH CAROLINA.
ABOUT ONCE AN HOUR A CAR WOULD APPEAR, ONLY TO PASS US BY.
BASTARD!
I WAS READY TO GIVE UP.
EITHER WE GET A RIDE OR I DIE HERE, WHICHEVER COMES FIRST. I NO LONGER CARE.
IT WAS BEGINNING TO LOOK LIKE THE LATTER.
THEN....
CHRIST, I'VE SEEN DRIER FISH THAN YOU BOYS!
GET IN

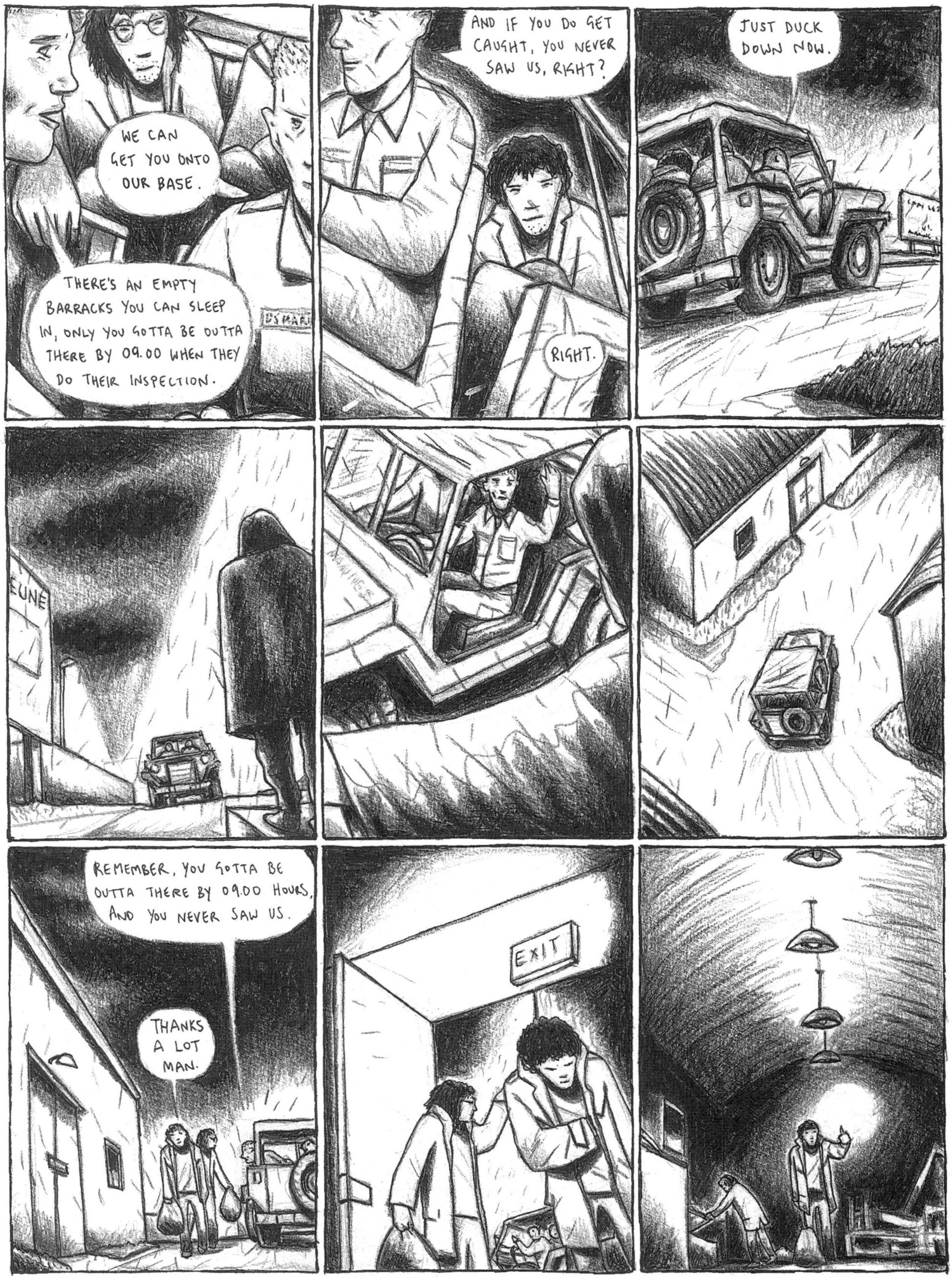
WE CAN GET YOU ONTO OUR BASE.
THERE'S AN EMPTY BARRACKS YOU CAN SLEEP IN, ONLY YOU GOTTA BE OUTTA THERE BY 09.00 WHEN THEY DO THEIR INSPECTION.
AND IF YOU DO GET CAUGHT, YOU NEVER SAW US, RIGHT?
RIGHT.
JUST DUCK DOWN NOW.
REMEMBER, YOU GOTTA BE OUTTA THERE BY 09.00 HOURS, AND YOU NEVER SAW US.
THANKS A LOT MAN.
EXIT

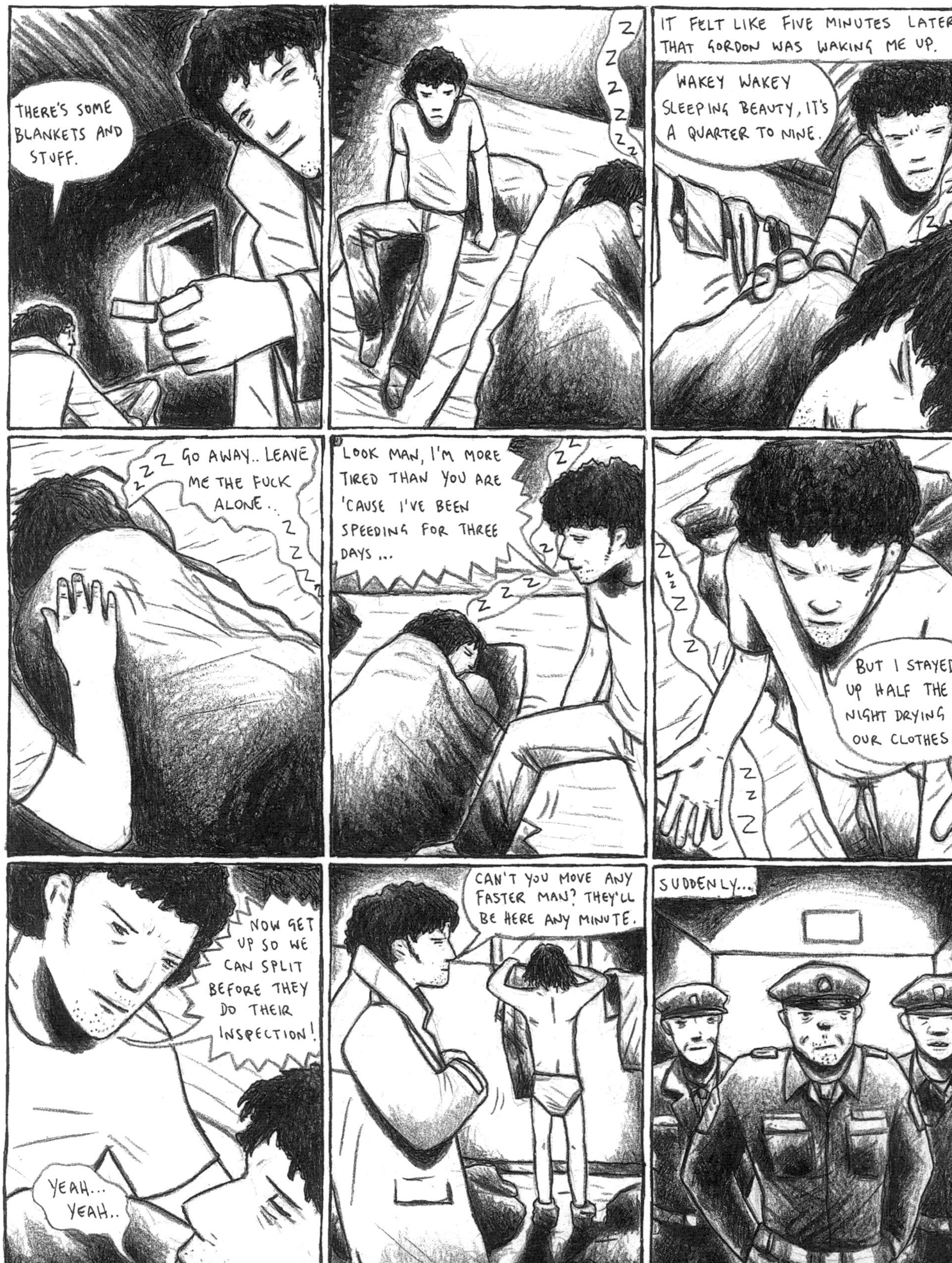
THERE'S SOME BLANKETS AND STUFF.
IT FELT LIKE FIVE MINUTES LATER THAT GORDON WAS WAKING ME UP.
WAKEY WAKEY SLEEPING BEAUTY, IT'S A QUARTER TO NINE.
GO AWAY.. LEAVE ME THE FUCK ALONE...
LOOK MAN, I'M MORE TIRED THAN YOU ARE 'CAUSE I'VE BEEN SPEEDING FOR THREE DAYS...
BUT I STAYED UP HALF THE NIGHT DRYING OUR CLOTHES.
NOW GET UP SO WE CAN SPLIT BEFORE THEY DO THEIR INSPECTION!
YEAH... YEAH..
CAN'T YOU MOVE ANY FASTER MAN? THEY'LL BE HERE ANY MINUTE.
SUDDENLY...

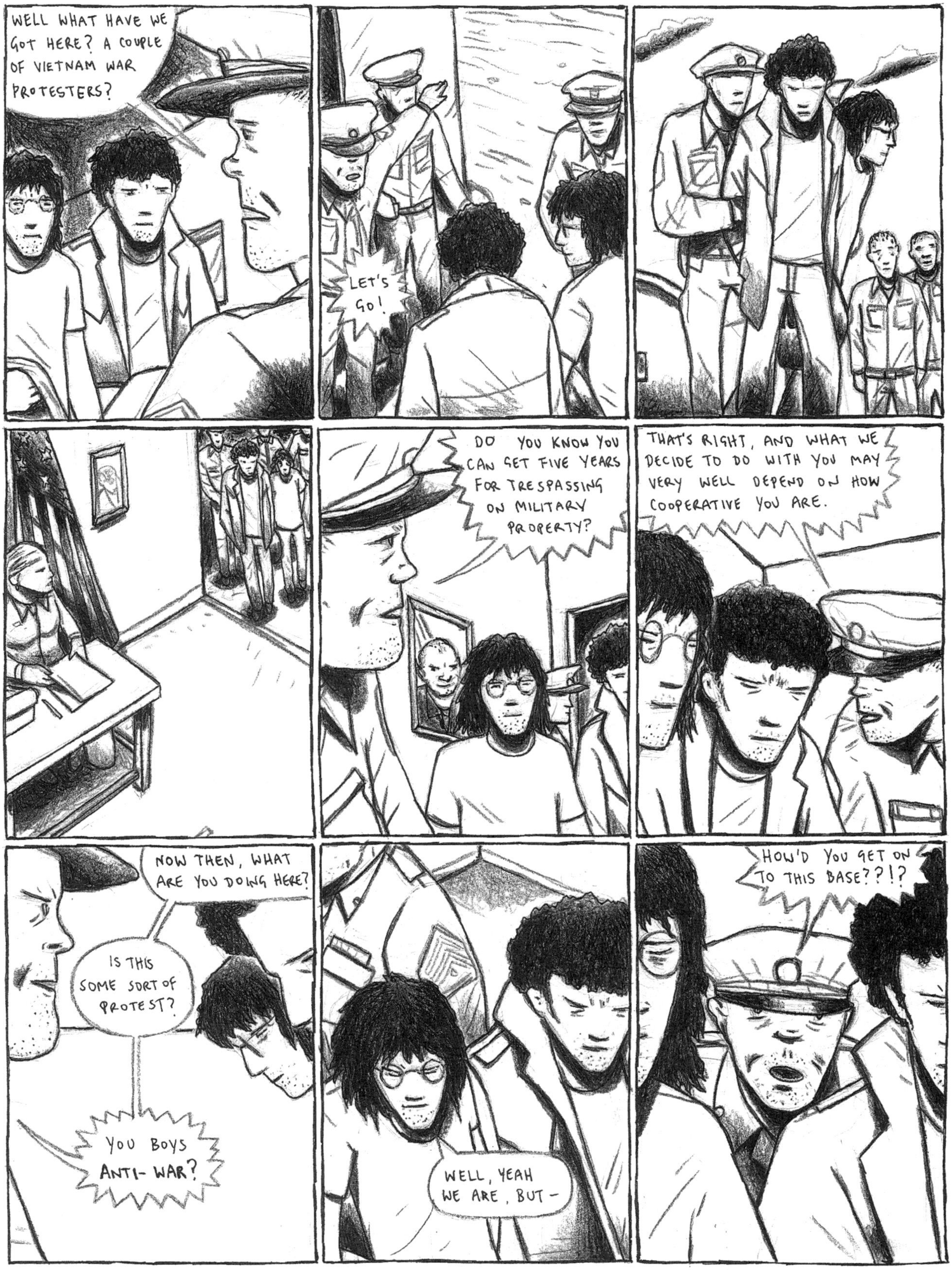
WELL WHAT HAVE WE GOT HERE? A COUPLE OF VIETNAM WAR PROTESTERS?
LET'S GO!
DO YOU KNOW YOU CAN GET FIVE YEARS FOR TRESPASSING ON MILITARY PROPERTY?
THAT'S RIGHT, AND WHAT WE DECIDE TO DO WITH YOU MAY VERY WELL DEPEND ON HOW COOPERATIVE YOU ARE.
NOW THEN, WHAT ARE YOU DOING HERE?
IS THIS SOME SORT OF PROTEST?
YOU BOYS ANTI-WAR?
WELL, YEAH WE ARE, BUT-
HOW'D YOU GET ON TO THIS BASE??!?

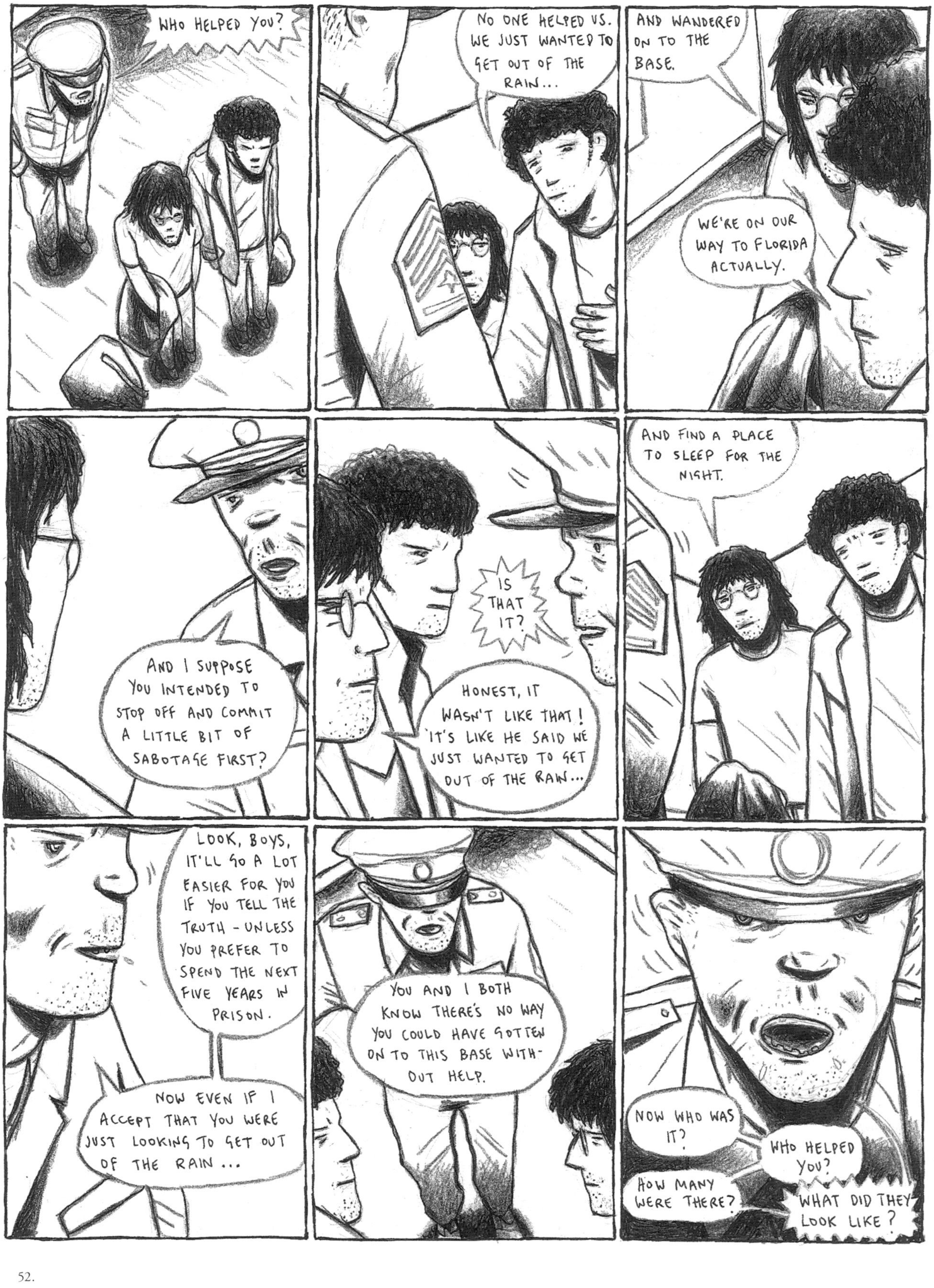
WHO HELPED YOU?
NO ONE HELPED US. WE JUST WANTED TO GET OUT OF THE RAIN...
AND WANDERED ON TO THE BASE.
WE'RE ON OUR WAY TO FLORIDA ACTUALLY.
AND I SUPPOSE YOU INTENDED TO STOP OFF AND COMMIT A LITTLE BIT OF SABOTAGE FIRST?
IS THAT IT?
HONEST, IT WASN'T LIKE THAT! IT'S LIKE HE SAID WE JUST WANTED TO GET OUT OF THE RAIN...
AND FIND A PLACE TO SLEEP FOR THE NIGHT.
LOOK, BOYS, IT'LL GO A LOT EASIER FOR YOU IF YOU TELL THE TRUTH - UNLESS YOU PREFER TO SPEND THE NEXT FIVE YEARS IN PRISON.
NOW EVEN IF I ACCEPT THAT YOU WERE JUST LOOKING TO GET OUT OF THE RAIN...
YOU AND I BOTH KNOW THERE'S NO WAY YOU COULD HAVE GOTTEN ON TO THIS BASE WITH-OUT HELP.
NOW WHO WAS IT?
WHO HELPED YOU?
HOW MANY WERE THERE?
WHAT DID THEY LOOK LIKE?

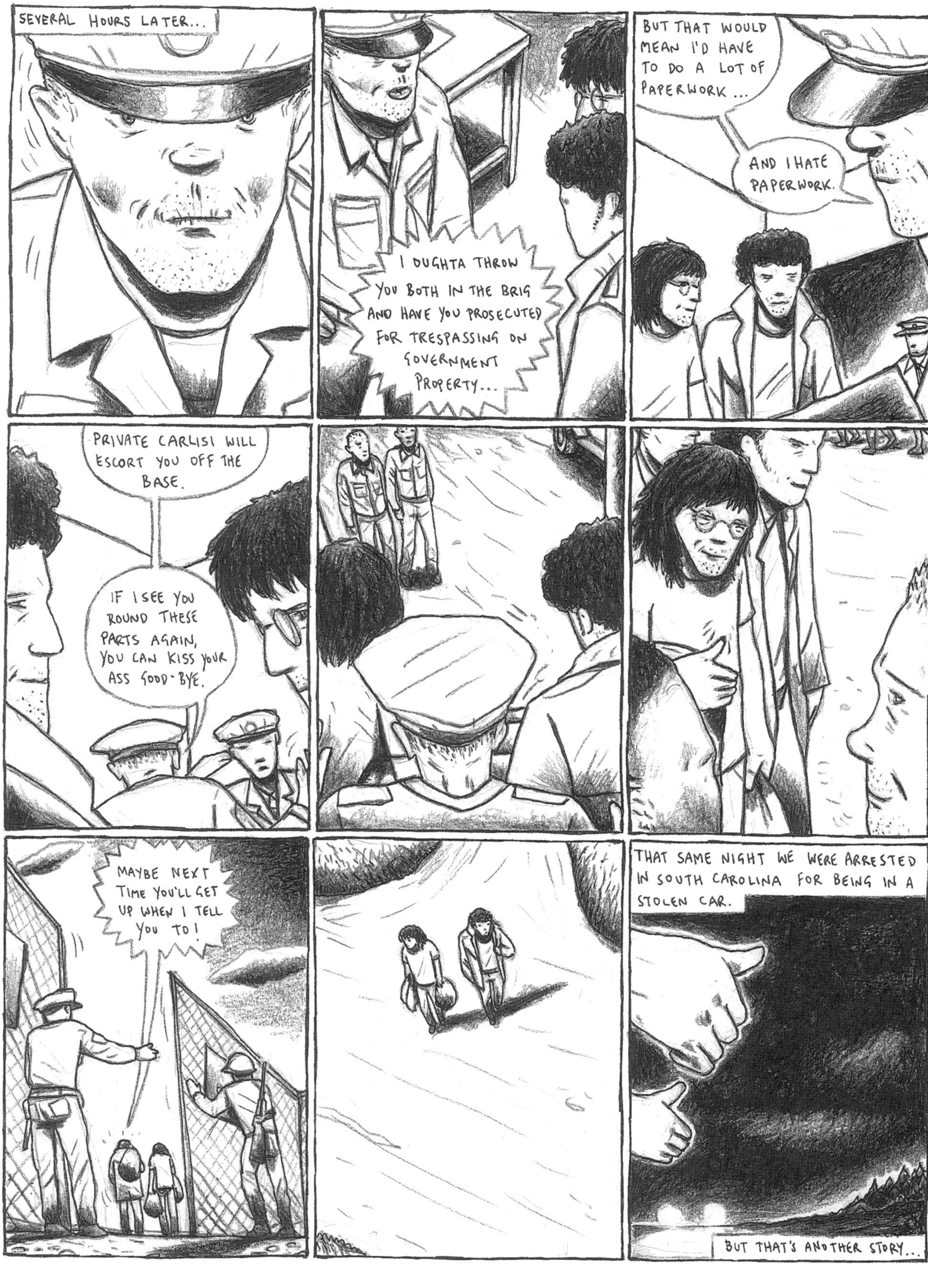
SEVERAL HOURS LATER...
I OUGHTA THROW YOU BOTH IN THE BRIG AND HAVE YOU PROSECUTED FOR TRESPASSING ON GOVERNMENT PROPERTY...
BUT THAT WOULD MEAN I'D HAVE TO DO A LOT OF PAPERWORK...
AND I HATE PAPERWORK.
PRIVATE CARLISI WILL ESCORT YOU OFF THE BASE.
IF I SEE YOU ROUND THESE PARTS AGAIN, YOU CAN KISS YOUR ASS GOOD-BYE.
MAYBE NEXT TIME YOU'LL GET UP WHEN I TELL YOU TO!
THAT SAME NIGHT WE WERE ARRESTED IN SOUTH CAROLINA FOR BEING IN A STOLEN CAR.
BUT THAT'S ANOTHER STORY...

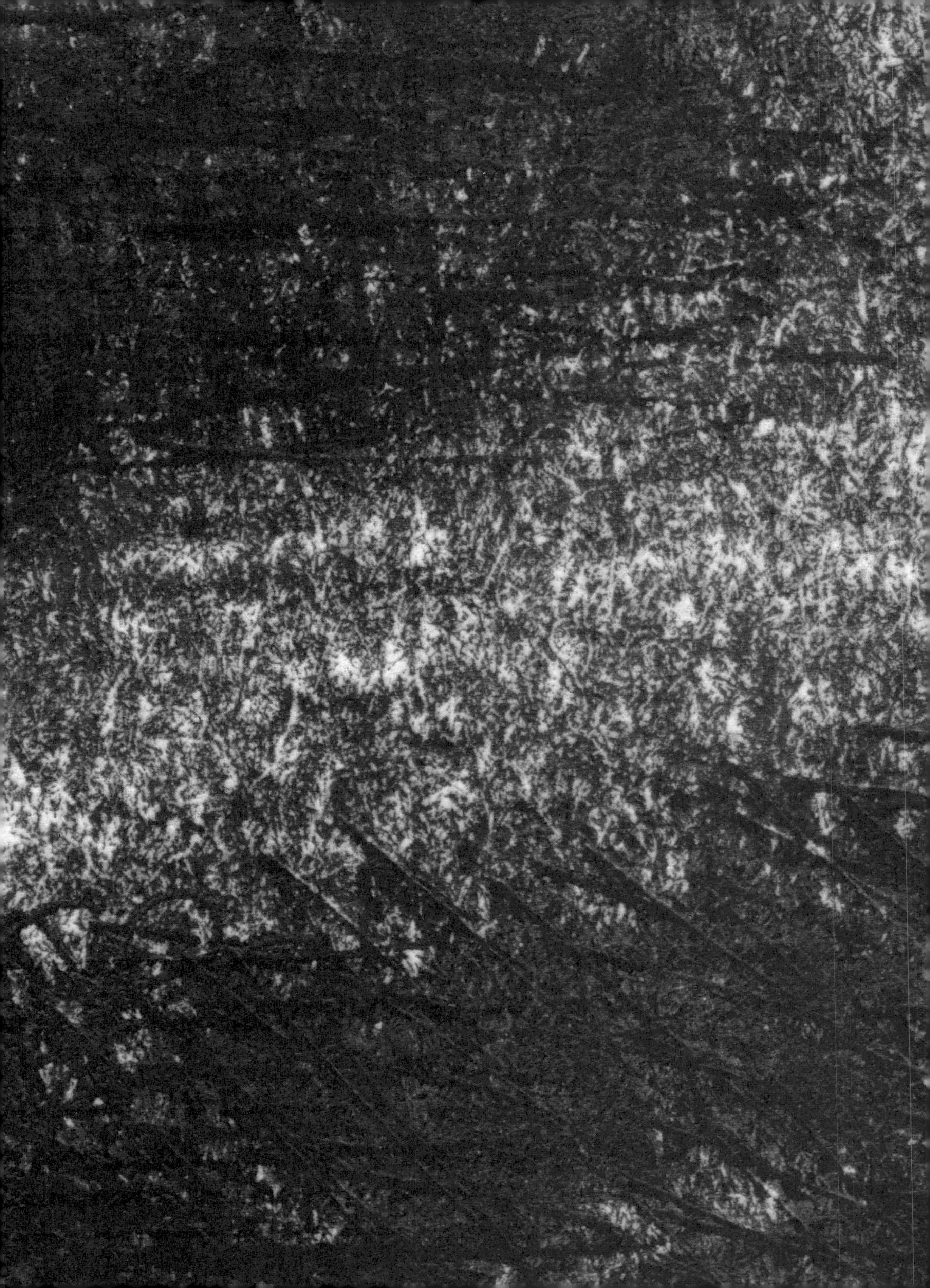

The Magic Kingdom

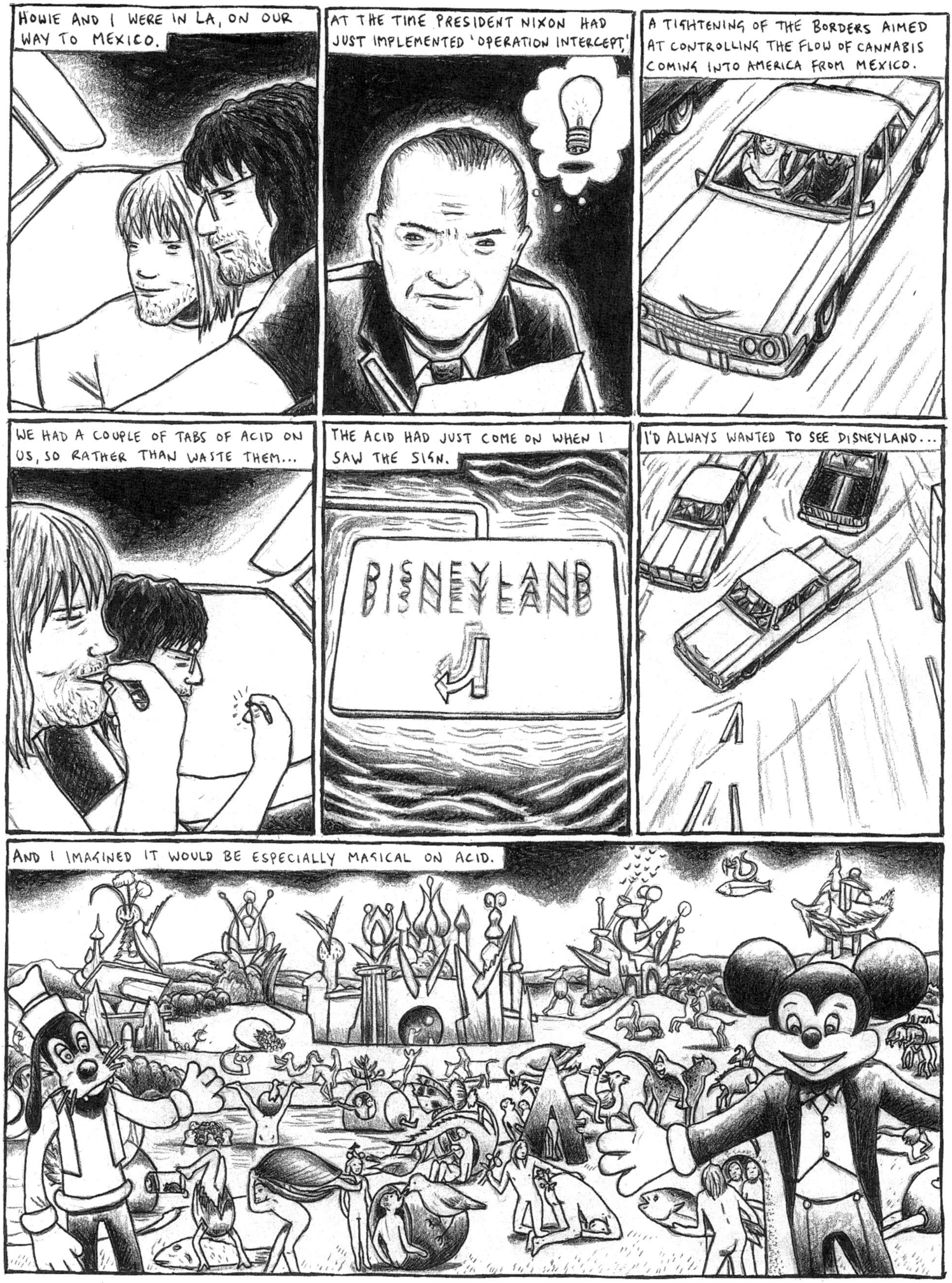
HOWIE AND I WERE IN LA, ON OUR WAY TO MEXICO.
AT THE TIME PRESIDENT NIXON HAD JUST IMPLEMENTED 'OPERATION INTERCEPT,'
A TIGHTENING OF THE BORDERS AIMED AT CONTROLLING THE FLOW OF CANNABIS COMING INTO AMERICA FROM MEXICO.
WE HAD A COUPLE OF TABS OF ACID ON US, SO RATHER THAN WASTE THEM...
THE ACID HAD JUST COME ON WHEN I SAW THE SIGN.
DISNEYLAND
I'D ALWAYS WANTED TO SEE DISNEYLAND...
AND I IMAGINED IT WOULD BE ESPECIALLY MAGICAL ON ACID.

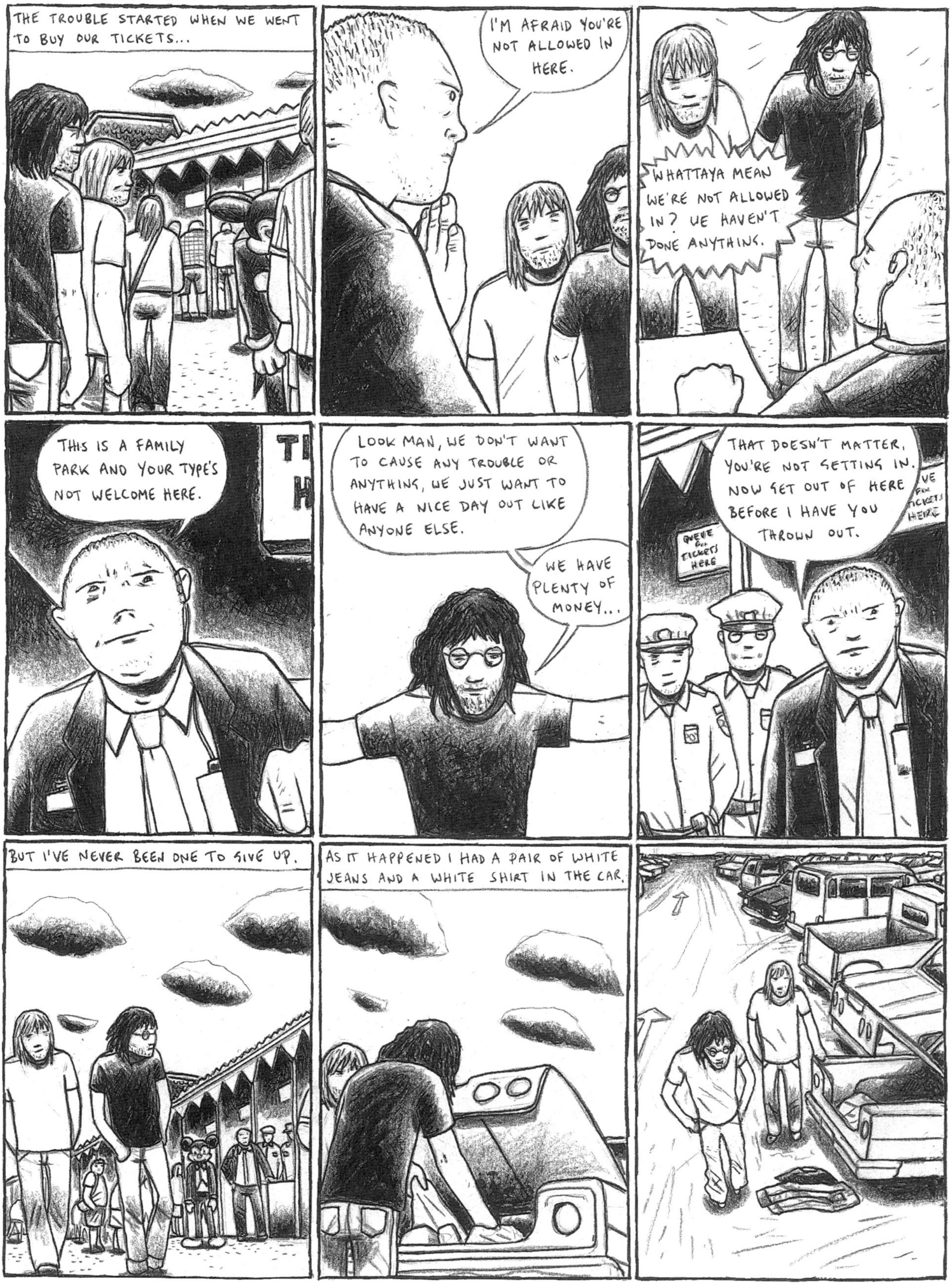
THE TROUBLE STARTED WHEN WE WENT TO BUY OUR TICKETS...
I'M AFRAID YOU'RE NOT ALLOWED IN HERE.
WHATTAYA MEAN WE'RE NOT ALLOWED IN? WE HAVEN'T DONE ANYTHING.
THIS IS A FAMILY PARK AND YOUR TYPE'S NOT WELCOME HERE.
LOOK MAN, WE DON'T WANT TO CAUSE ANY TROUBLE OR ANYTHING, WE JUST WANT TO HAVE A NICE DAY OUT LIKE ANYONE ELSE.
WE HAVE PLENTY OF MONEY...
THAT DOESN'T MATTER. YOU'RE NOT GETTING IN. NOW GET OUT OF HERE BEFORE I HAVE YOU THROWN OUT.
BUT I'VE NEVER BEEN ONE TO GIVE UP.
AS IT HAPPENED I HAD A PAIR OF WHITE JEANS AND A WHITE SHIRT IN THE CAR.

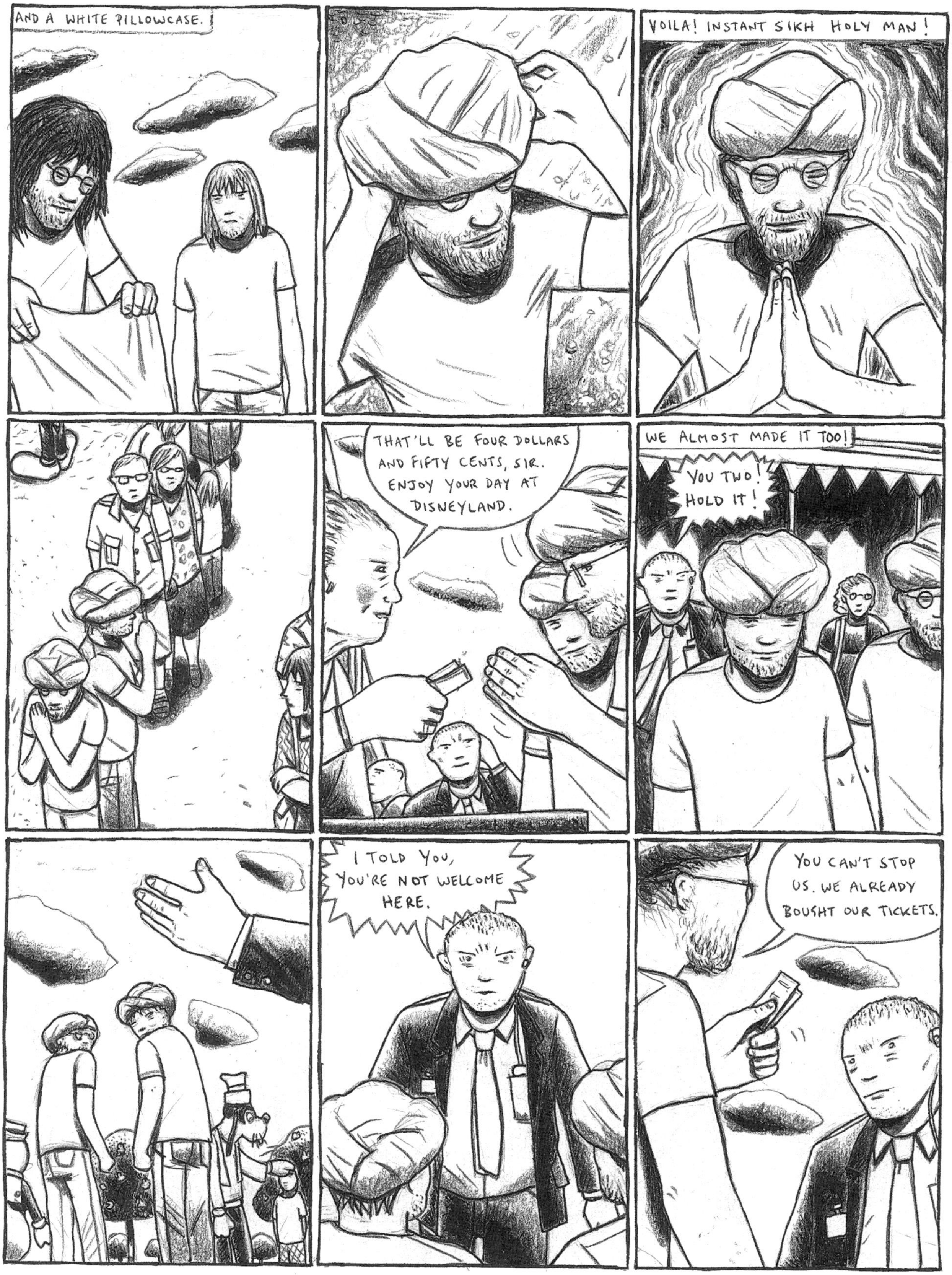

AND A WHITE PILLOWCASE.
VOILA! INSTANT SIKH HOLY MAN!
THAT'LL BE FOUR DOLLARS AND FIFTY CENTS, SIR. ENJOY YOUR DAY AT DISNEYLAND.
WE ALMOST MADE IT TOO!
YOU TWO! HOLD IT!
I TOLD YOU, YOU'RE NOT WELCOME HERE.
YOU CAN'T STOP US. WE ALREADY BOUGHT OUR TICKETS.

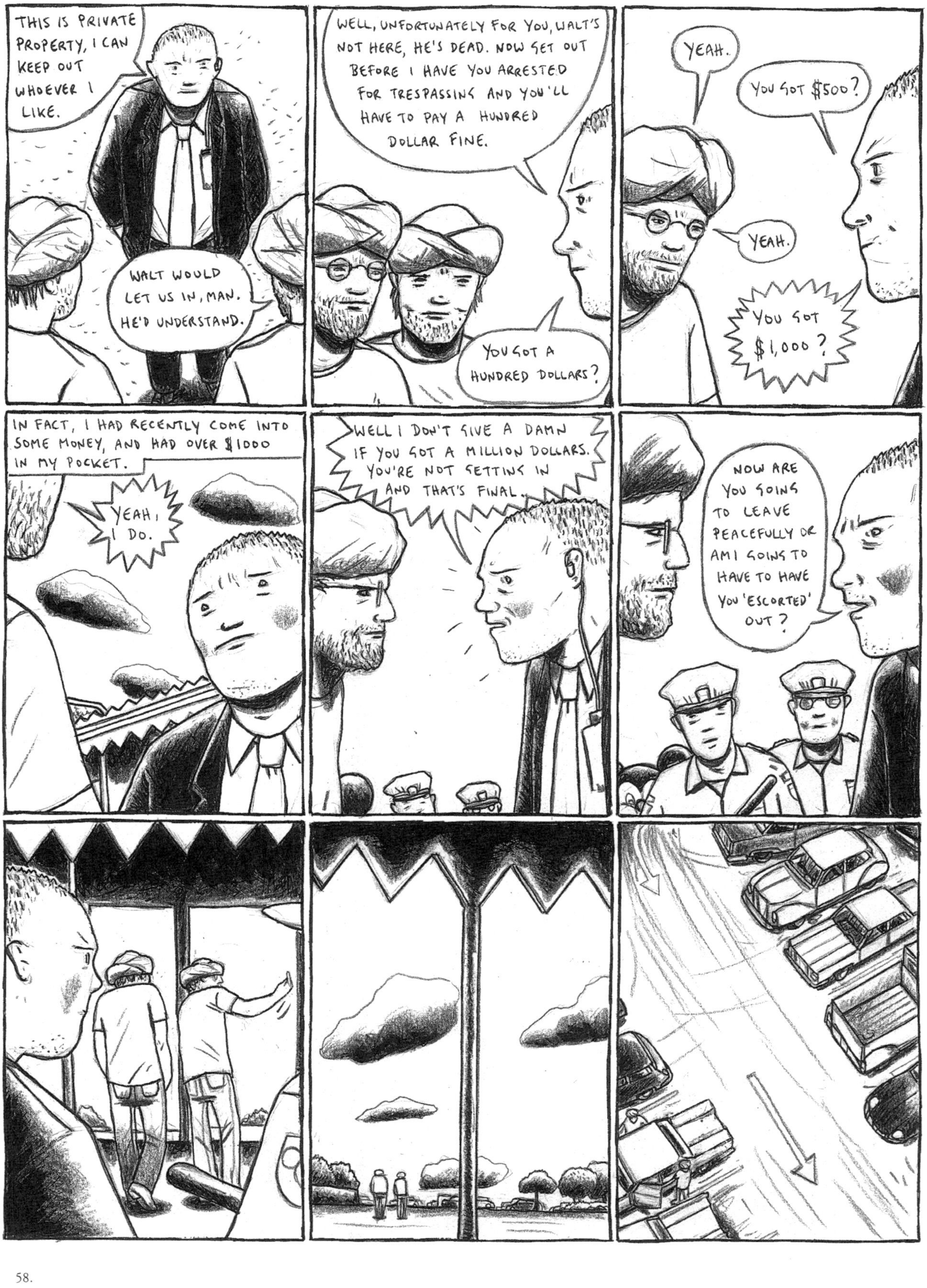
THIS IS PRIVATE PROPERTY, I CAN KEEP OUT WHOEVER I LIKE.
WALT WOULD LET US IN, MAN. HE'D UNDERSTAND.
WELL, UNFORTUNATELY FOR YOU, WALT'S NOT HERE, HE'S DEAD. NOW GET OUT BEFORE I HAVE YOU ARRESTED FOR TRESPASSING AND YOU'LL HAVE TO PAY A HUNDRED DOLLAR FINE.
YOU GOT A HUNDRED DOLLARS?
YEAH.
YOU GOT $500?
YEAH.
YOU GOT $1,000?
IN FACT, I HAD RECENTLY COME INTO SOME MONEY, AND HAD OVER $1000 IN MY POCKET.
YEAH, I DO.
WELL I DON'T GIVE A DAMN IF YOU GOT A MILLION DOLLARS. YOU'RE NOT GETTING IN AND THAT'S FINAL.
NOW ARE YOU GOING TO LEAVE PEACEFULLY OR AM I GOING TO HAVE TO HAVE YOU 'ESCORTED' OUT?

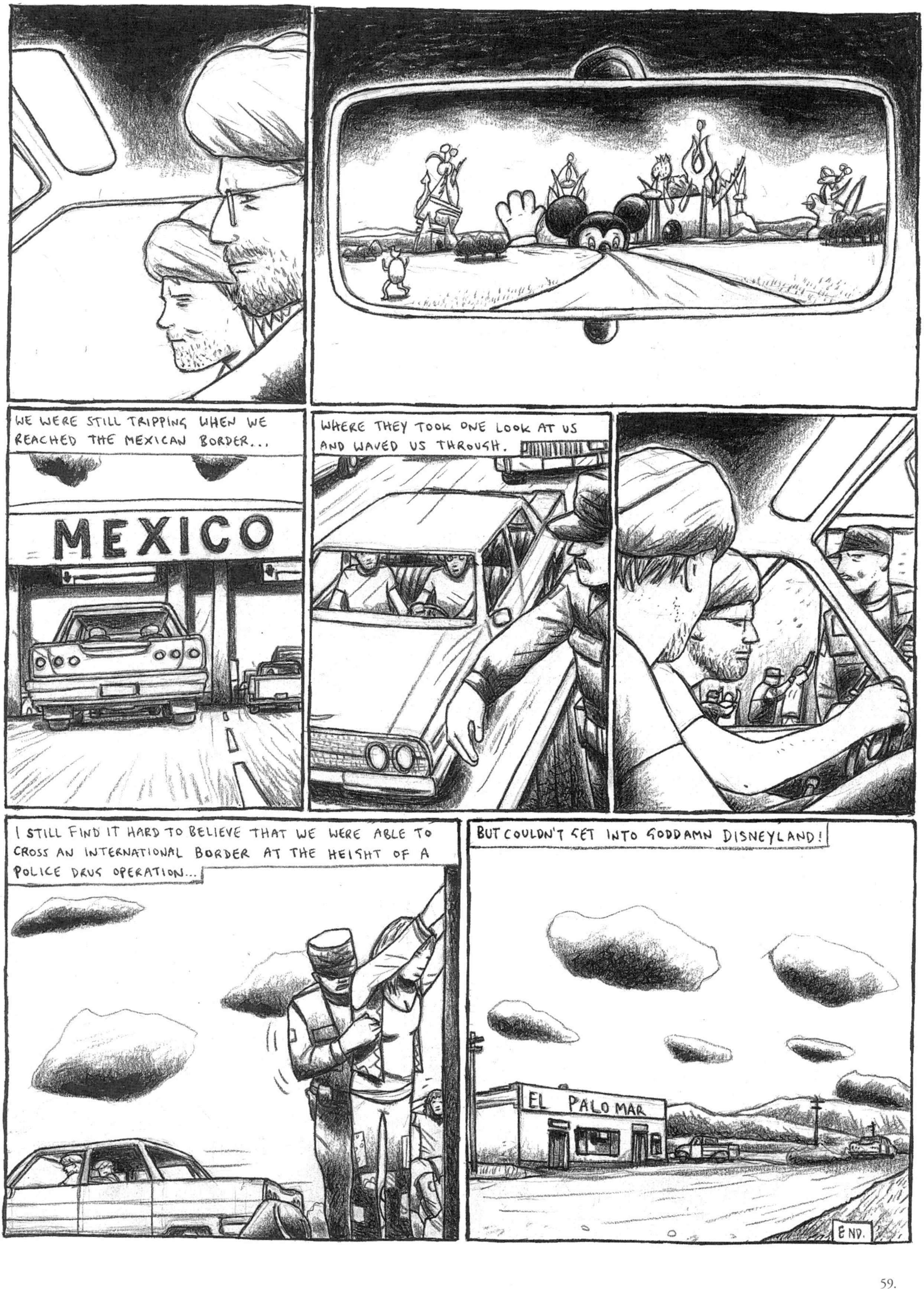
WE WERE STILL TRIPPING WHEN WE REACHED THE MEXICAN BORDER...
MEXICO
WHERE THEY TOOK ONE LOOK AT US AND WAVED US THROUGH.
I STILL FIND IT HARD TO BELIEVE THAT WE WERE ABLE TO CROSS AN INTERNATIONAL BORDER AT THE HEIGHT OF A POLICE DRUG OPERATION...
BUT COULDN'T GET INTO GODDAMN DISNEYLAND!
EL PALOMAR
END.

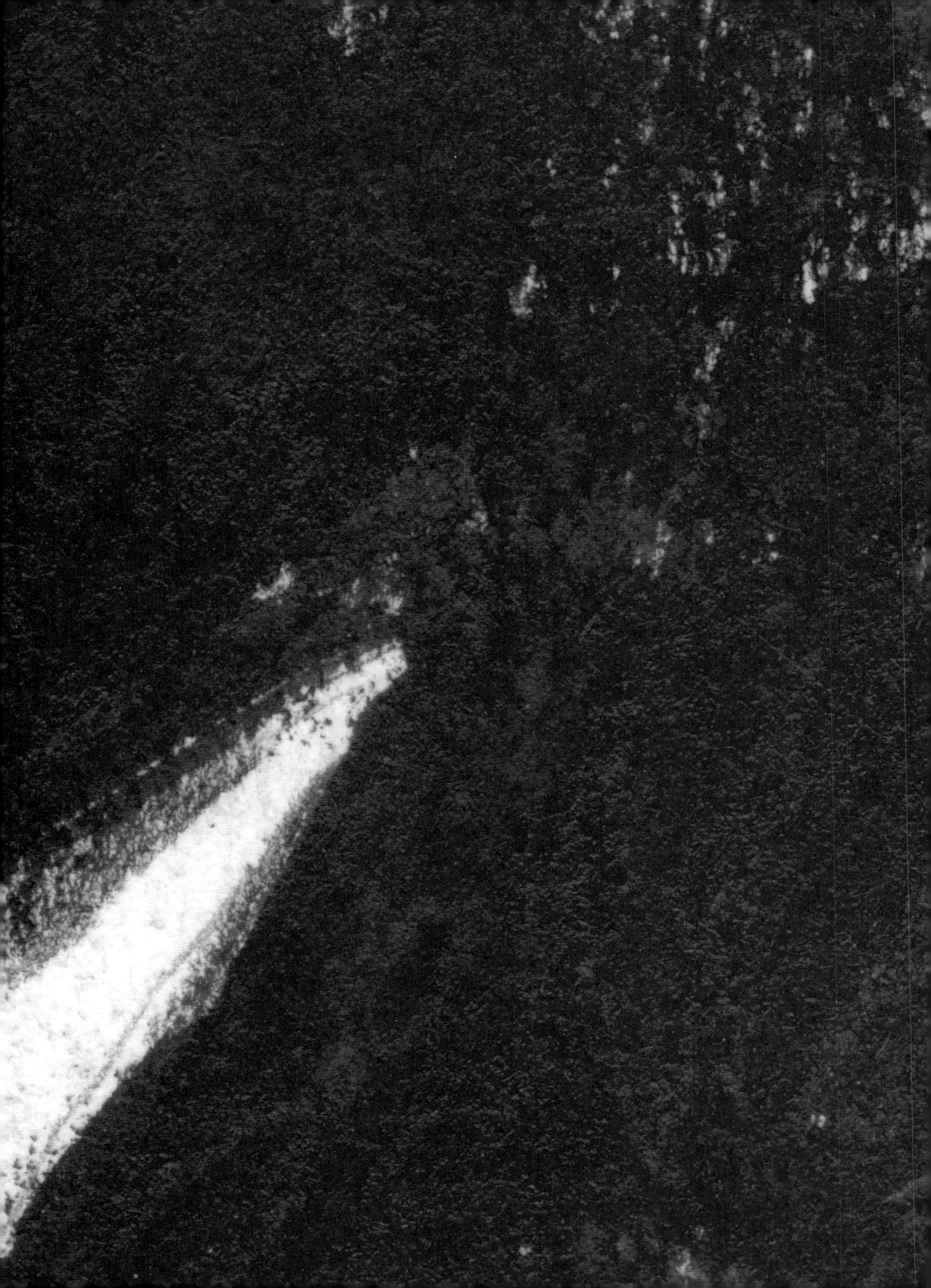

"Never goin' back to Georgia"

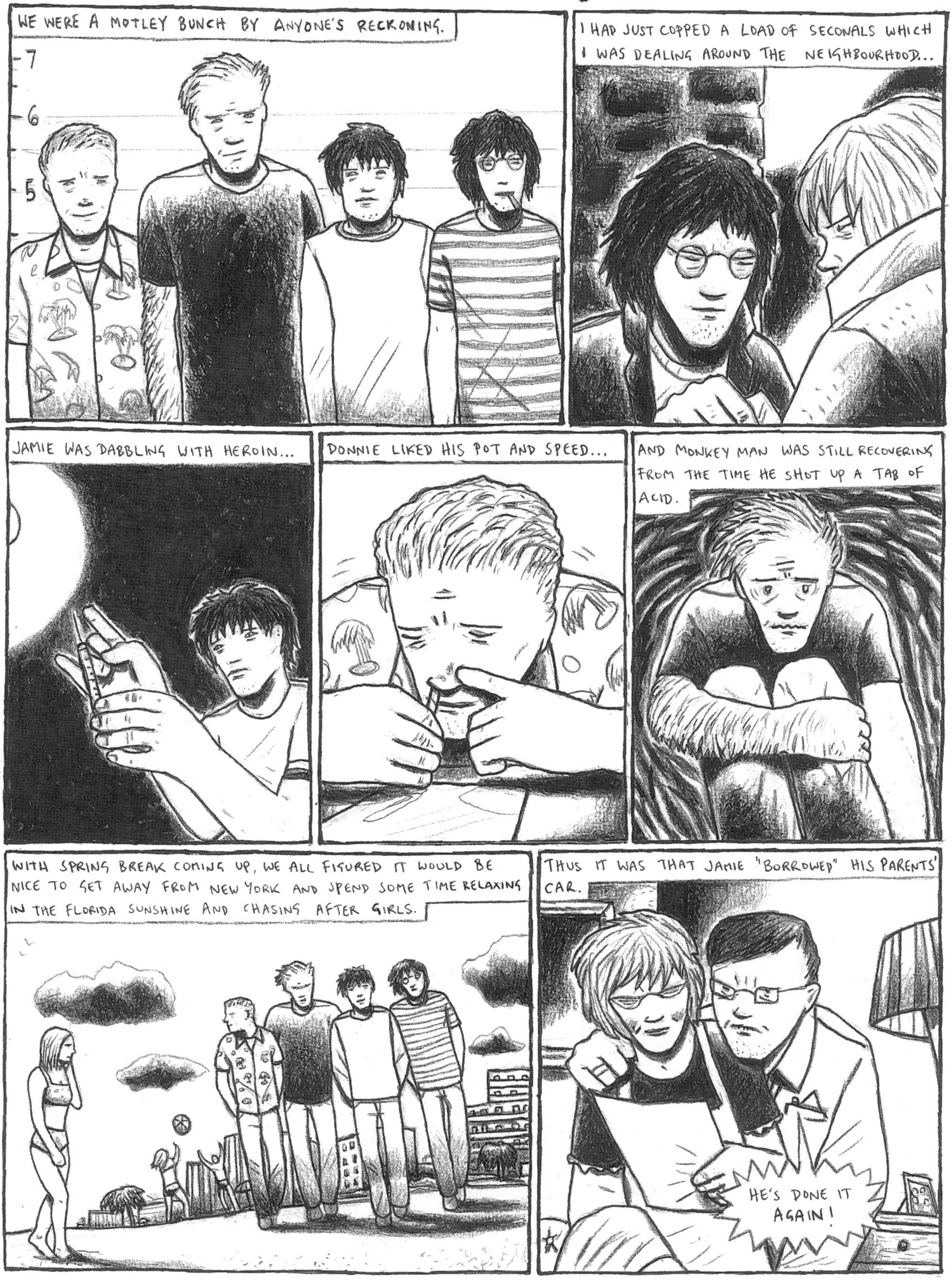
WE WERE A MOTLEY BUNCH BY ANYONE'S RECKONING.
7
6
5
I HAD JUST COPPED A LOAD OF SECONALS WHICH I WAS DEALING AROUND THE NEIGHBOURHOOD...
JAMIE WAS DABBLING WITH HEROIN...
DONNIE LIKED HIS POT AND SPEED...
AND MONKEY MAN WAS STILL RECOVERING FROM THE TIME HE SHOT UP A TAB OF ACID.
WITH SPRING BREAK COMING UP, WE ALL FIGURED IT WOULD BE NICE TO GET AWAY FROM NEW YORK AND SPEND SOME TIME RELAXING IN THE FLORIDA SUNSHINE AND CHASING AFTER GIRLS.
THUS IT WAS THAT JAMIE "BORROWED" HIS PARENTS' CAR.
HE'S DONE IT AGAIN!

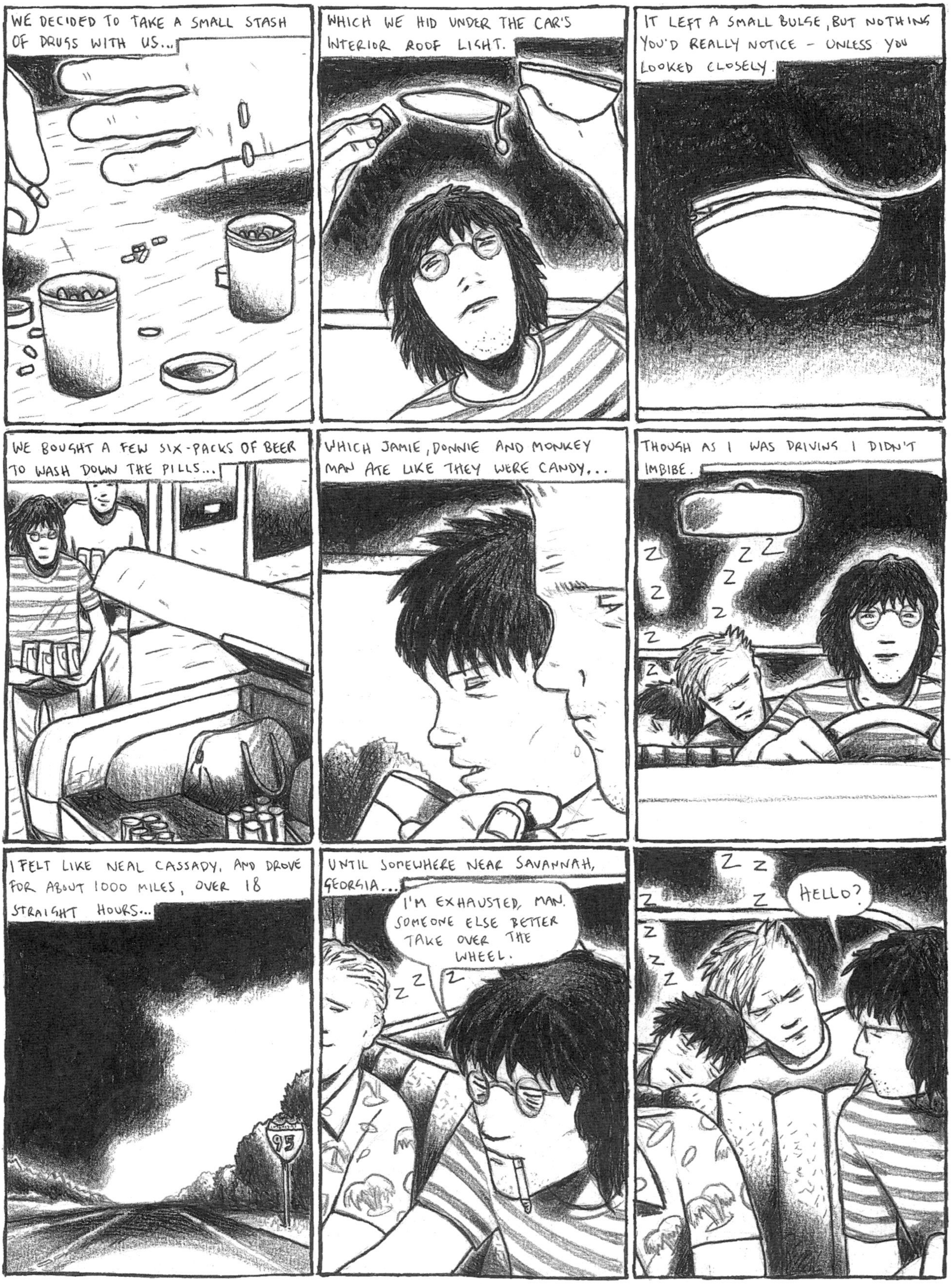

WE DECIDED TO TAKE A SMALL STASH OF DRUGS WITH US...
WHICH WE HID UNDER THE CAR'S INTERIOR ROOF LIGHT.
IT LEFT A SMALL BULGE, BUT NOTHING YOU'D REALLY NOTICE - UNLESS YOU LOOKED CLOSELY.
WE BOUGHT A FEW SIX-PACKS OF BEER TO WASH DOWN THE PILLS...
WHICH JAMIE, DONNIE AND MONKEY MAN ATE LIKE THEY WERE CANDY...
THOUGH AS I WAS DRIVING I DIDN'T IMBIBE.
Z Z Z Z Z Z Z
I FELT LIKE NEAL CASSADY, AND DROVE FOR ABOUT 1000 MILES, OVER 18 STRAIGHT HOURS...
95
UNTIL SOMEWHERE NEAR SAVANNAH, GEORGIA...
I'M EXHAUSTED, MAN. SOMEONE ELSE BETTER TAKE OVER THE WHEEL.
Z Z Z
Z Z Z Z Z Z Z Z
HELLO?

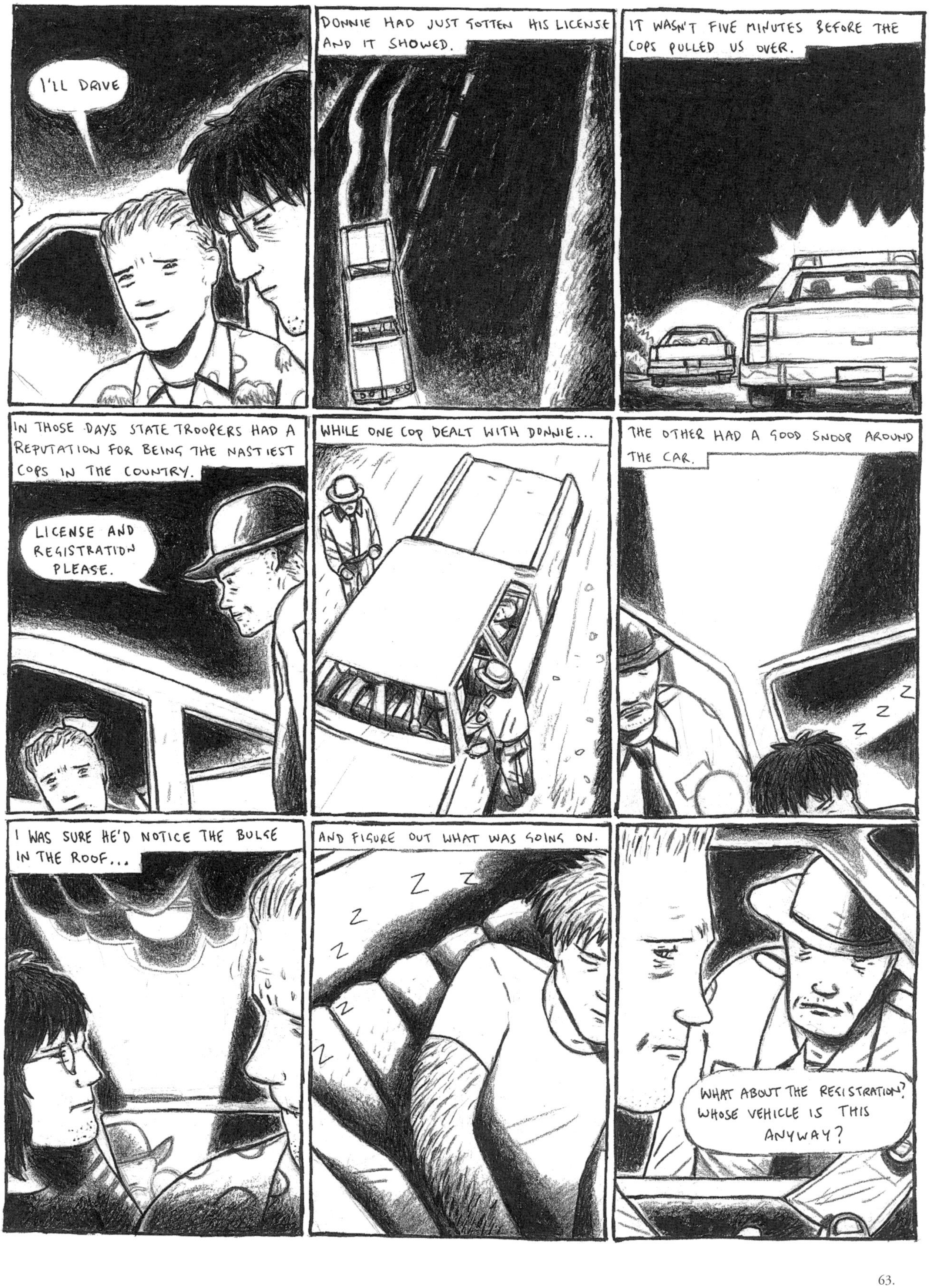
I'LL DRIVE
DONNIE HAD JUST GOTTEN HIS LICENSE AND IT SHOWED.
IT WASN'T FIVE MINUTES BEFORE THE COPS PULLED US OVER.
IN THOSE DAYS STATE TROOPERS HAD A REPUTATION FOR BEING THE NASTIEST COPS IN THE COUNTRY.
LICENSE AND REGISTRATION PLEASE.
WHILE ONE COP DEALT WITH DONNIE...
THE OTHER HAD A GOOD SNOOP AROUND THE CAR.
Z Z Z
I WAS SURE HE'D NOTICE THE BULGE IN THE ROOF...
AND FIGURE OUT WHAT WAS GOING ON.
Z Z Z Z Z Z
WHAT ABOUT THE REGISTRATION? WHOSE VEHICLE IS THIS ANYWAY?

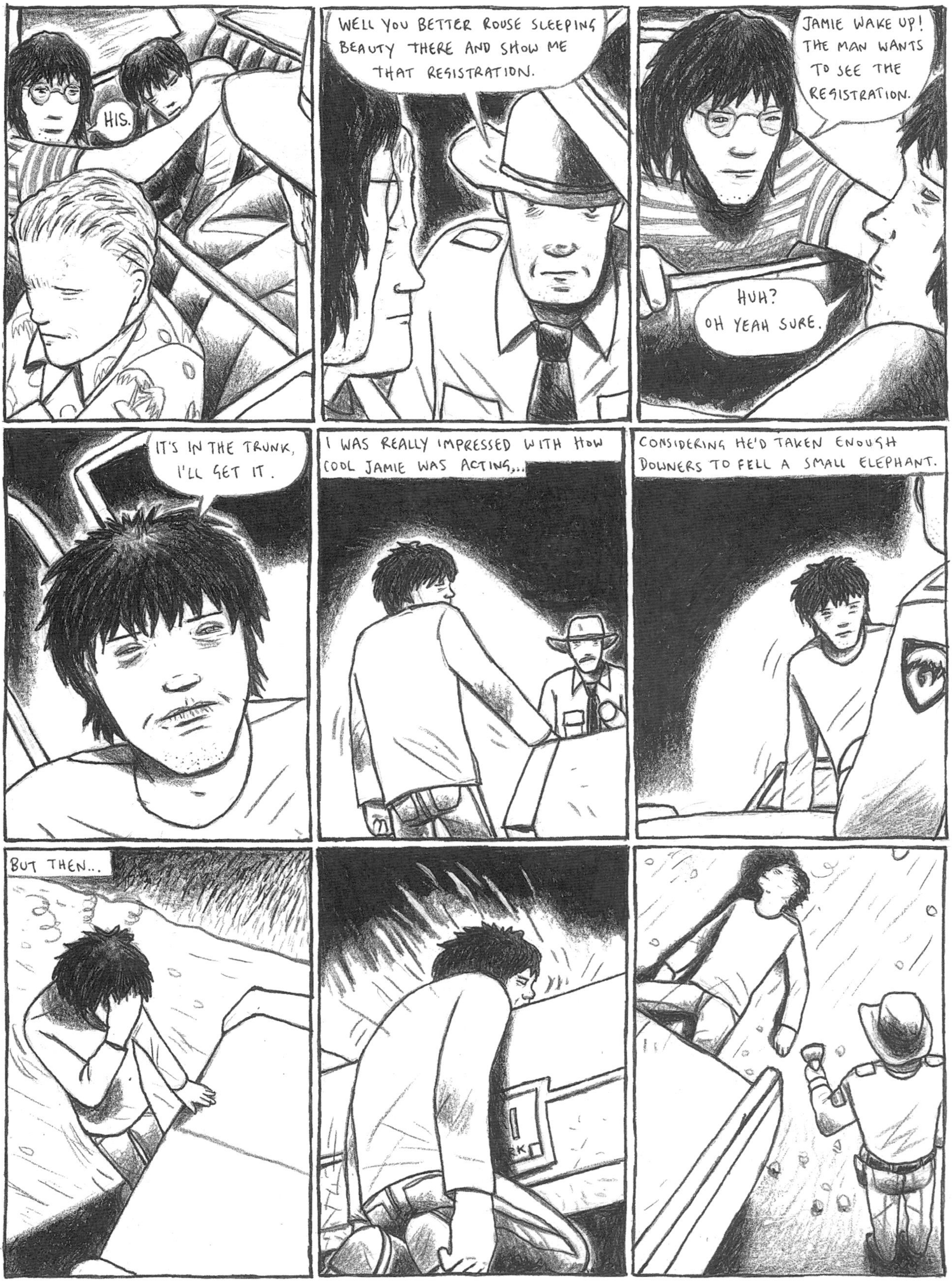
HIS.
WELL YOU BETTER ROUSE SLEEPING BEAUTY THERE AND SHOW ME THAT REGISTRATION.
JAMIE WAKE UP! THE MAN WANTS TO SEE THE REGISTRATION.
HUH? OH YEAH SURE.
IT'S IN THE TRUNK, I'LL GET IT.
I WAS REALLY IMPRESSED WITH HOW COOL JAMIE WAS ACTING...
CONSIDERING HE'D TAKEN ENOUGH DOWNERS TO FELL A SMALL ELEPHANT.
BUT THEN...

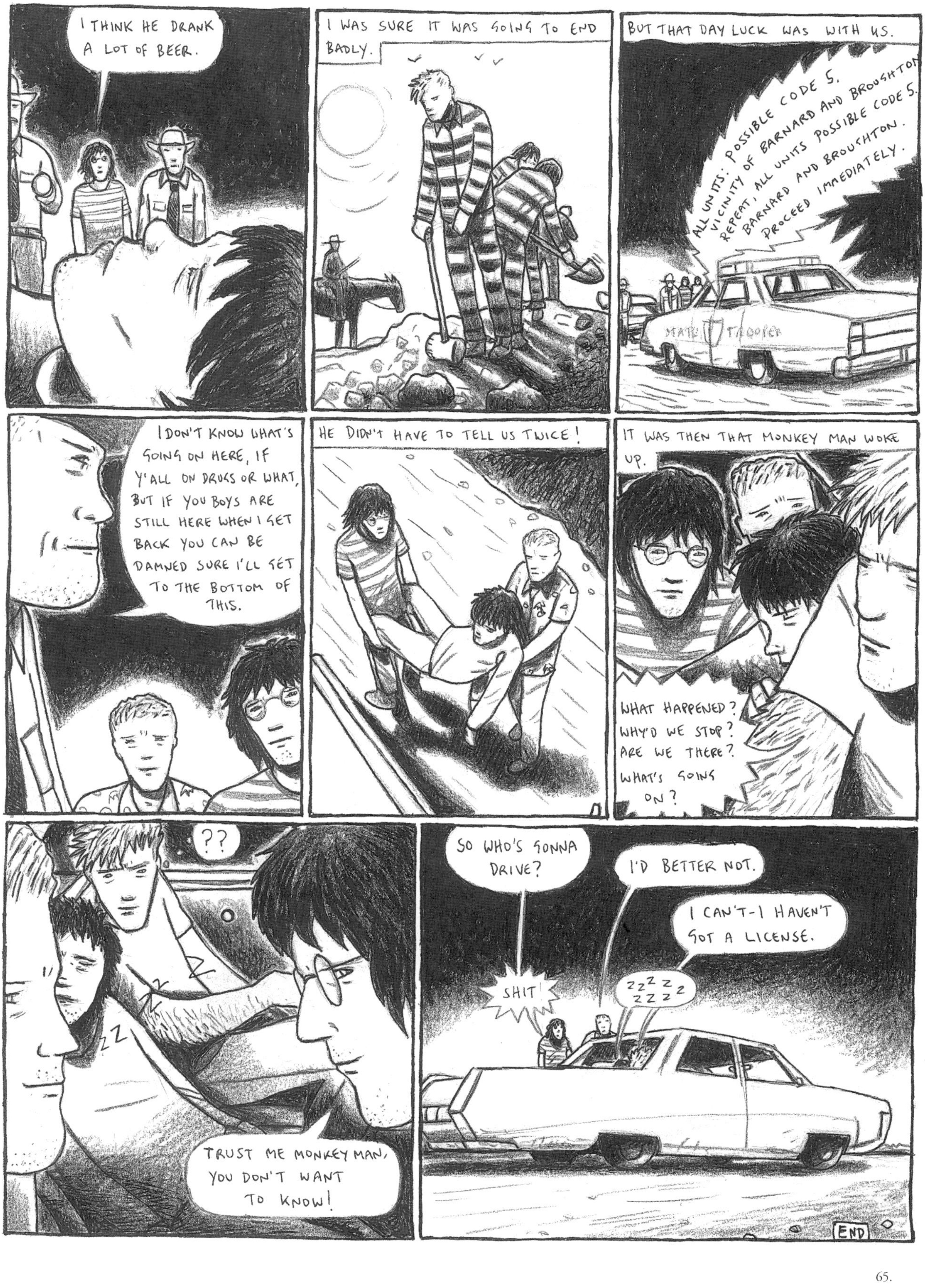
I THINK HE DRANK A LOT OF BEER.
I WAS SURE IT WAS GOING TO END BADLY.
BUT THAT DAY LUCK WAS WITH US.
ALL UNITS: POSSIBLE CODE 5. VICINITY OF BARNARD AND BROUGHTON. REPEAT, ALL UNITS POSSIBLE CODE 5. BARNARD AND BROUGHTON. PROCEED IMMEDIATELY.
STATE TROOPER
I DON'T KNOW WHAT'S GOING ON HERE, IF Y'ALL ON DRUGS OR WHAT, BUT IF YOU BOYS ARE STILL HERE WHEN I GET BACK YOU CAN BE DAMNED SURE I'LL GET TO THE BOTTOM OF THIS.
HE DIDN'T HAVE TO TELL US TWICE!
IT WAS THEN THAT MONKEY MAN WOKE UP.
WHAT HAPPENED? WHY'D WE STOP? ARE WE THERE? WHAT'S GOING ON?
??
TRUST ME MONKEY MAN, YOU DON'T WANT TO KNOW!
SO WHO'S GONNA DRIVE?
I'D BETTER NOT.
I CAN'T-I HAVEN'T GOT A LICENSE.
SHIT!
END

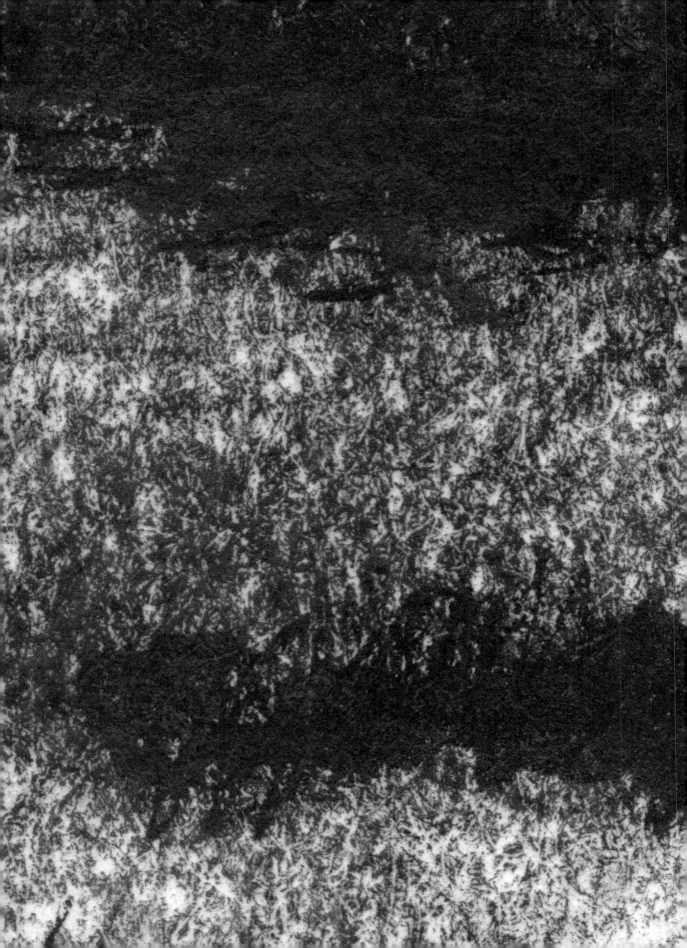

If it seems too good to be true...

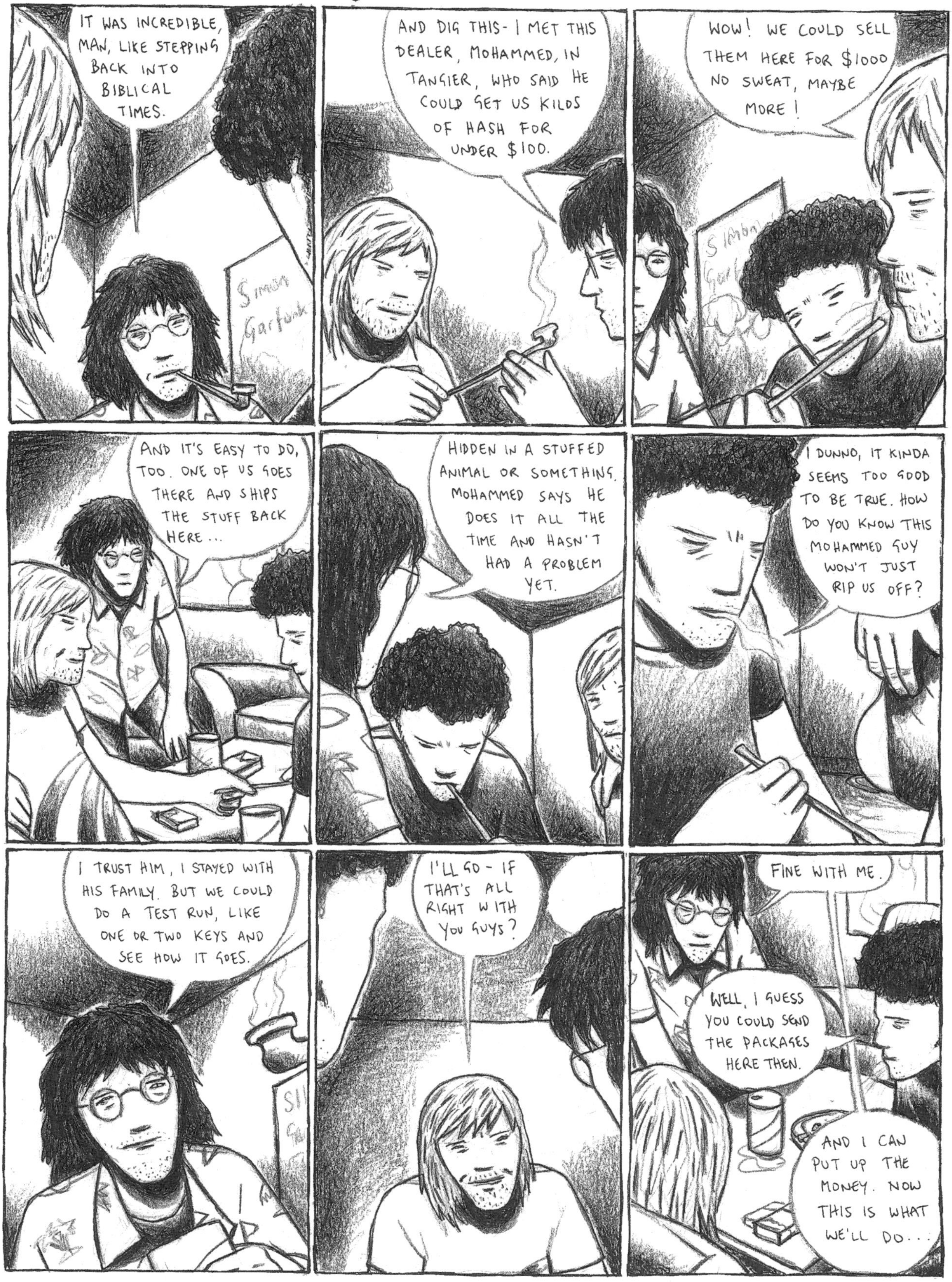
IT WAS INCREDIBLE, MAN, LIKE STEPPING BACK INTO BIBLICAL TIMES.
AND DIG THIS - I MET THIS DEALER, MOHAMMED, IN TANGIER, WHO SAID HE COULD GET US KILOS OF HASH FOR UNDER $100.
WOW! WE COULD SELL THEM HERE FOR $1000 NO SWEAT, MAYBE MORE!
AND IT'S EASY TO DO, TOO. ONE OF US GOES THERE AND SHIPS THE STUFF BACK HERE...
HIDDEN IN A STUFFED ANIMAL OR SOMETHING. MOHAMMED SAYS HE DOES IT ALL THE TIME AND HASN'T HAD A PROBLEM YET.
I DUNNO, IT KINDA SEEMS TOO GOOD TO BE TRUE. HOW DO YOU KNOW THIS MOHAMMED GUY WON'T JUST RIP US OFF?
I TRUST HIM, I STAYED WITH HIS FAMILY. BUT WE COULD DO A TEST RUN, LIKE ONE OR TWO KEYS AND SEE HOW IT GOES.
I'LL GO - IF THAT'S ALL RIGHT WITH YOU GUYS?
FINE WITH ME.
WELL, I GUESS YOU COULD SEND THE PACKAGES HERE THEN.
AND I CAN PUT UP THE MONEY. NOW THIS IS WHAT WE'LL DO...

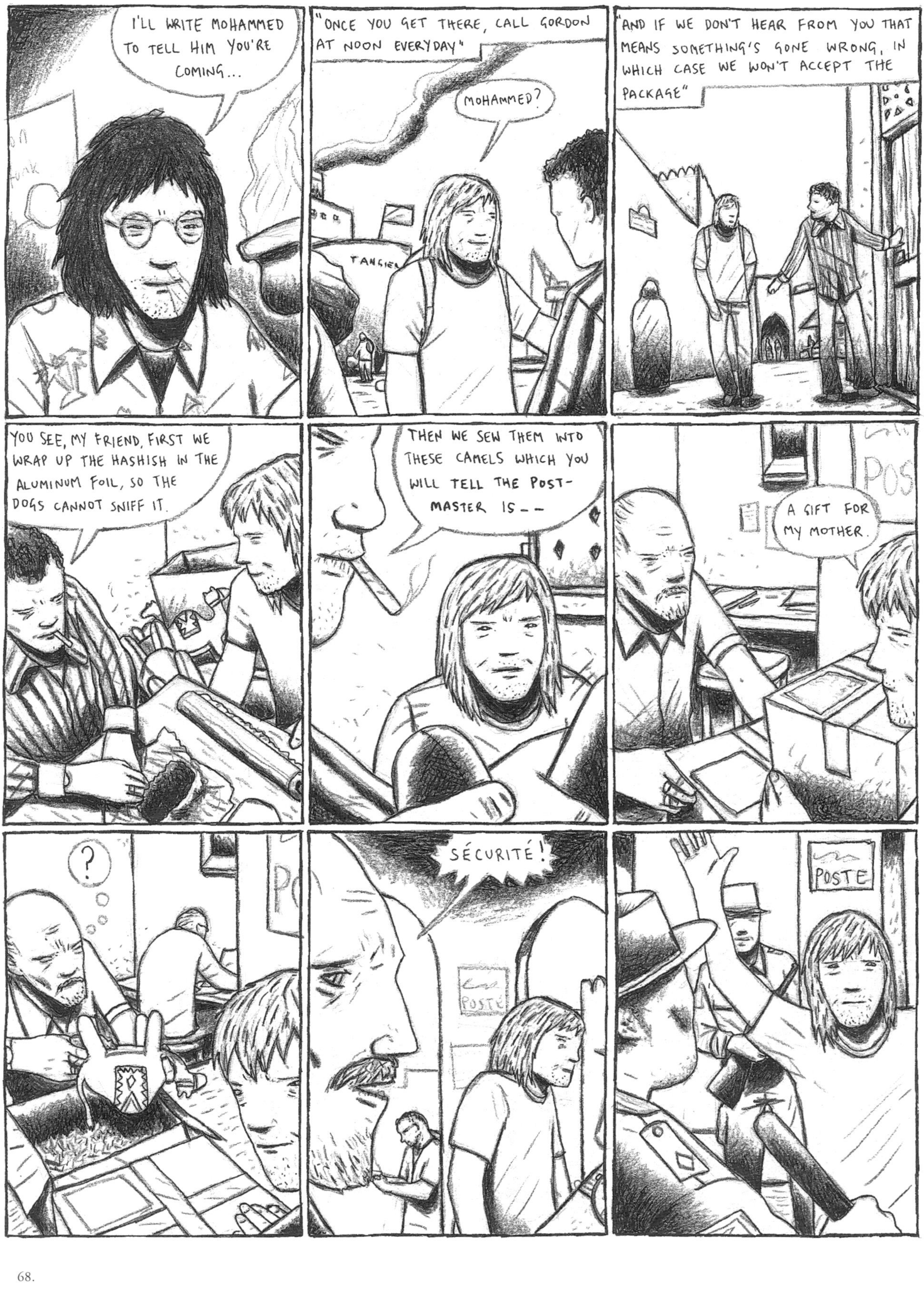
I'LL WRITE MOHAMMED TO TELL HIM YOU'RE COMING...
"ONCE YOU GET THERE, CALL GORDON AT NOON EVERYDAY"
MOHAMMED?
TANGIER
"AND IF WE DON'T HEAR FROM YOU THAT MEANS SOMETHING'S GONE WRONG, IN WHICH CASE WE WON'T ACCEPT THE PACKAGE"
YOU SEE, MY FRIEND, FIRST WE WRAP UP THE HASHISH IN THE ALUMINUM FOIL, SO THE DOGS CANNOT SNIFF IT.
THEN WE SEW THEM INTO THESE CAMELS WHICH YOU WILL TELL THE POST-MASTER IS--
A GIFT FOR MY MOTHER.
?
SÉCURITÉ!
POSTE
POSTE

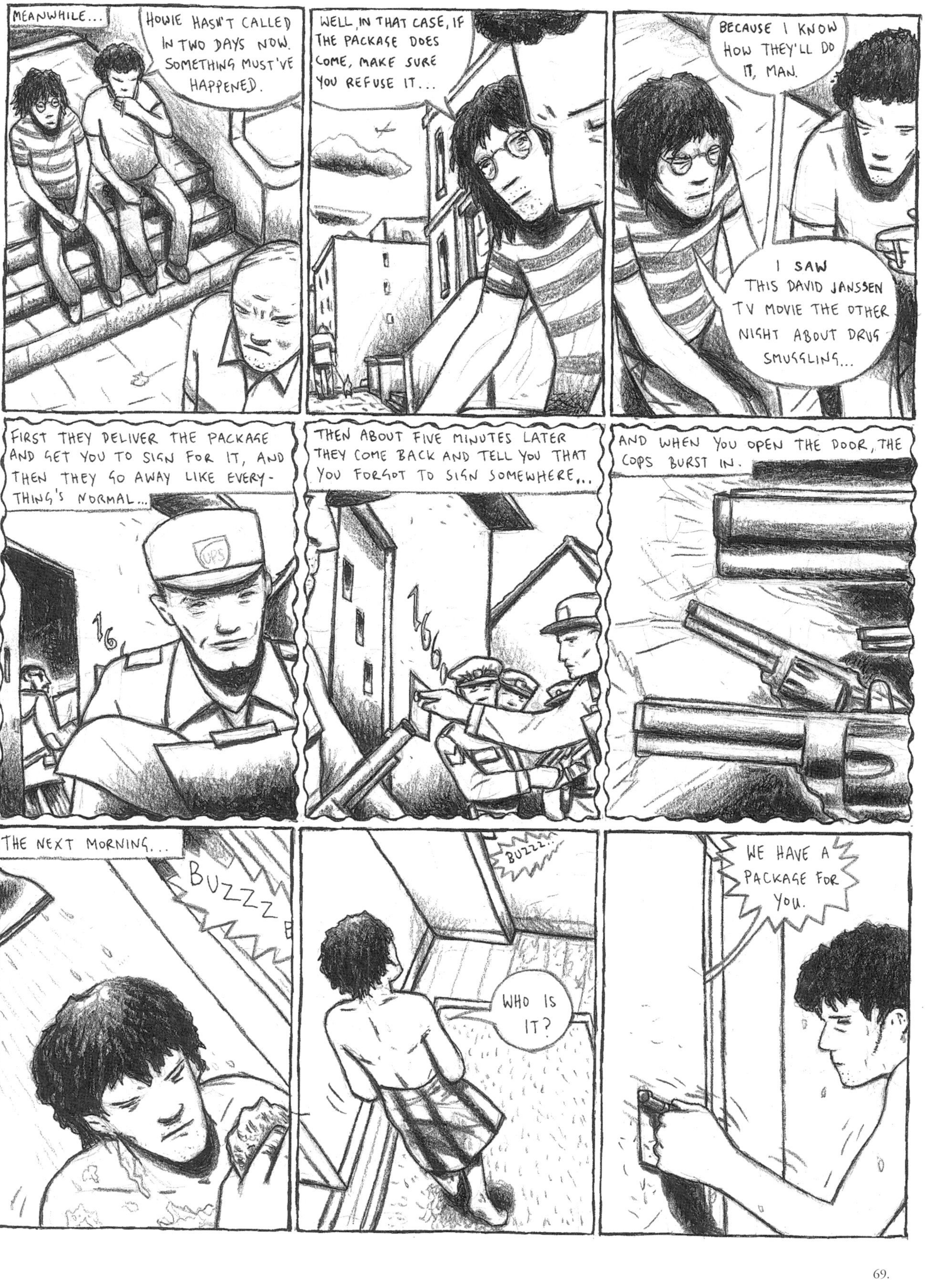
MEANWHILE...
HOWIE HASN'T CALLED IN TWO DAYS NOW. SOMETHING MUST'VE HAPPENED.
WELL, IN THAT CASE, IF THE PACKAGE DOES COME, MAKE SURE YOU REFUSE IT...
BECAUSE I KNOW HOW THEY'LL DO IT, MAN.
I SAW THIS DAVID JANSSEN TV MOVIE THE OTHER NIGHT ABOUT DRUG SMUGGLING...
FIRST THEY DELIVER THE PACKAGE AND GET YOU TO SIGN FOR IT, AND THEN THEY GO AWAY LIKE EVERY-THING'S NORMAL...
UPS
16
THEN ABOUT FIVE MINUTES LATER THEY COME BACK AND TELL YOU THAT YOU FORGOT TO SIGN SOMEWHERE...
AND WHEN YOU OPEN THE DOOR, THE COPS BURST IN.
THE NEXT MORNING...
BUZZZ
BUZZZ...
WHO IS IT?
WE HAVE A PACKAGE FOR YOU.

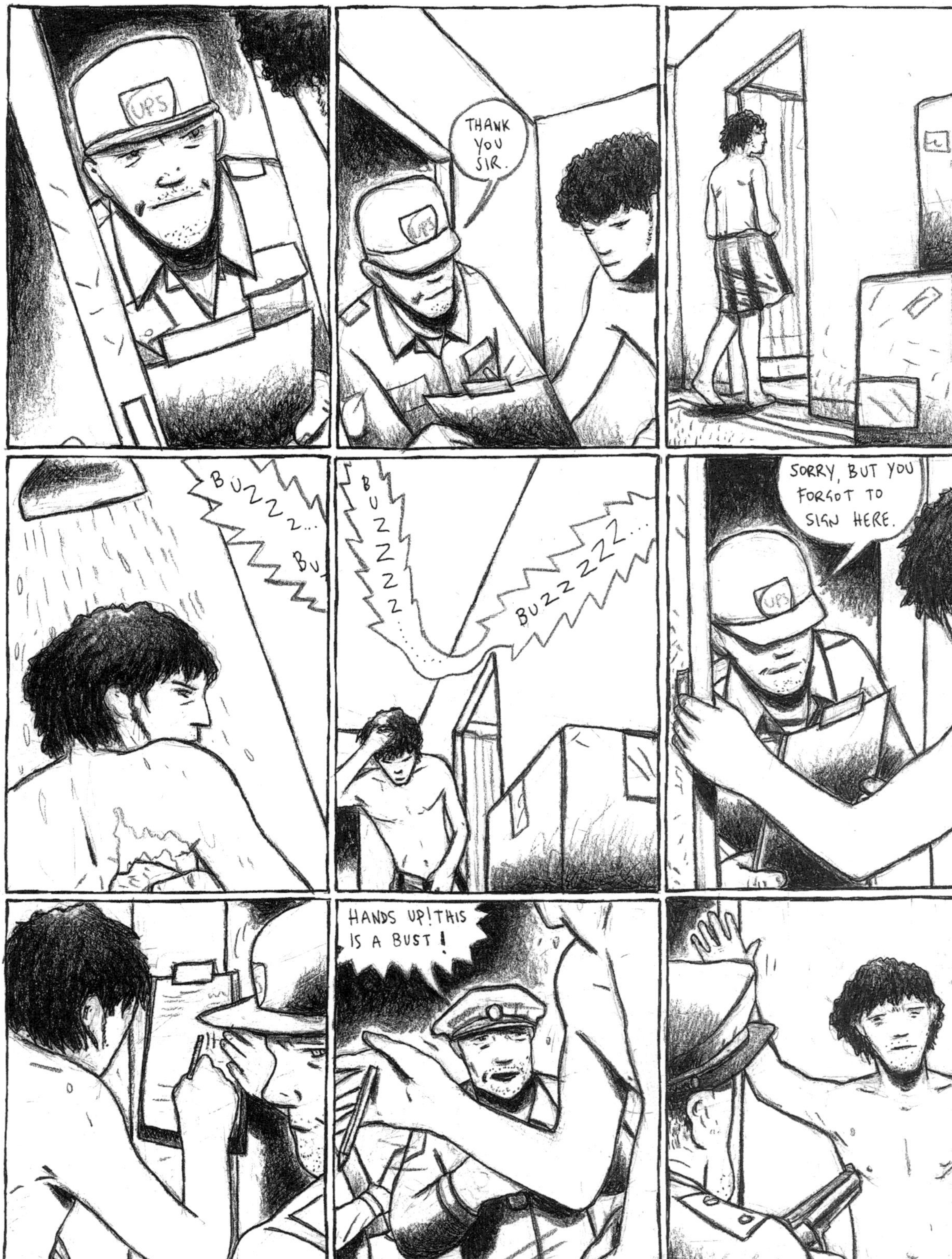
THANK YOU SIR.
BUZZz...
BU
BUZZZZ...
BUZZZZZ...
SORRY, BUT YOU FORGOT TO SIGN HERE.
HANDS UP! THIS IS A BUST!
POLICE

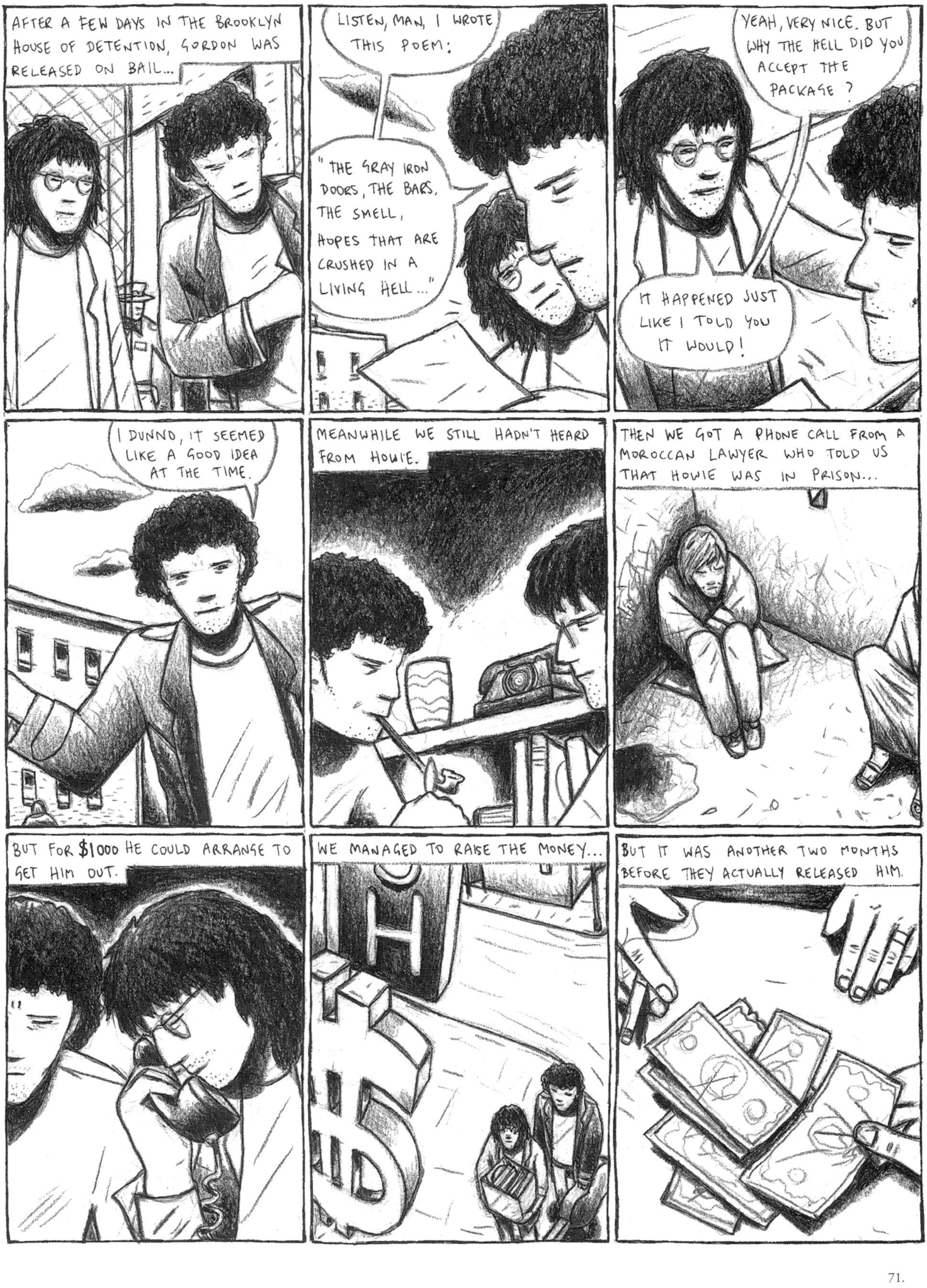
AFTER A FEW DAYS IN THE BROOKLYN HOUSE OF DETENTION, GORDON WAS RELEASED ON BAIL...
LISTEN, MAN, I WROTE THIS POEM:
"THE GRAY IRON DOORS, THE BARS, THE SMELL, HOPES THAT ARE CRUSHED IN A LIVING HELL..."
YEAH, VERY NICE. BUT WHY THE HELL DID YOU ACCEPT THE PACKAGE ?
IT HAPPENED JUST LIKE I TOLD YOU IT WOULD!
I DUNNO, IT SEEMED LIKE A GOOD IDEA AT THE TIME.
MEANWHILE WE STILL HADN'T HEARD FROM HOWIE.
THEN WE GOT A PHONE CALL FROM A MOROCCAN LAWYER WHO TOLD US THAT HOWIE WAS IN PRISON...
BUT FOR $1000 HE COULD ARRANGE TO GET HIM OUT.
WE MANAGED TO RAISE THE MONEY...
BUT IT WAS ANOTHER TWO MONTHS BEFORE THEY ACTUALLY RELEASED HIM.

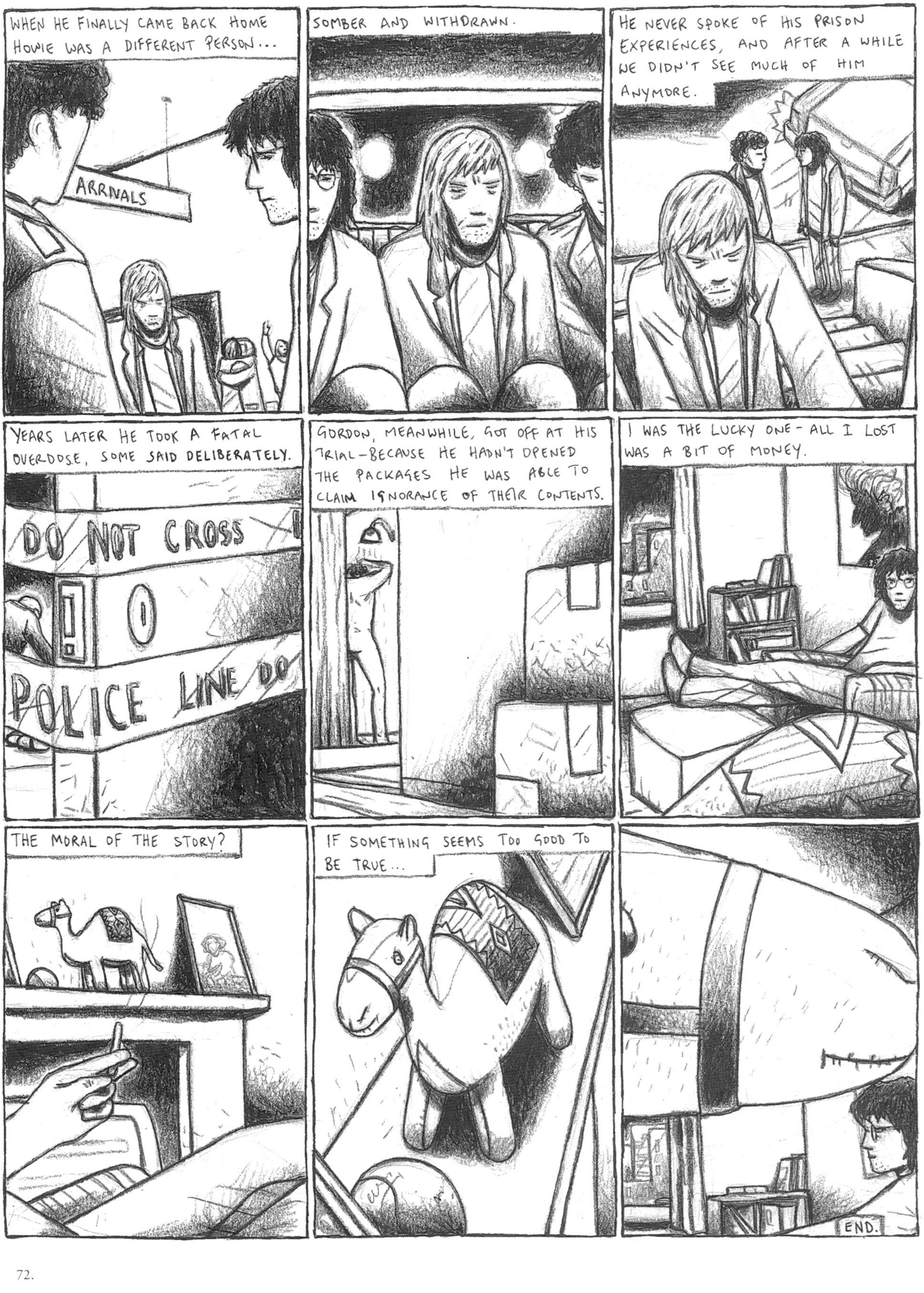
WHEN HE FINALLY CAME BACK HOME HOWIE WAS A DIFFERENT PERSON...
ARRIVALS
SOMBER AND WITHDRAWN.
HE NEVER SPOKE OF HIS PRISON EXPERIENCES, AND AFTER A WHILE WE DIDN'T SEE MUCH OF HIM ANYMORE.
YEARS LATER HE TOOK A FATAL OVERDOSE, SOME SAID DELIBERATELY.
DO NOT CROSS
POLICE LINE DO
GORDON, MEANWHILE, GOT OFF AT HIS TRIAL—BECAUSE HE HADN'T OPENED THE PACKAGES HE WAS ABLE TO CLAIM IGNORANCE OF THEIR CONTENTS.
I WAS THE LUCKY ONE—ALL I LOST WAS A BIT OF MONEY.
THE MORAL OF THE STORY?
IF SOMETHING SEEMS TOO GOOD TO BE TRUE...
END.

daphne

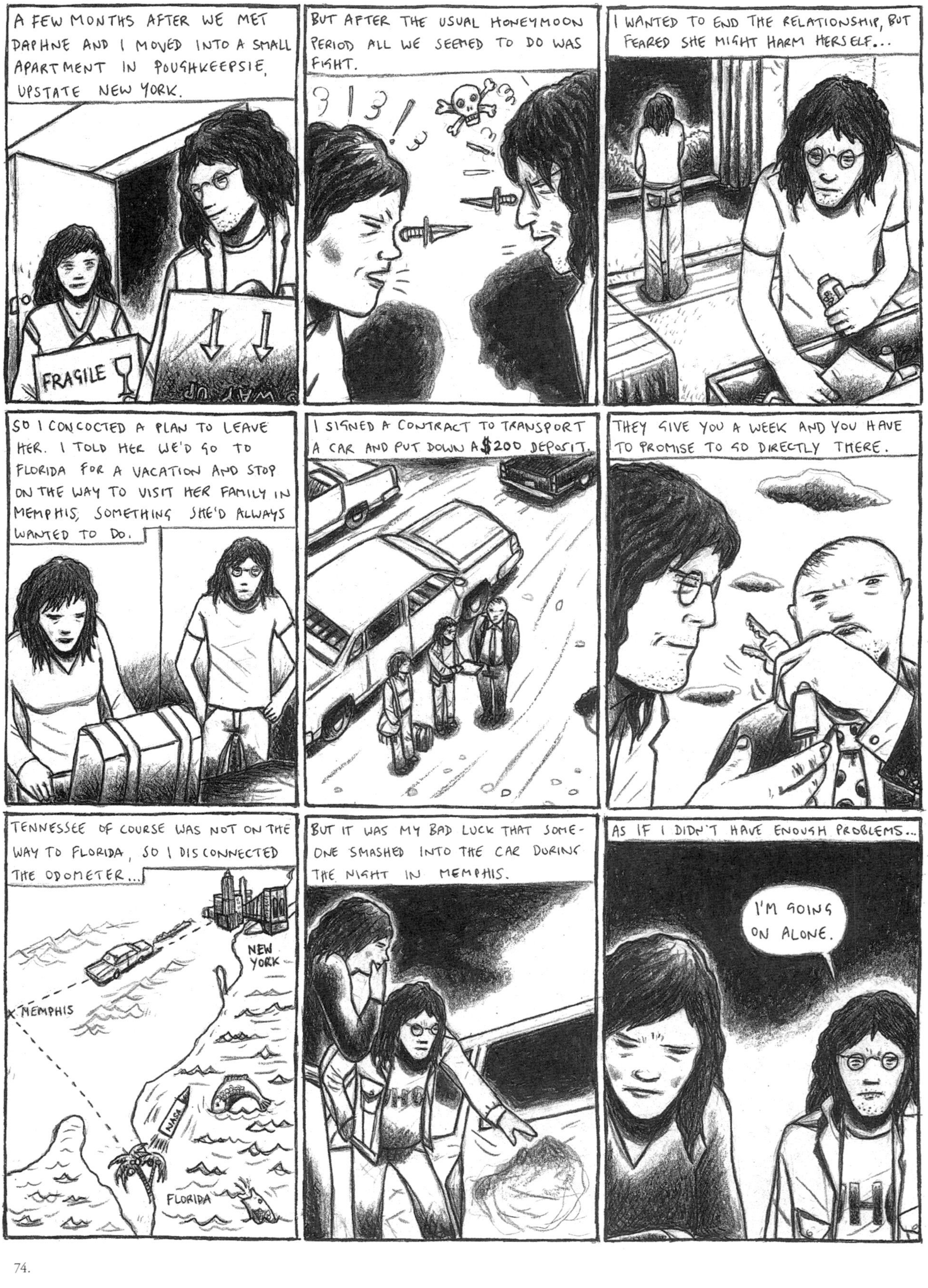
A FEW MONTHS AFTER WE MET DAPHNE AND I MOVED INTO A SMALL APARTMENT IN POUGHKEEPSIE, UPSTATE NEW YORK.
FRAGILE
BUT AFTER THE USUAL HONEYMOON PERIOD ALL WE SEEMED TO DO WAS FIGHT.
I WANTED TO END THE RELATIONSHIP, BUT FEARED SHE MIGHT HARM HERSELF...
SO I CONCOCTED A PLAN TO LEAVE HER. I TOLD HER WE'D GO TO FLORIDA FOR A VACATION AND STOP ON THE WAY TO VISIT HER FAMILY IN MEMPHIS, SOMETHING SHE'D ALWAYS WANTED TO DO.
I SIGNED A CONTRACT TO TRANSPORT A CAR AND PUT DOWN A $200 DEPOSIT.
THEY GIVE YOU A WEEK AND YOU HAVE TO PROMISE TO GO DIRECTLY THERE.
TENNESSEE OF COURSE WAS NOT ON THE WAY TO FLORIDA, SO I DISCONNECTED THE ODOMETER...
NEW YORK
MEMPHIS
FLORIDA
BUT IT WAS MY BAD LUCK THAT SOME-ONE SMASHED INTO THE CAR DURING THE NIGHT IN MEMPHIS.
AS IF I DIDN'T HAVE ENOUGH PROBLEMS...
I'M GOING ON ALONE.

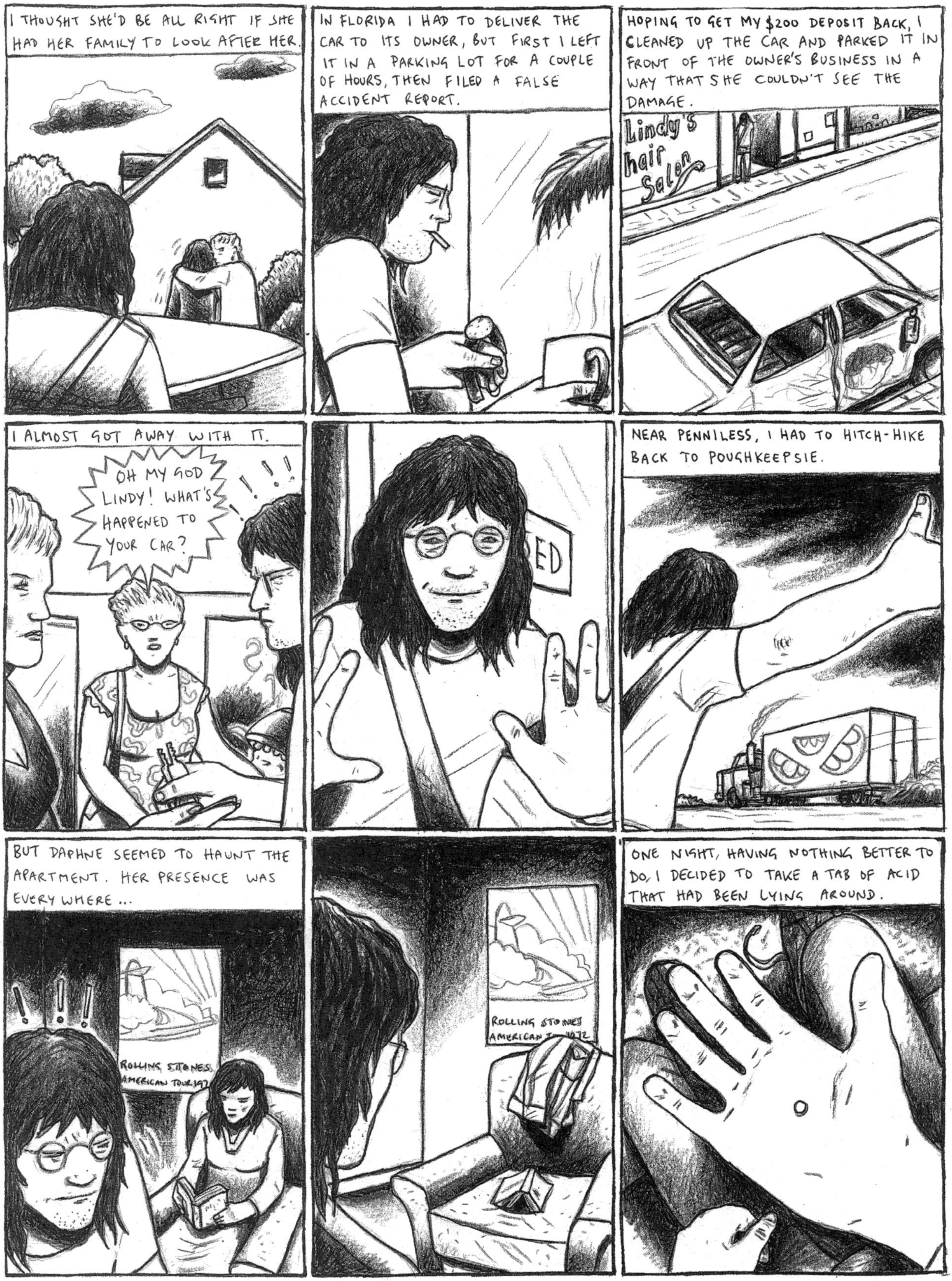
I THOUGHT SHE'D BE ALL RIGHT IF SHE HAD HER FAMILY TO LOOK AFTER HER.
IN FLORIDA I HAD TO DELIVER THE CAR TO ITS OWNER, BUT FIRST I LEFT IT IN A PARKING LOT FOR A COUPLE OF HOURS, THEN FILED A FALSE ACCIDENT REPORT.
HOPING TO GET MY $200 DEPOSIT BACK, I CLEANED UP THE CAR AND PARKED IT IN FRONT OF THE OWNER'S BUSINESS IN A WAY THAT SHE COULDN'T SEE THE DAMAGE.
Lindy's hair Salon
I ALMOST GOT AWAY WITH IT.
OH MY GOD LINDY! WHAT'S HAPPENED TO YOUR CAR?
!!!
NEAR PENNILESS, I HAD TO HITCH-HIKE BACK TO POUGHKEEPSIE.
BUT DAPHNE SEEMED TO HAUNT THE APARTMENT. HER PRESENCE WAS EVERYWHERE...
!!!
ROLLING STONES AMERICAN TOUR 1972
ROLLING STONES AMERICAN TOUR 1972
ONE NIGHT, HAVING NOTHING BETTER TO DO, I DECIDED TO TAKE A TAB OF ACID THAT HAD BEEN LYING AROUND.

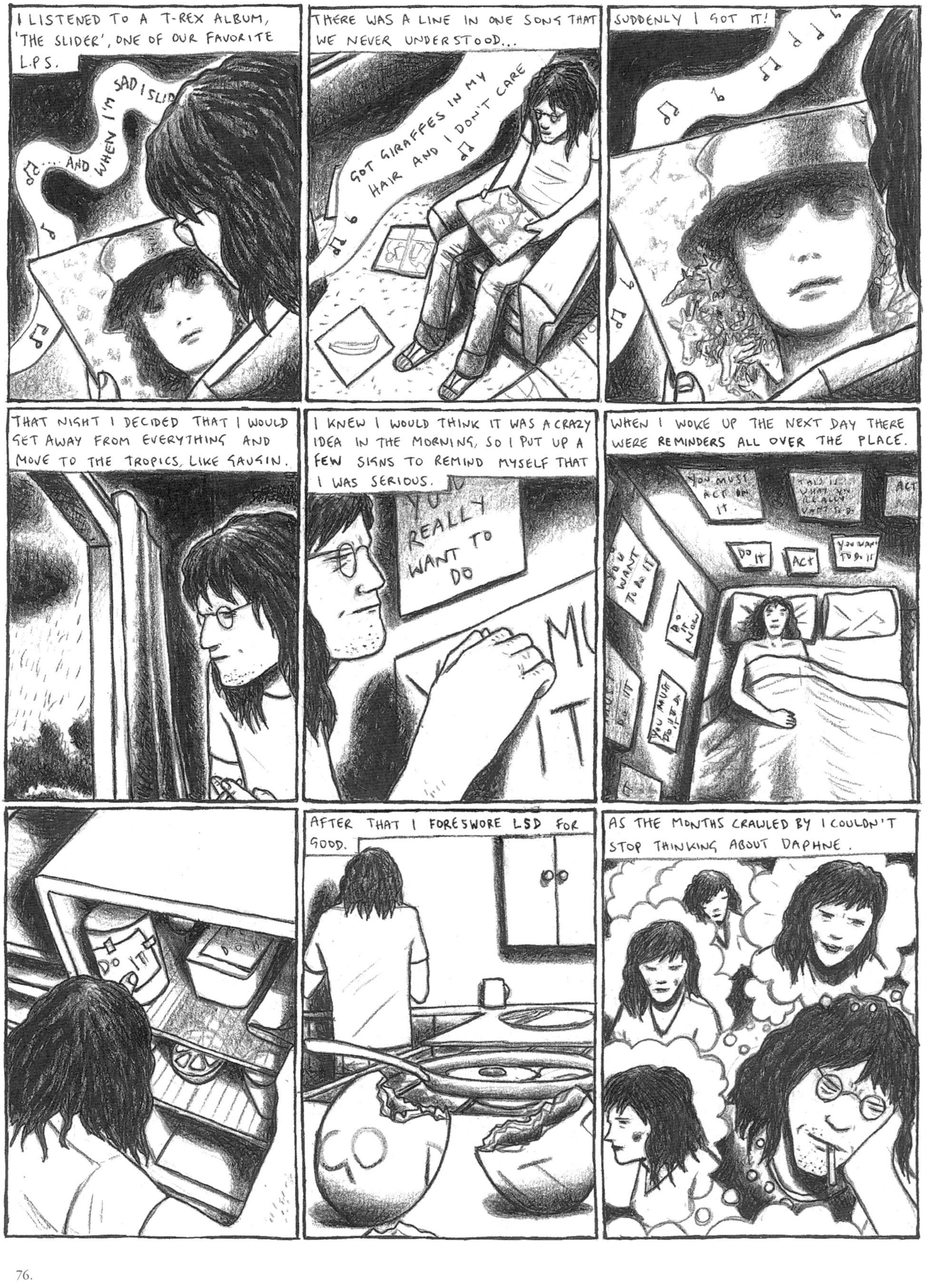
I LISTENED TO A T-REX ALBUM, 'THE SLIDER', ONE OF OUR FAVORITE L.P.S.
... AND WHEN I'M SAD I SLID
THERE WAS A LINE IN ONE SONG THAT WE NEVER UNDERSTOOD...
GOT GIRAFFES IN MY HAIR AND I DON'T CARE
SUDDENLY I GOT IT!
THAT NIGHT I DECIDED THAT I WOULD GET AWAY FROM EVERYTHING AND MOVE TO THE TROPICS, LIKE GAUGIN.
I KNEW I WOULD THINK IT WAS A CRAZY IDEA IN THE MORNING, SO I PUT UP A FEW SIGNS TO REMIND MYSELF THAT I WAS SERIOUS.
REALLY WANT TO DO
WHEN I WOKE UP THE NEXT DAY THERE WERE REMINDERS ALL OVER THE PLACE.
YOU MUST ACT ON IT.
ACT
DO IT
ACT
DO IT NOW
DO IT
AFTER THAT I FORESWORE LSD FOR GOOD.
AS THE MONTHS CRAWLED BY I COULDN'T STOP THINKING ABOUT DAPHNE.

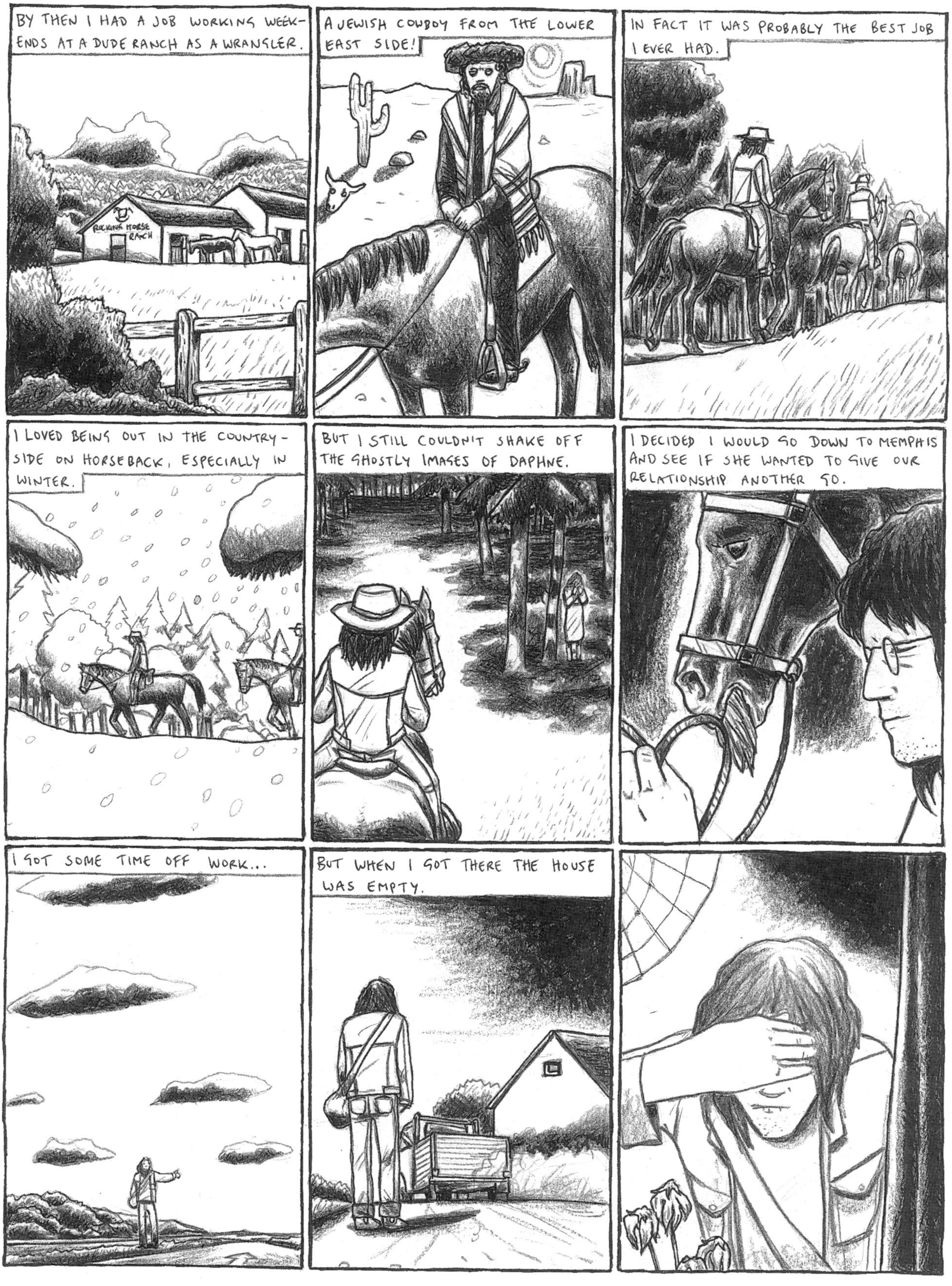
BY THEN I HAD A JOB WORKING WEEK-ENDS AT A DUDE RANCH AS A WRANGLER.
ROCKING HORSE RANCH
A JEWISH COWBOY FROM THE LOWER EAST SIDE!
IN FACT IT WAS PROBABLY THE BEST JOB I EVER HAD.
I LOVED BEING OUT IN THE COUNTRY-SIDE ON HORSEBACK, ESPECIALLY IN WINTER.
BUT I STILL COULDN'T SHAKE OFF THE GHOSTLY IMAGES OF DAPHNE.
I DECIDED I WOULD GO DOWN TO MEMPHIS AND SEE IF SHE WANTED TO GIVE OUR RELATIONSHIP ANOTHER GO.
I GOT SOME TIME OFF WORK...
BUT WHEN I GOT THERE THE HOUSE WAS EMPTY.

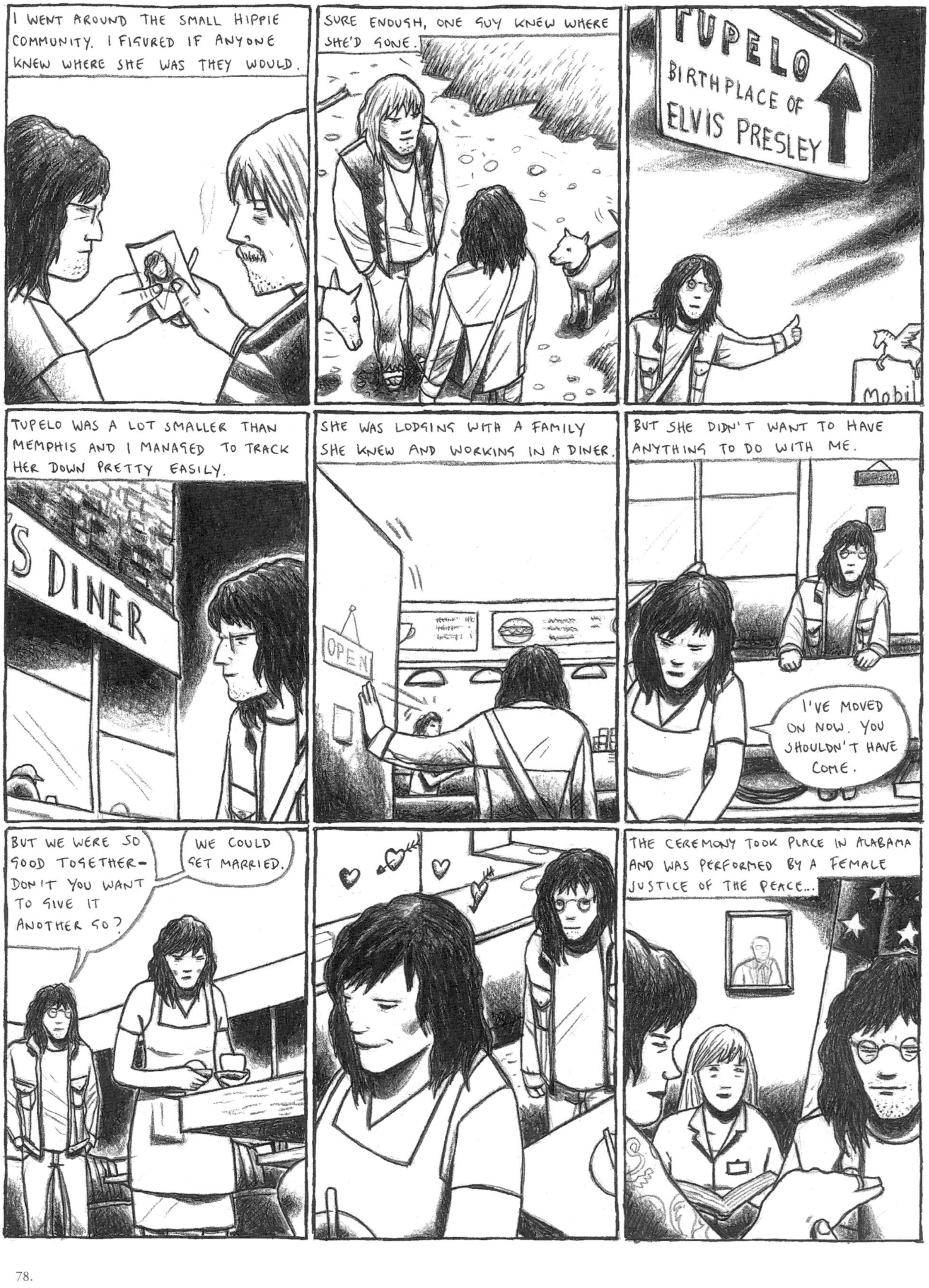
I WENT AROUND THE SMALL HIPPIE COMMUNITY. I FIGURED IF ANYONE KNEW WHERE SHE WAS THEY WOULD.
SURE ENOUGH, ONE GUY KNEW WHERE SHE'D GONE.
TUPELO
BIRTHPLACE OF ELVIS PRESLEY
Mobil
TUPELO WAS A LOT SMALLER THAN MEMPHIS AND I MANAGED TO TRACK HER DOWN PRETTY EASILY.
DINER
SHE WAS LODGING WITH A FAMILY SHE KNEW AND WORKING IN A DINER.
OPEN
BUT SHE DIDN'T WANT TO HAVE ANYTHING TO DO WITH ME.
I'VE MOVED ON NOW. YOU SHOULDN'T HAVE COME.
BUT WE WERE SO GOOD TOGETHER- DON'T YOU WANT TO GIVE IT ANOTHER GO?
WE COULD GET MARRIED.
THE CEREMONY TOOK PLACE IN ALABAMA AND WAS PERFORMED BY A FEMALE JUSTICE OF THE PEACE...

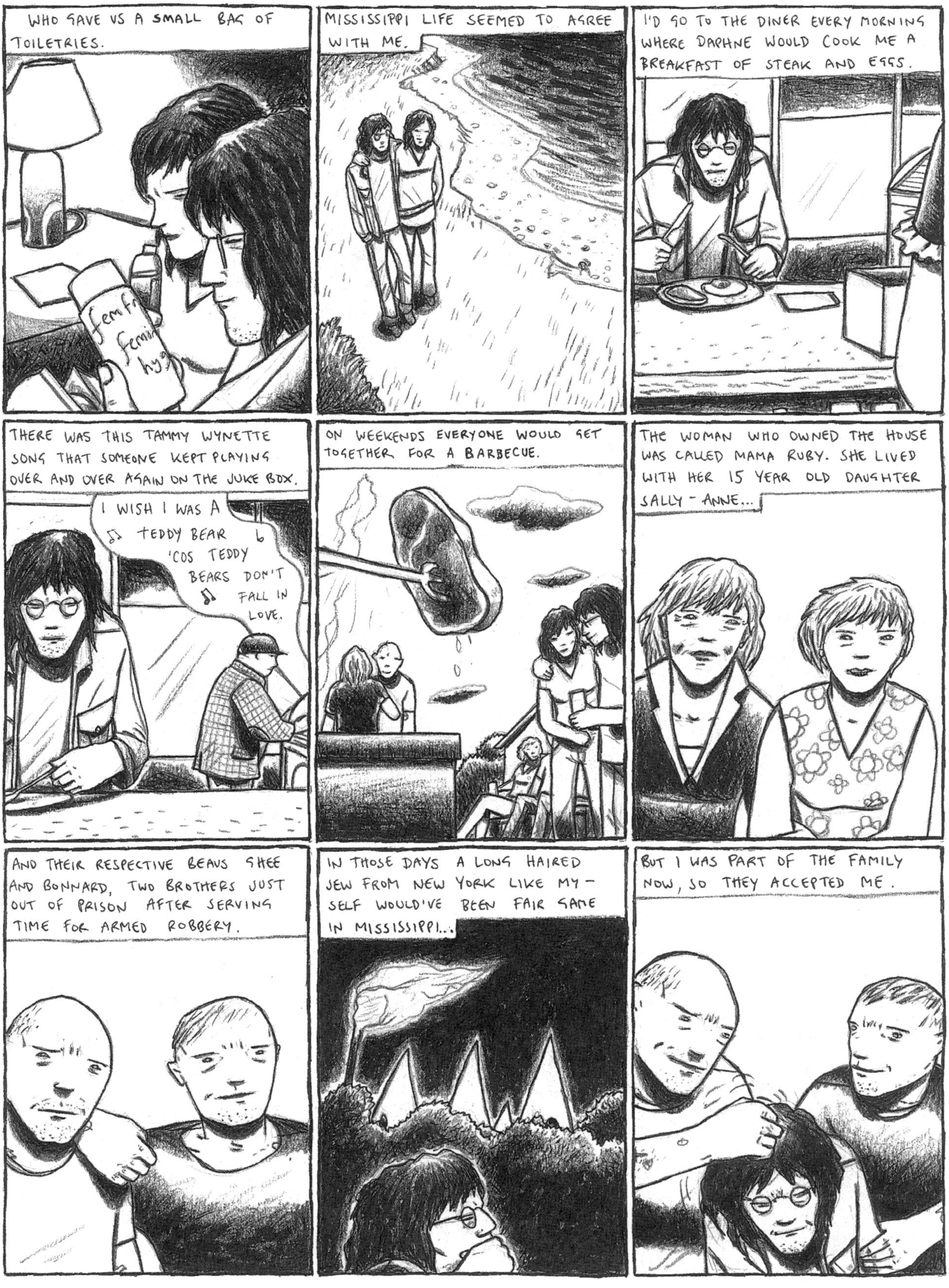
WHO GAVE US A SMALL BAG OF TOILETRIES.
MISSISSIPPI LIFE SEEMED TO AGREE WITH ME.
I'D GO TO THE DINER EVERY MORNING WHERE DAPHNE WOULD COOK ME A BREAKFAST OF STEAK AND EGGS.
THERE WAS THIS TAMMY WYNETTE SONG THAT SOMEONE KEPT PLAYING OVER AND OVER AGAIN ON THE JUKE BOX.
I WISH I WAS A TEDDY BEAR 'COS TEDDY BEARS DON'T FALL IN LOVE.
ON WEEKENDS EVERYONE WOULD GET TOGETHER FOR A BARBECUE.
THE WOMAN WHO OWNED THE HOUSE WAS CALLED MAMA RUBY. SHE LIVED WITH HER 15 YEAR OLD DAUGHTER SALLY-ANNE...
AND THEIR RESPECTIVE BEAUS SHEE AND BONNARD, TWO BROTHERS JUST OUT OF PRISON AFTER SERVING TIME FOR ARMED ROBBERY.
IN THOSE DAYS A LONG HAIRED JEW FROM NEW YORK LIKE MY-SELF WOULD'VE BEEN FAIR GAME IN MISSISSIPPI...
BUT I WAS PART OF THE FAMILY NOW, SO THEY ACCEPTED ME.

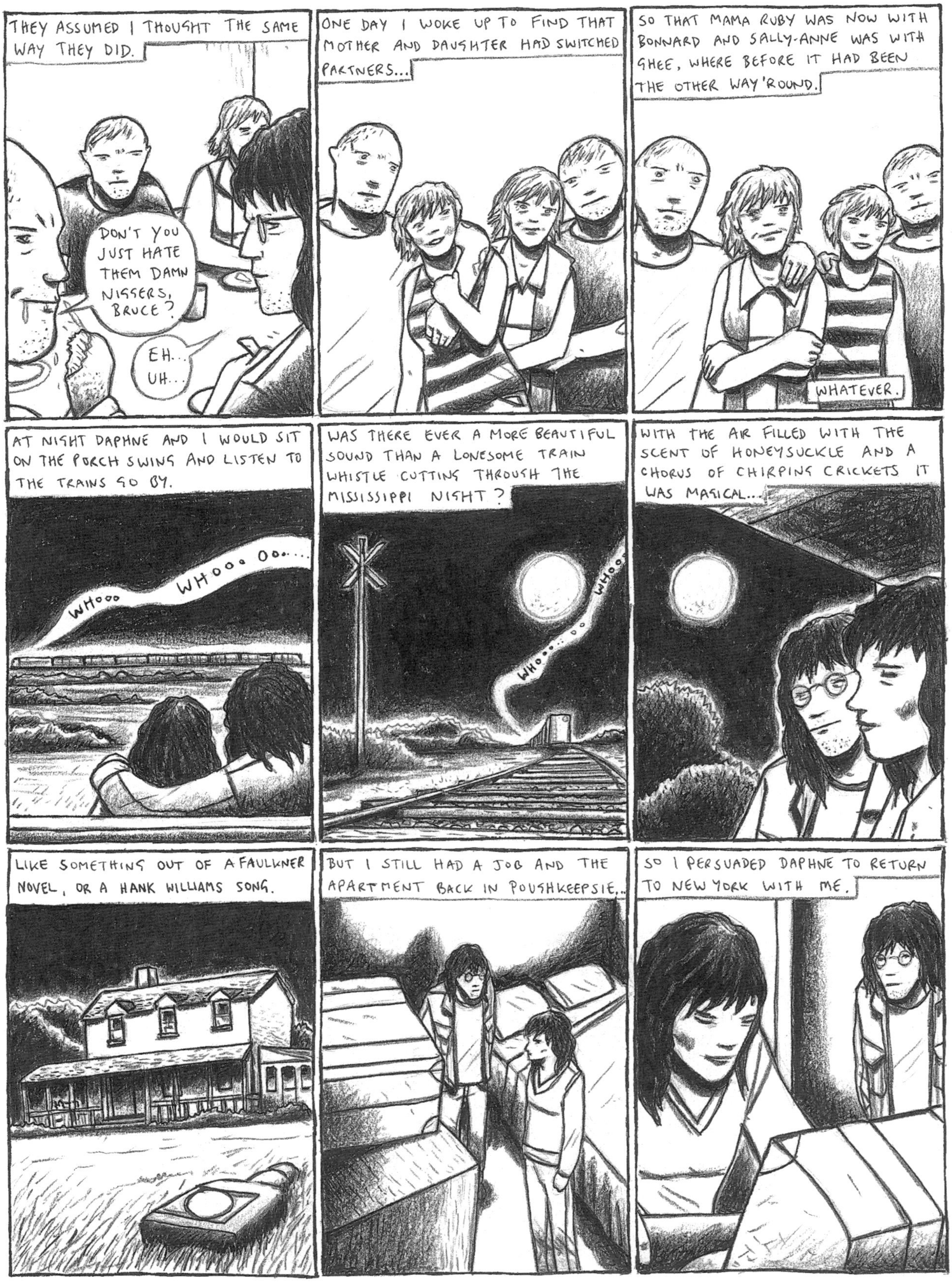
THEY ASSUMED I THOUGHT THE SAME WAY THEY DID.
DON'T YOU JUST HATE THEM DAMN NIGGERS, BRUCE?
EH... UH...
ONE DAY I WOKE UP TO FIND THAT MOTHER AND DAUGHTER HAD SWITCHED PARTNERS...
SO THAT MAMA RUBY WAS NOW WITH BONNARD AND SALLY-ANNE WAS WITH GHEE, WHERE BEFORE IT HAD BEEN THE OTHER WAY 'ROUND.
WHATEVER.
AT NIGHT DAPHNE AND I WOULD SIT ON THE PORCH SWING AND LISTEN TO THE TRAINS GO BY.
WHOOO WHOOO OO....
WAS THERE EVER A MORE BEAUTIFUL SOUND THAN A LONESOME TRAIN WHISTLE CUTTING THROUGH THE MISSISSIPPI NIGHT?
WHOOO... OO WHOOO
WITH THE AIR FILLED WITH THE SCENT OF HONEYSUCKLE AND A CHORUS OF CHIRPING CRICKETS IT WAS MAGICAL...
LIKE SOMETHING OUT OF A FAULKNER NOVEL, OR A HANK WILLIAMS SONG.
BUT I STILL HAD A JOB AND THE APARTMENT BACK IN POUGHKEEPSIE...
SO I PERSUADED DAPHNE TO RETURN TO NEW YORK WITH ME.

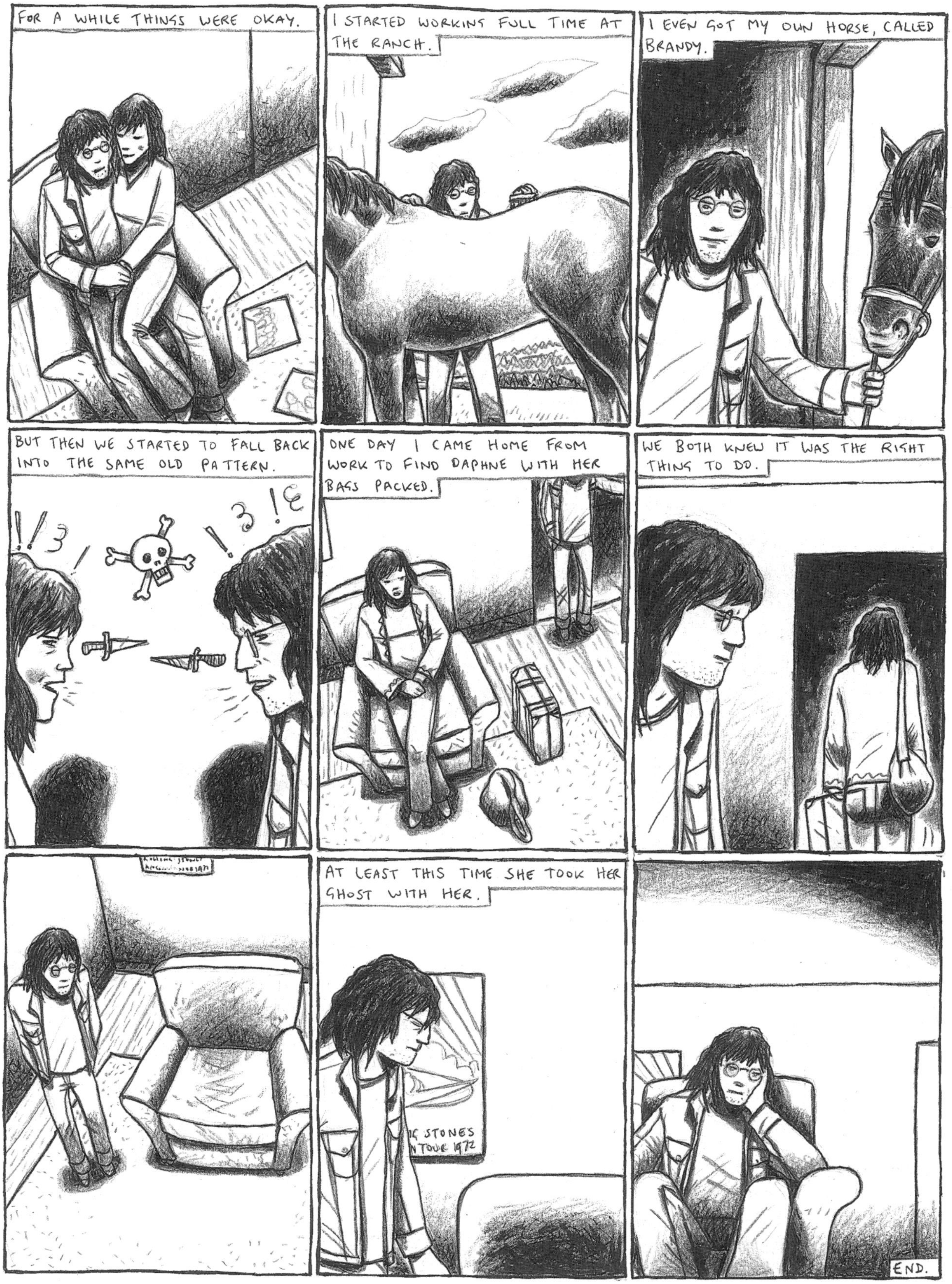
FOR A WHILE THINGS WERE OKAY.
I STARTED WORKING FULL TIME AT THE RANCH.
I EVEN GOT MY OWN HORSE, CALLED BRANDY.
BUT THEN WE STARTED TO FALL BACK INTO THE SAME OLD PATTERN.
ONE DAY I CAME HOME FROM WORK TO FIND DAPHNE WITH HER BAGS PACKED.
WE BOTH KNEW IT WAS THE RIGHT THING TO DO.
AT LEAST THIS TIME SHE TOOK HER GHOST WITH HER.
END.

Mardi Gras Part 1

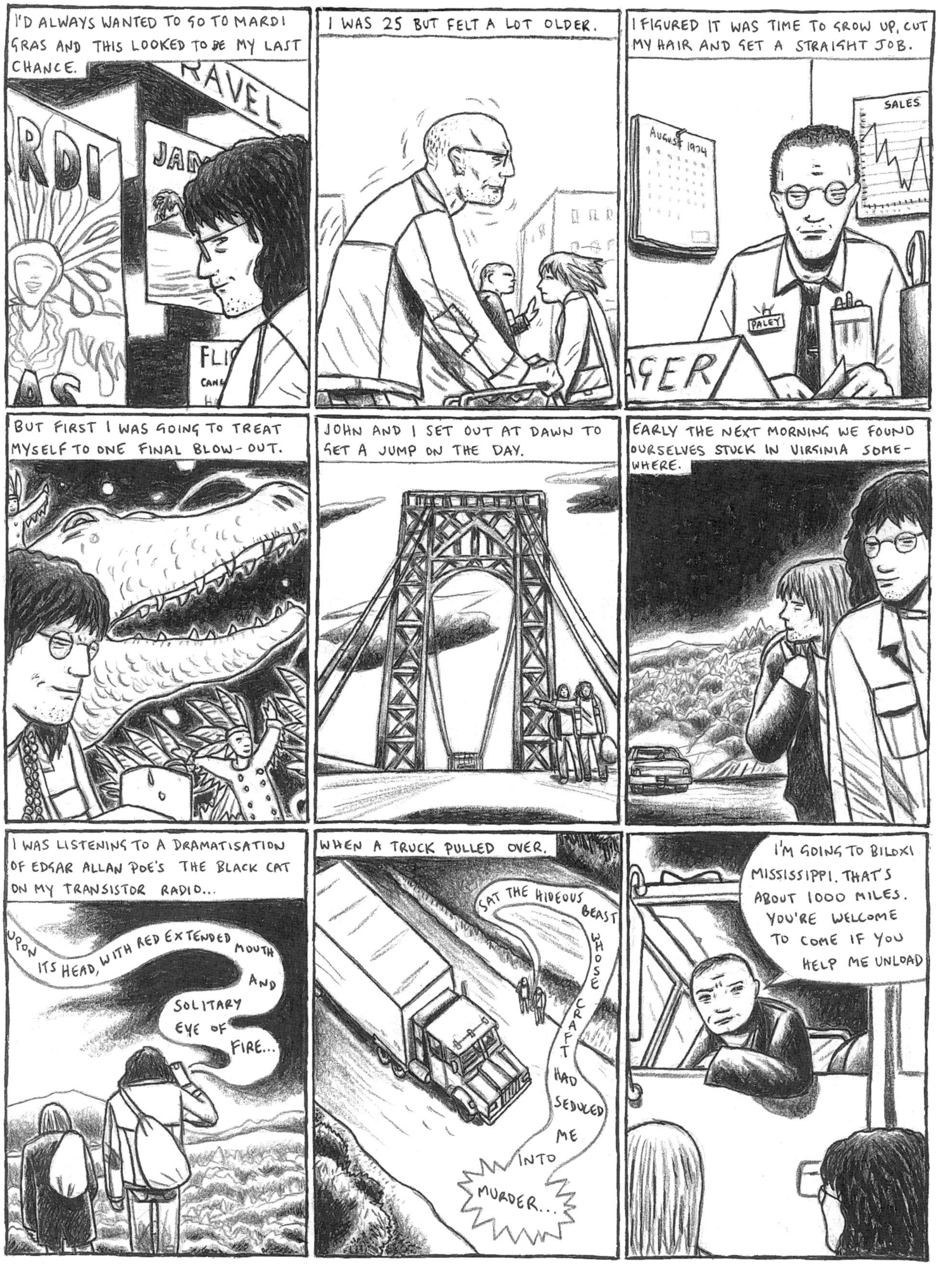

I'D ALWAYS WANTED TO GO TO MARDI GRAS AND THIS LOOKED TO BE MY LAST CHANCE.
RAVEL
RDI
I WAS 25 BUT FELT A LOT OLDER.
I FIGURED IT WAS TIME TO GROW UP, CUT MY HAIR AND GET A STRAIGHT JOB.
SALES
AUGUST 1974
PALEY
AGER
BUT FIRST I WAS GOING TO TREAT MYSELF TO ONE FINAL BLOW-OUT.
JOHN AND I SET OUT AT DAWN TO GET A JUMP ON THE DAY.
EARLY THE NEXT MORNING WE FOUND OURSELVES STUCK IN VIRGINIA SOMEWHERE.
I WAS LISTENING TO A DRAMATISATION OF EDGAR ALLAN POE'S THE BLACK CAT ON MY TRANSISTOR RADIO...
UPON ITS HEAD, WITH RED EXTENDED MOUTH AND SOLITARY EYE OF FIRE...
WHEN A TRUCK PULLED OVER.
SAT THE HIDEOUS BEAST WHOSE CRAFT HAD SEDUCED ME INTO MURDER...
I'M GOING TO BILOXI MISSISSIPPI. THAT'S ABOUT 1000 MILES. YOU'RE WELCOME TO COME IF YOU HELP ME UNLOAD

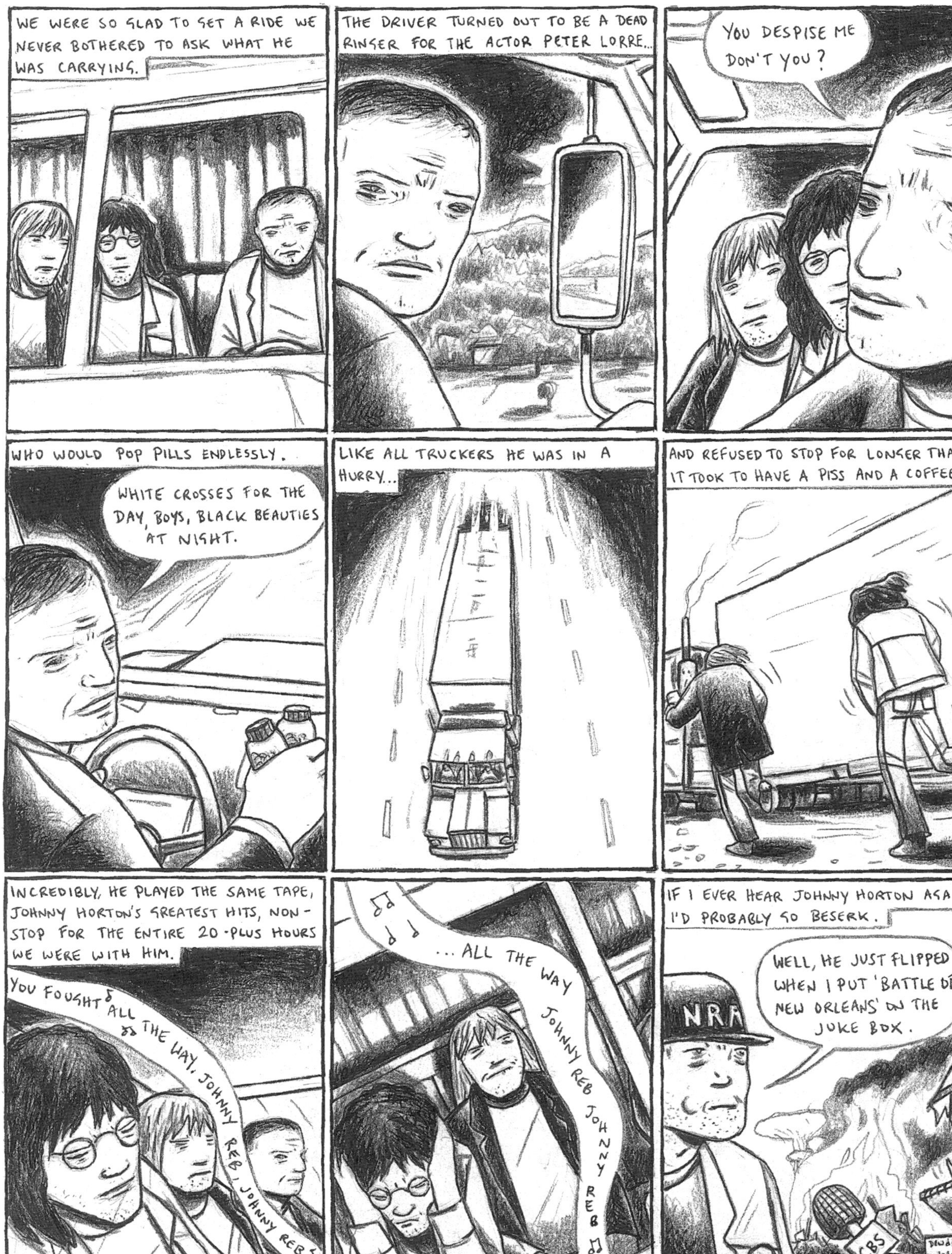
WE WERE SO GLAD TO GET A RIDE WE NEVER BOTHERED TO ASK WHAT HE WAS CARRYING.
THE DRIVER TURNED OUT TO BE A DEAD RINGER FOR THE ACTOR PETER LORRE...
YOU DESPISE ME DON'T YOU?
WHO WOULD POP PILLS ENDLESSLY.
WHITE CROSSES FOR THE DAY, BOYS, BLACK BEAUTIES AT NIGHT.
LIKE ALL TRUCKERS HE WAS IN A HURRY...
AND REFUSED TO STOP FOR LONGER THAN IT TOOK TO HAVE A PISS AND A COFFEE.
INCREDIBLY, HE PLAYED THE SAME TAPE, JOHNNY HORTON'S GREATEST HITS, NON-STOP FOR THE ENTIRE 20-PLUS HOURS WE WERE WITH HIM.
YOU FOUGHT ALL THE WAY, JOHNNY REB, JOHNNY REB...
...ALL THE WAY JOHNNY REB JOHNNY REB
IF I EVER HEAR JOHNNY HORTON AGAIN I'D PROBABLY GO BESERK.
NRA
WELL, HE JUST FLIPPED WHEN I PUT 'BATTLE OF NEW ORLEANS' ON THE JUKE BOX.
CBS
DEWDROP INN

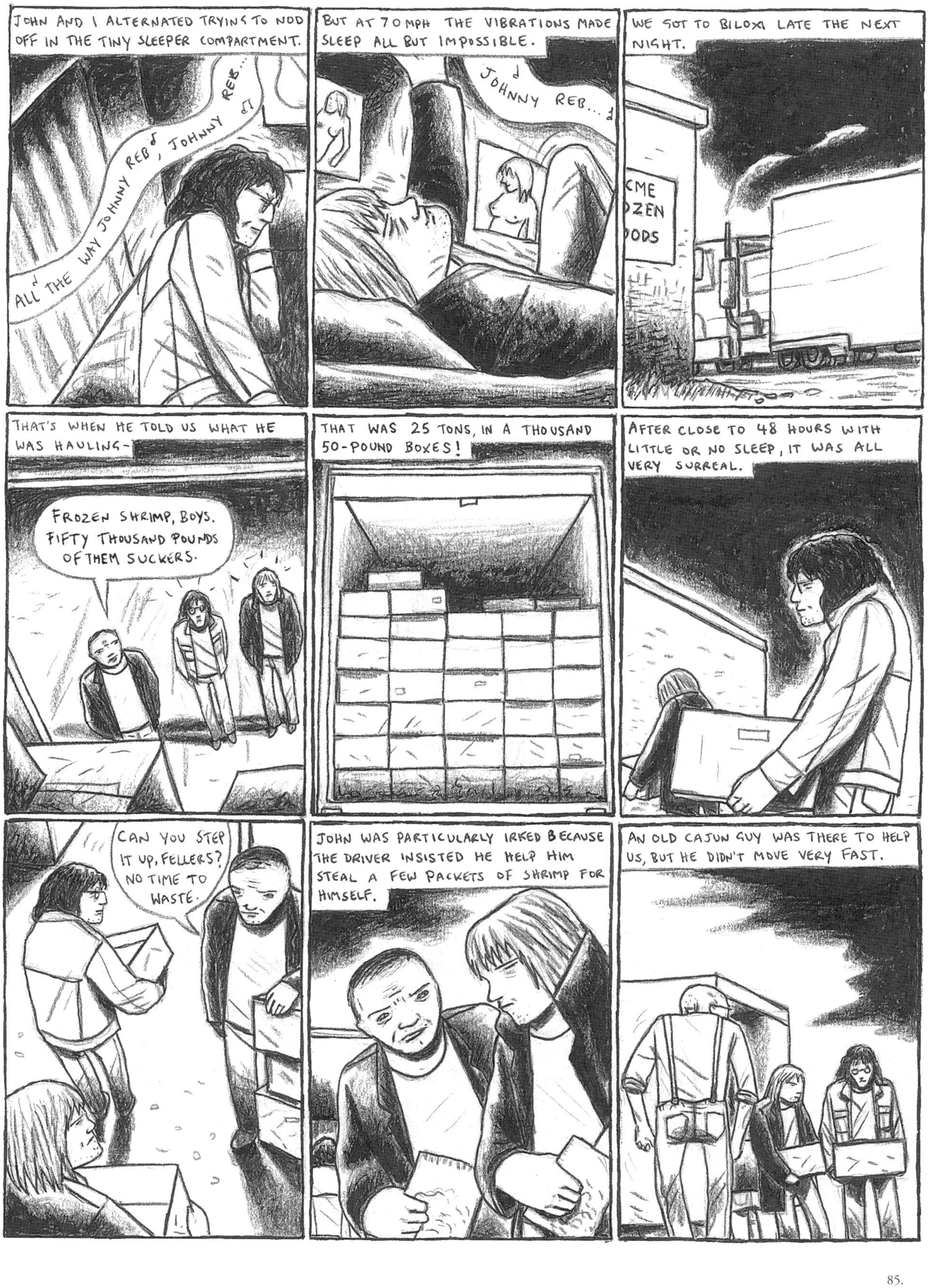
John and I alternated trying to nod off in the tiny sleeper compartment.
All the way Johnny Reb, Johnny Reb...
But at 70 mph the vibrations made sleep all but impossible.
Johnny Reb...
We got to Biloxi late the next night.
CME
ZEN
ODS
That's when he told us what he was hauling-
Frozen shrimp, boys. Fifty thousand pounds of them suckers.
That was 25 tons, in a thousand 50-pound boxes!
After close to 48 hours with little or no sleep, it was all very surreal.
Can you step it up, fellers? No time to waste.
John was particularly irked because the driver insisted he help him steal a few packets of shrimp for himself.
An old Cajun guy was there to help us, but he didn't move very fast.

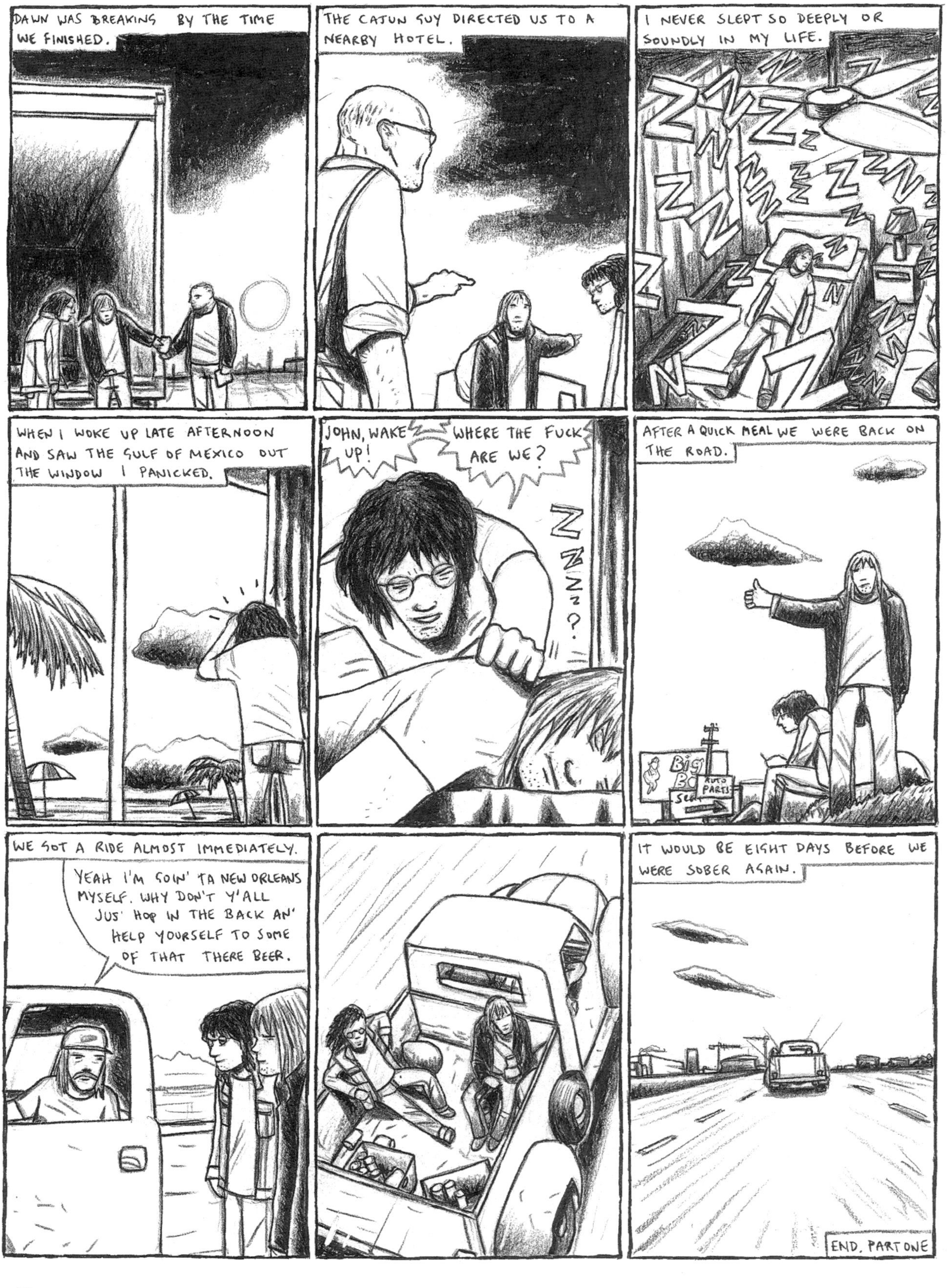
DAWN WAS BREAKING BY THE TIME WE FINISHED.
THE CAJUN GUY DIRECTED US TO A NEARBY HOTEL.
I NEVER SLEPT SO DEEPLY OR SOUNDLY IN MY LIFE.
WHEN I WOKE UP LATE AFTERNOON AND SAW THE GULF OF MEXICO OUT THE WINDOW I PANICKED.
JOHN, WAKE UP!
WHERE THE FUCK ARE WE?
ZZZ?
AFTER A QUICK MEAL WE WERE BACK ON THE ROAD.
AUTO PARTS
WE GOT A RIDE ALMOST IMMEDIATELY.
YEAH I'M GOIN' TA NEW ORLEANS MYSELF. WHY DON'T Y'ALL JUS' HOP IN THE BACK AN' HELP YOURSELF TO SOME OF THAT THERE BEER.
IT WOULD BE EIGHT DAYS BEFORE WE WERE SOBER AGAIN.
END, PART ONE

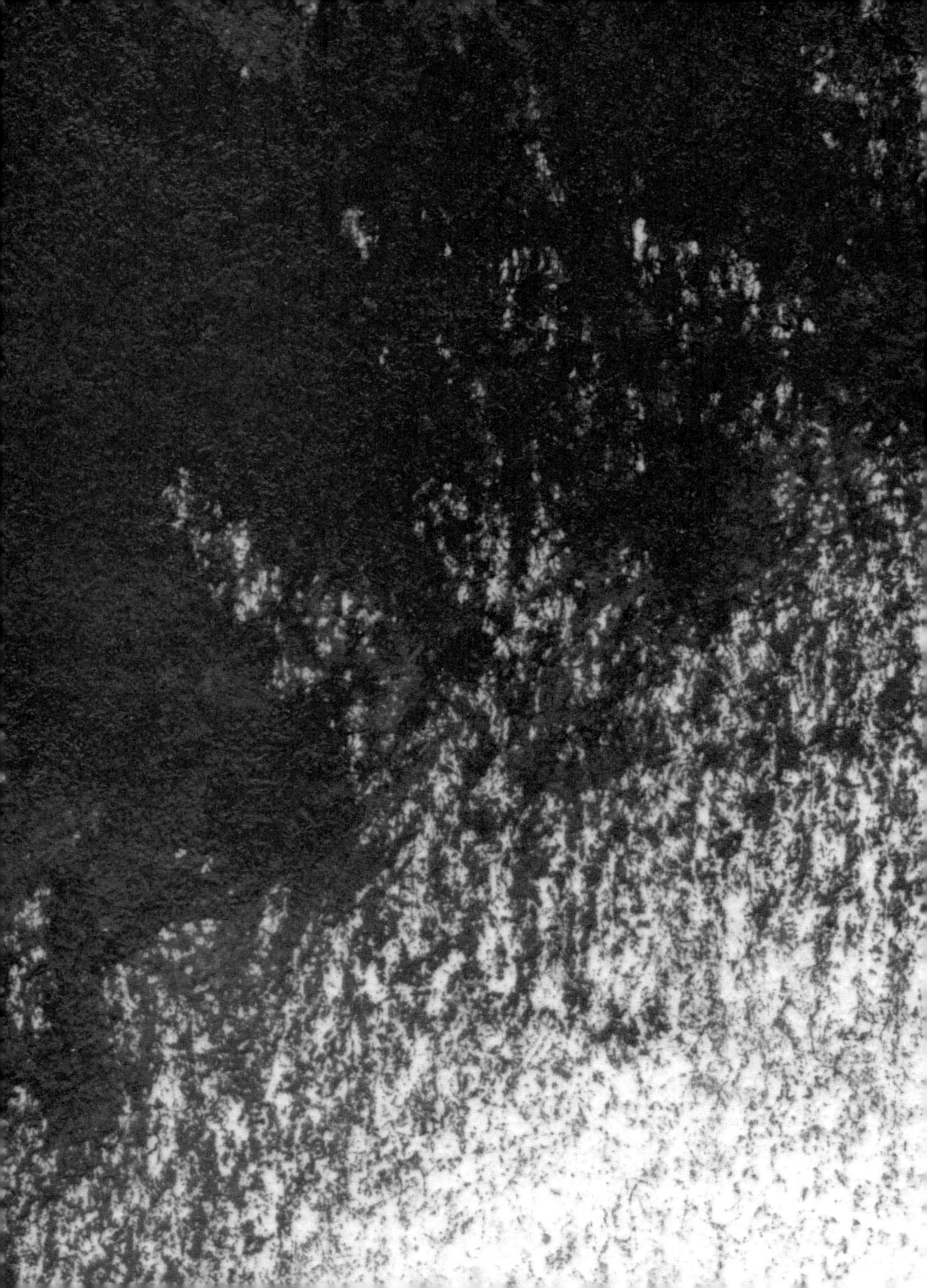

Ol' Man river, Mardi Gras part 2

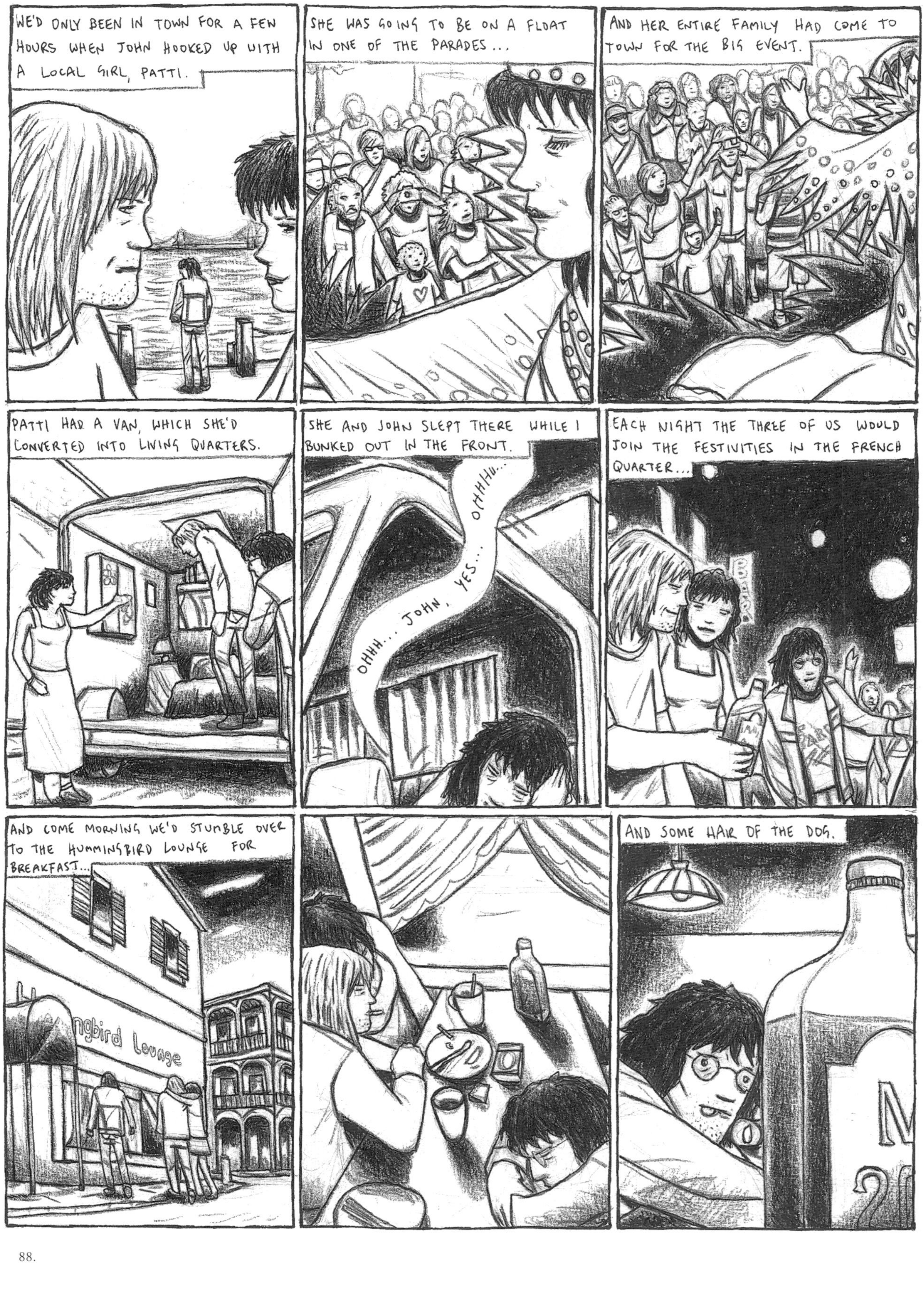

WE'D ONLY BEEN IN TOWN FOR A FEW HOURS WHEN JOHN HOOKED UP WITH A LOCAL GIRL, PATTI.
SHE WAS GOING TO BE ON A FLOAT IN ONE OF THE PARADES...
AND HER ENTIRE FAMILY HAD COME TO TOWN FOR THE BIG EVENT.
PATTI HAD A VAN, WHICH SHE'D CONVERTED INTO LIVING QUARTERS.
SHE AND JOHN SLEPT THERE WHILE I BUNKED OUT IN THE FRONT.
OHHH... JOHN, YES... OHHHH...
EACH NIGHT THE THREE OF US WOULD JOIN THE FESTIVITIES IN THE FRENCH QUARTER...
AND COME MORNING WE'D STUMBLE OVER TO THE HUMMINGBIRD LOUNGE FOR BREAKFAST...
ngbird Lounge
AND SOME HAIR OF THE DOG.

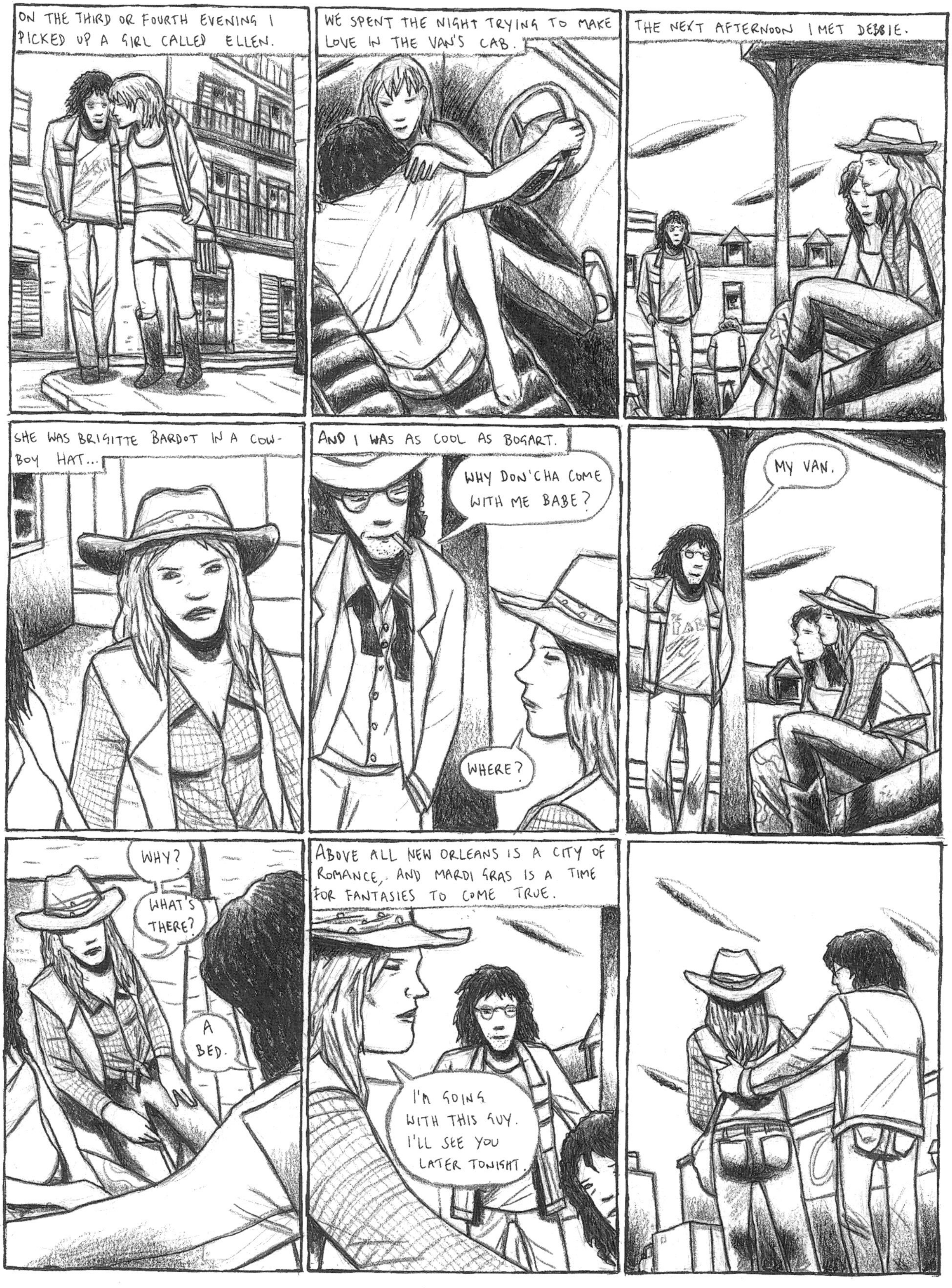
ON THE THIRD OR FOURTH EVENING I PICKED UP A GIRL CALLED ELLEN.
WE SPENT THE NIGHT TRYING TO MAKE LOVE IN THE VAN'S CAB.
THE NEXT AFTERNOON I MET DEBBIE.
SHE WAS BRIGITTE BARDOT IN A COW-BOY HAT...
AND I WAS AS COOL AS BOGART.
WHY DON'CHA COME WITH ME BABE?
WHERE?
MY VAN.
WHY?
WHAT'S THERE?
A BED.
ABOVE ALL NEW ORLEANS IS A CITY OF ROMANCE, AND MARDI GRAS IS A TIME FOR FANTASIES TO COME TRUE.
I'M GOING WITH THIS GUY. I'LL SEE YOU LATER TONIGHT.

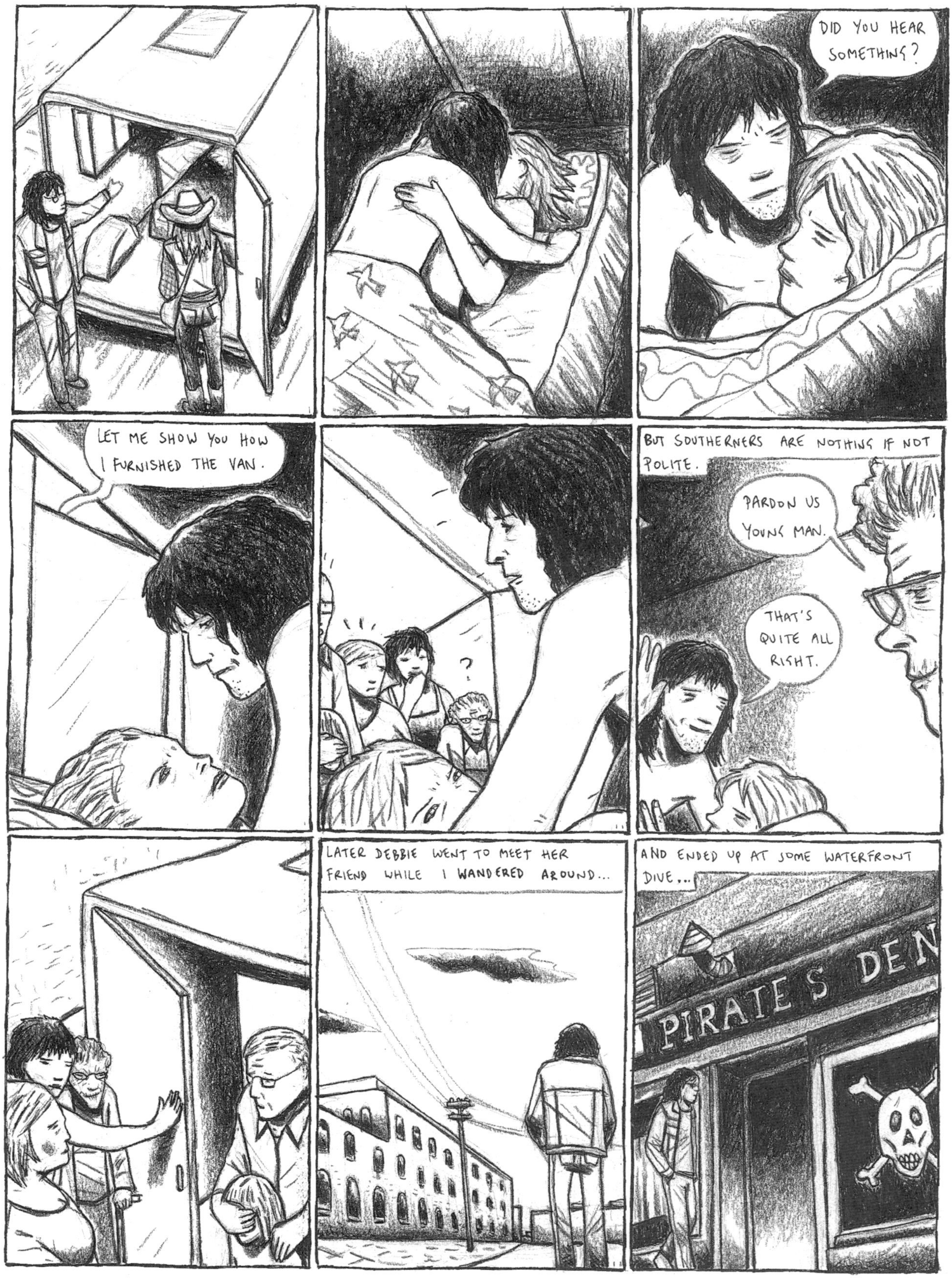
DID YOU HEAR SOMETHING?
LET ME SHOW YOU HOW I FURNISHED THE VAN.
?
BUT SOUTHERNERS ARE NOTHING IF NOT POLITE.
PARDON US YOUNG MAN.
THAT'S QUITE ALL RIGHT.
LATER DEBBIE WENT TO MEET HER FRIEND WHILE I WANDERED AROUND...
AND ENDED UP AT SOME WATERFRONT DIVE...
PIRATE'S DEN

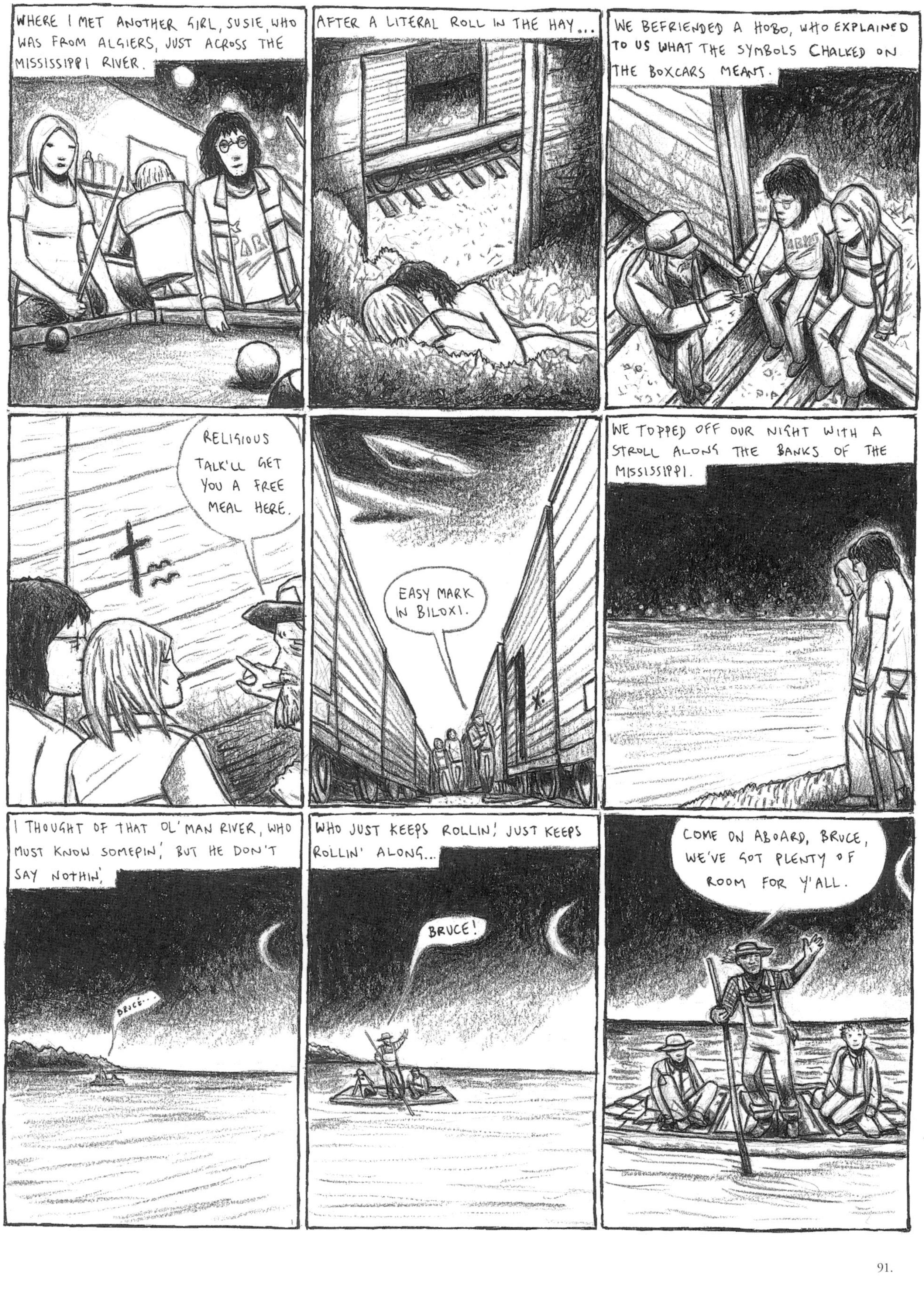
WHERE I MET ANOTHER GIRL, SUSIE, WHO WAS FROM ALGIERS, JUST ACROSS THE MISSISSIPPI RIVER.
AFTER A LITERAL ROLL IN THE HAY...
WE BEFRIENDED A HOBO, WHO EXPLAINED TO US WHAT THE SYMBOLS CHALKED ON THE BOXCARS MEANT.
RELIGIOUS TALK'LL GET YOU A FREE MEAL HERE.
EASY MARK IN BILOXI.
WE TOPPED OFF OUR NIGHT WITH A STROLL ALONG THE BANKS OF THE MISSISSIPPI.
I THOUGHT OF THAT OL' MAN RIVER, WHO MUST KNOW SOMEPIN', BUT HE DON'T SAY NOTHIN',
BRUCE...
WHO JUST KEEPS ROLLIN', JUST KEEPS ROLLIN' ALONG...
BRUCE!
COME ON ABOARD, BRUCE, WE'VE GOT PLENTY OF ROOM FOR Y'ALL.

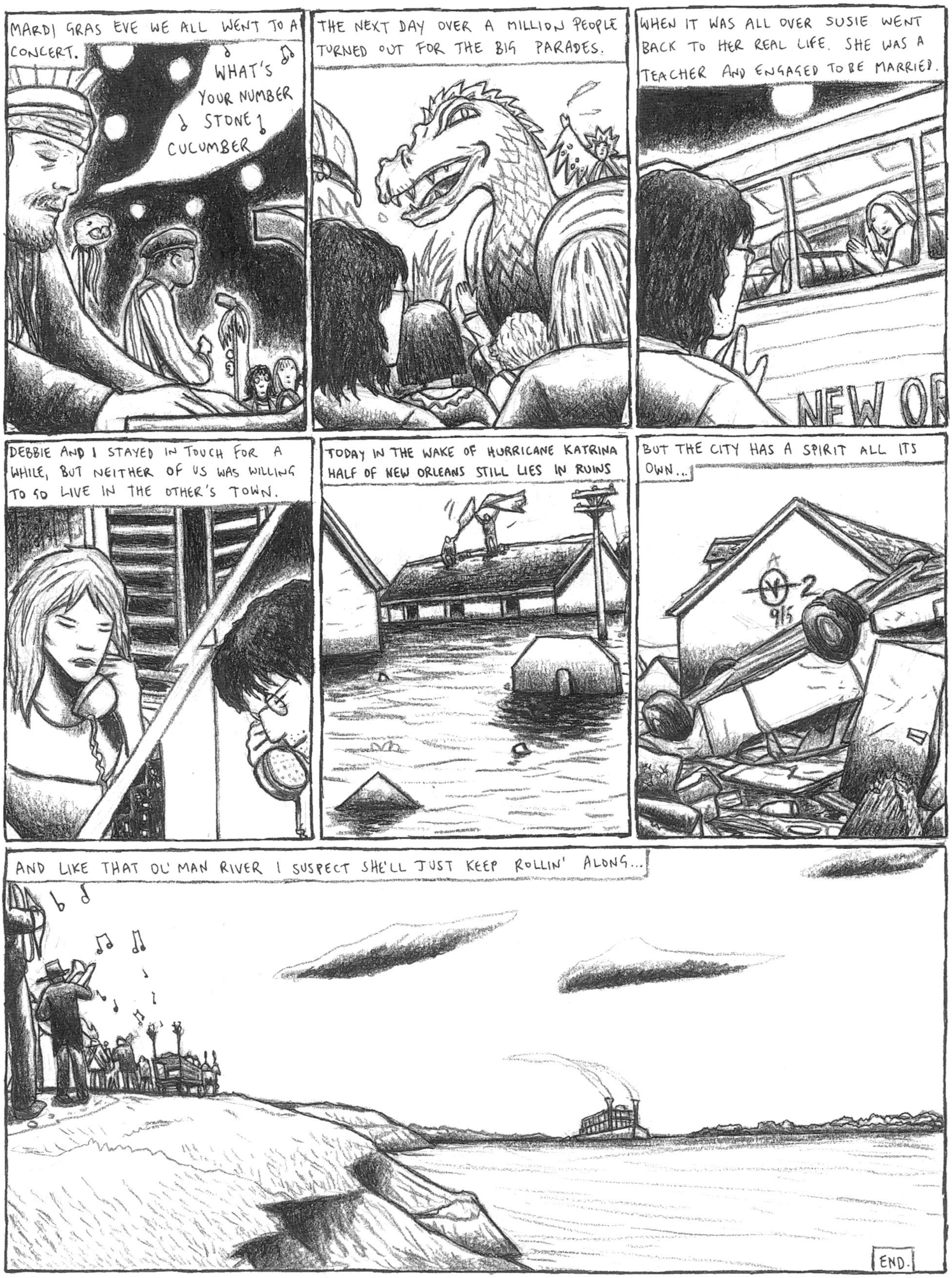
MARDI GRAS EVE WE ALL WENT TO A CONCERT.
WHAT'S YOUR NUMBER STONE CUCUMBER
THE NEXT DAY OVER A MILLION PEOPLE TURNED OUT FOR THE BIG PARADES.
WHEN IT WAS ALL OVER SUSIE WENT BACK TO HER REAL LIFE. SHE WAS A TEACHER AND ENGAGED TO BE MARRIED.
NEW OR
DEBBIE AND I STAYED IN TOUCH FOR A WHILE, BUT NEITHER OF US WAS WILLING TO GO LIVE IN THE OTHER'S TOWN.
TODAY IN THE WAKE OF HURRICANE KATRINA HALF OF NEW ORLEANS STILL LIES IN RUINS
BUT THE CITY HAS A SPIRIT ALL ITS OWN...
AND LIKE THAT OL' MAN RIVER I SUSPECT SHE'LL JUST KEEP ROLLIN' ALONG...
END.

What would you do?

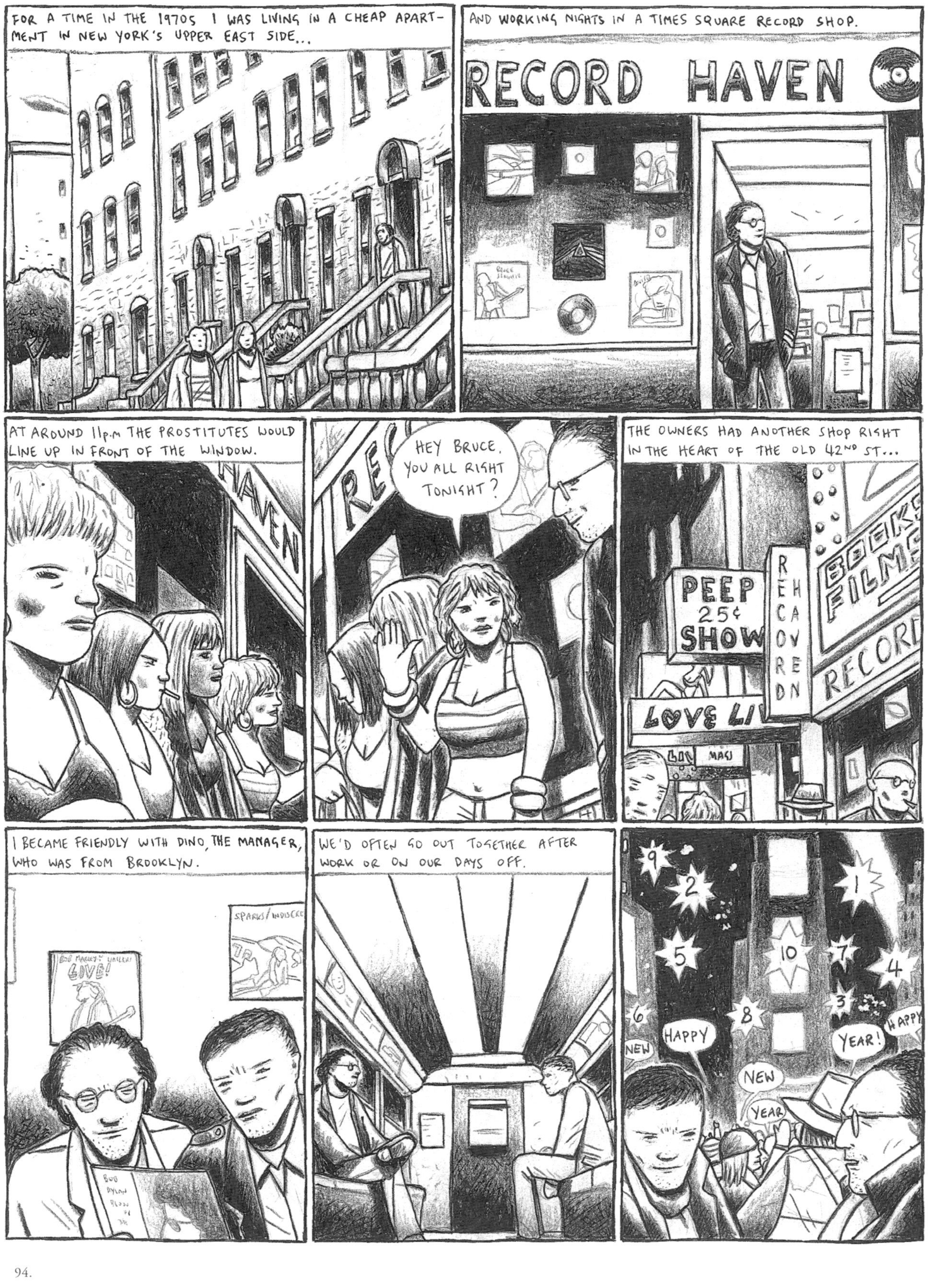

FOR A TIME IN THE 1970S I WAS LIVING IN A CHEAP APARTMENT IN NEW YORK'S UPPER EAST SIDE...
AND WORKING NIGHTS IN A TIMES SQUARE RECORD SHOP.
RECORD HAVEN
AT AROUND 11p.m THE PROSTITUTES WOULD LINE UP IN FRONT OF THE WINDOW.
HAVEN
HEY BRUCE, YOU ALL RIGHT TONIGHT?
THE OWNERS HAD ANOTHER SHOP RIGHT IN THE HEART OF THE OLD 42ND ST...
PEEP 25¢ SHOW
RECORD HAVEN
BOOKS FILMS
RECORD
LOVE LI
I BECAME FRIENDLY WITH DINO, THE MANAGER, WHO WAS FROM BROOKLYN.
BOB MARLEY & THE WAILERS LIVE!
SPARKS / INDISCREET
WE'D OFTEN GO OUT TOGETHER AFTER WORK OR ON OUR DAYS OFF.
9
2
1
5
10
7
4
3
6
8
NEW
HAPPY
YEAR!
HAPPY
NEW
YEAR

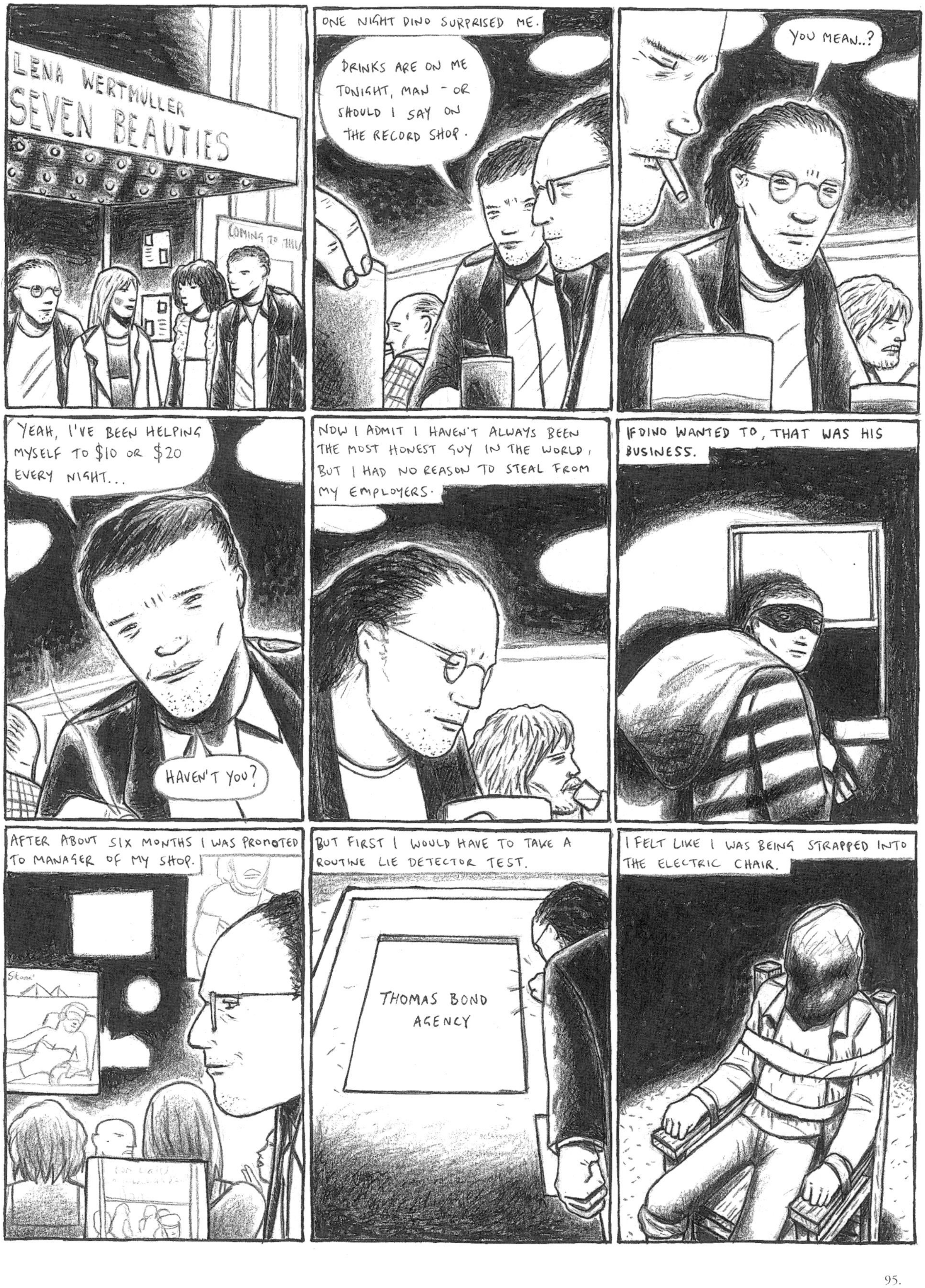
LENA WERTMULLER
SEVEN BEAUTIES
ONE NIGHT DINO SURPRISED ME.
DRINKS ARE ON ME TONIGHT, MAN - OR SHOULD I SAY ON THE RECORD SHOP.
YOU MEAN..?
YEAH, I'VE BEEN HELPING MYSELF TO $10 OR $20 EVERY NIGHT...
HAVEN'T YOU?
NOW I ADMIT I HAVEN'T ALWAYS BEEN THE MOST HONEST GUY IN THE WORLD, BUT I HAD NO REASON TO STEAL FROM MY EMPLOYERS.
IF DINO WANTED TO, THAT WAS HIS BUSINESS.
AFTER ABOUT SIX MONTHS I WAS PROMOTED TO MANAGER OF MY SHOP.
BUT FIRST I WOULD HAVE TO TAKE A ROUTINE LIE DETECTOR TEST.
THOMAS BOND AGENCY
I FELT LIKE I WAS BEING STRAPPED INTO THE ELECTRIC CHAIR.

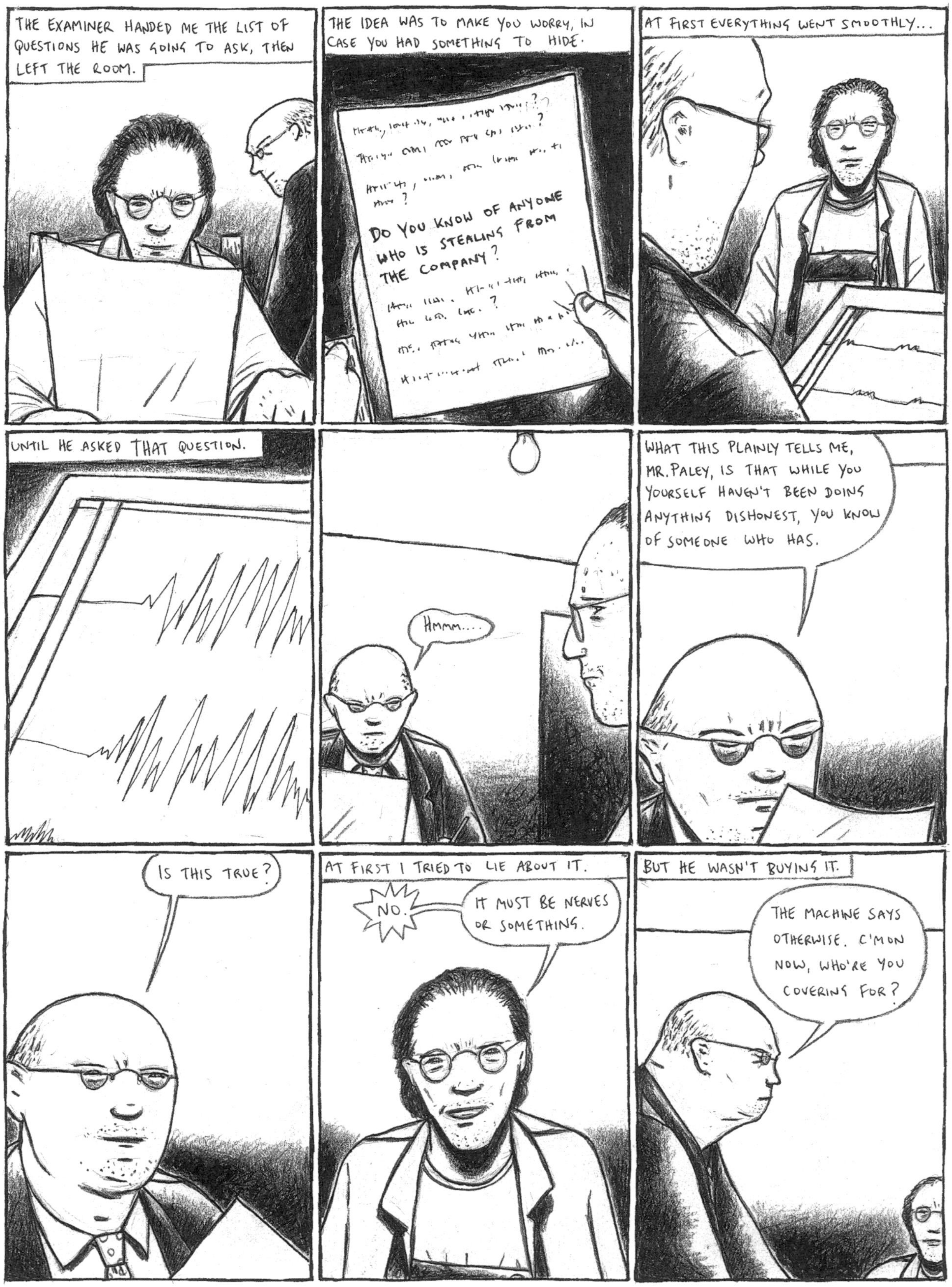
THE EXAMINER HANDED ME THE LIST OF QUESTIONS HE WAS GOING TO ASK, THEN LEFT THE ROOM.
THE IDEA WAS TO MAKE YOU WORRY, IN CASE YOU HAD SOMETHING TO HIDE.
DO YOU KNOW OF ANYONE WHO IS STEALING FROM THE COMPANY?
AT FIRST EVERYTHING WENT SMOOTHLY...
UNTIL HE ASKED THAT QUESTION.
Hmmm...
WHAT THIS PLAINLY TELLS ME, MR. PALEY, IS THAT WHILE YOU YOURSELF HAVEN'T BEEN DOING ANYTHING DISHONEST, YOU KNOW OF SOMEONE WHO HAS.
IS THIS TRUE?
AT FIRST I TRIED TO LIE ABOUT IT.
NO.
IT MUST BE NERVES OR SOMETHING.
BUT HE WASN'T BUYING IT.
THE MACHINE SAYS OTHERWISE. C'MON NOW, WHO'RE YOU COVERING FOR?

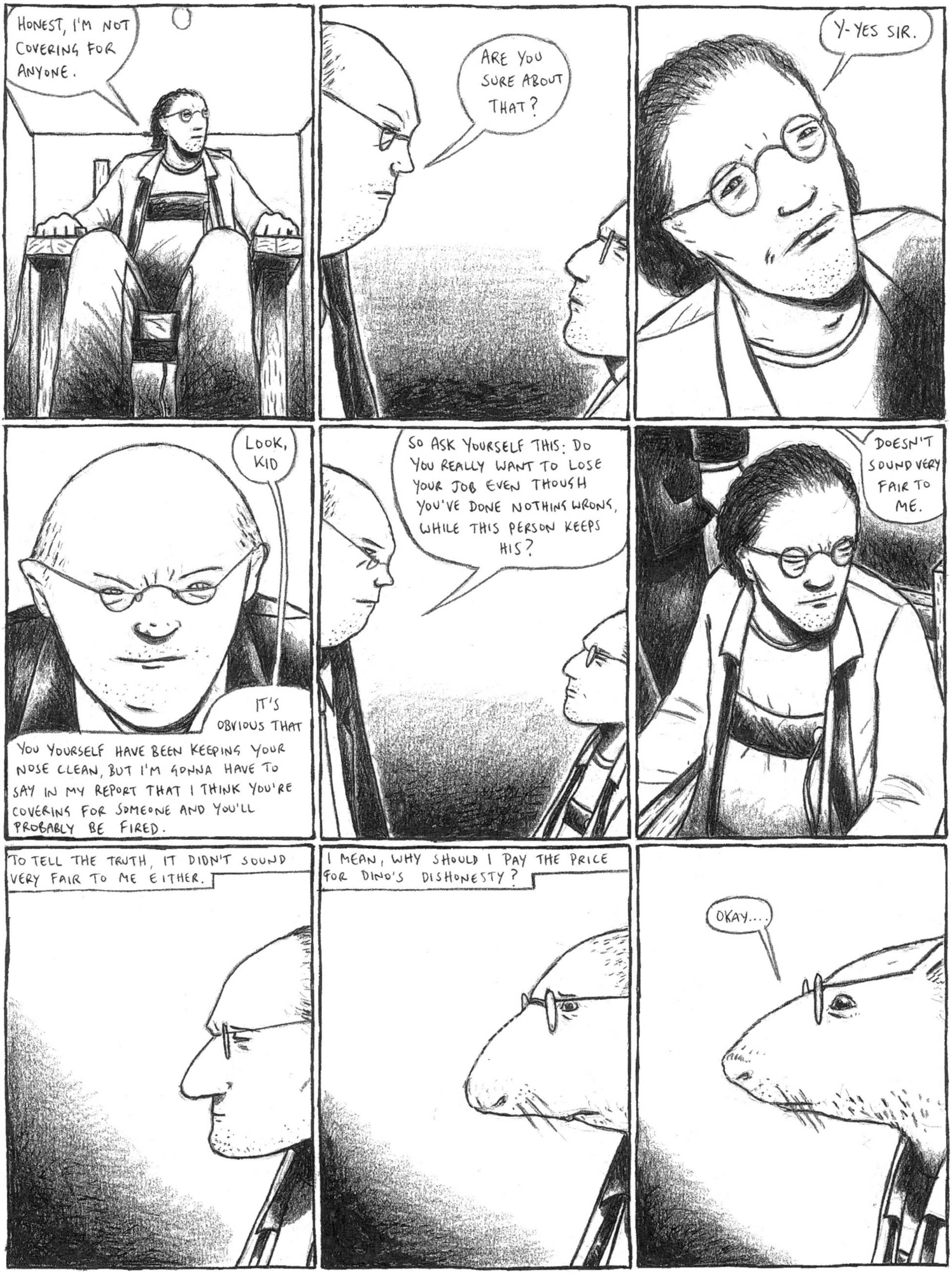
HONEST, I'M NOT COVERING FOR ANYONE.
ARE YOU SURE ABOUT THAT?
Y-YES SIR.
LOOK, KID
IT'S OBVIOUS THAT YOU YOURSELF HAVE BEEN KEEPING YOUR NOSE CLEAN, BUT I'M GONNA HAVE TO SAY IN MY REPORT THAT I THINK YOU'RE COVERING FOR SOMEONE AND YOU'LL PROBABLY BE FIRED.
SO ASK YOURSELF THIS: DO YOU REALLY WANT TO LOSE YOUR JOB EVEN THOUGH YOU'VE DONE NOTHING WRONG, WHILE THIS PERSON KEEPS HIS?
DOESN'T SOUND VERY FAIR TO ME.
TO TELL THE TRUTH, IT DIDN'T SOUND VERY FAIR TO ME EITHER.
I MEAN, WHY SHOULD I PAY THE PRICE FOR DINO'S DISHONESTY?
OKAY....

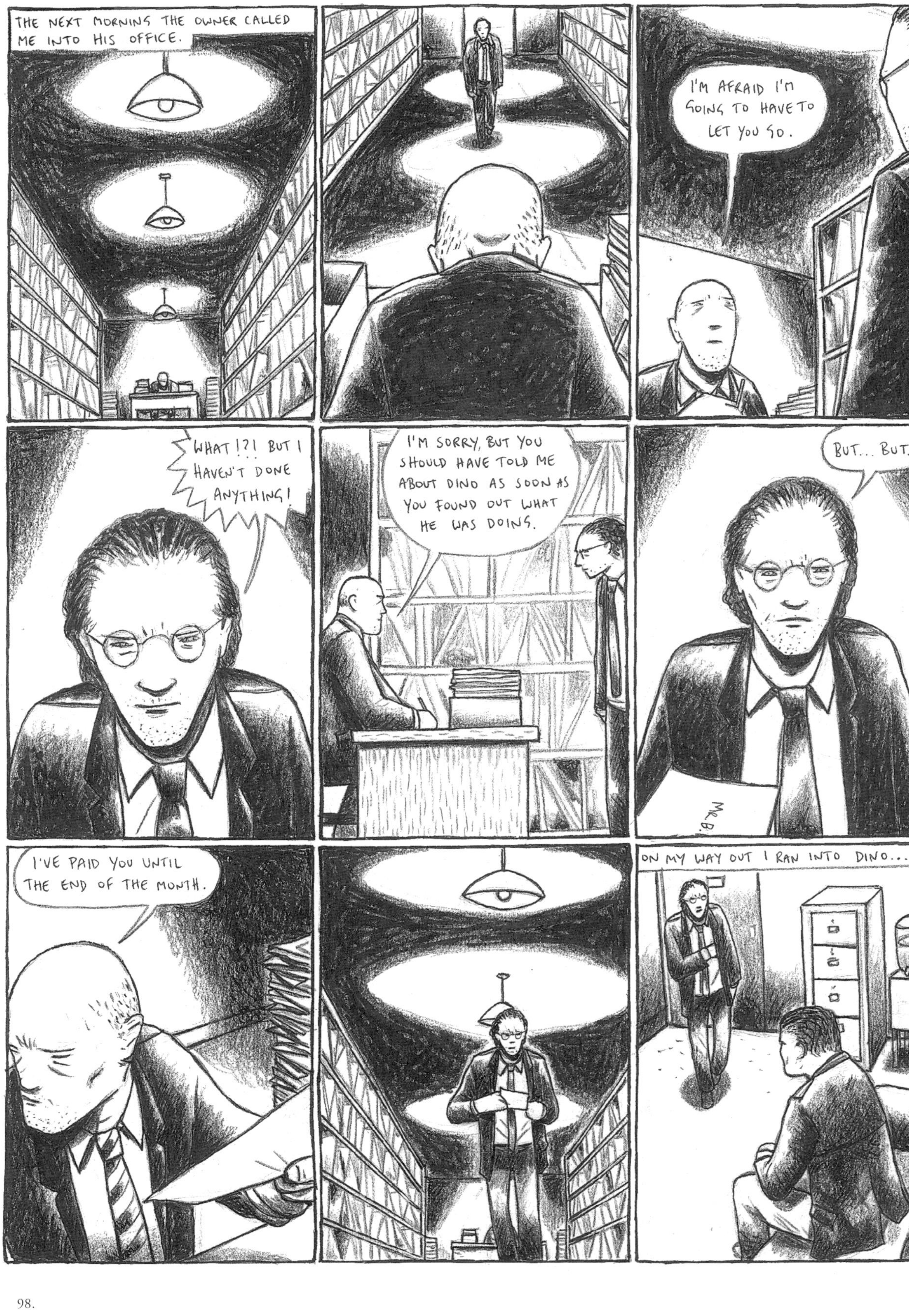
THE NEXT MORNING THE OWNER CALLED ME INTO HIS OFFICE.
I'M AFRAID I'M GOING TO HAVE TO LET YOU GO.
WHAT!?! BUT I HAVEN'T DONE ANYTHING!
I'M SORRY, BUT YOU SHOULD HAVE TOLD ME ABOUT DINO AS SOON AS YOU FOUND OUT WHAT HE WAS DOING.
BUT... BUT..
MR. B.
I'VE PAID YOU UNTIL THE END OF THE MONTH.
ON MY WAY OUT I RAN INTO DINO...

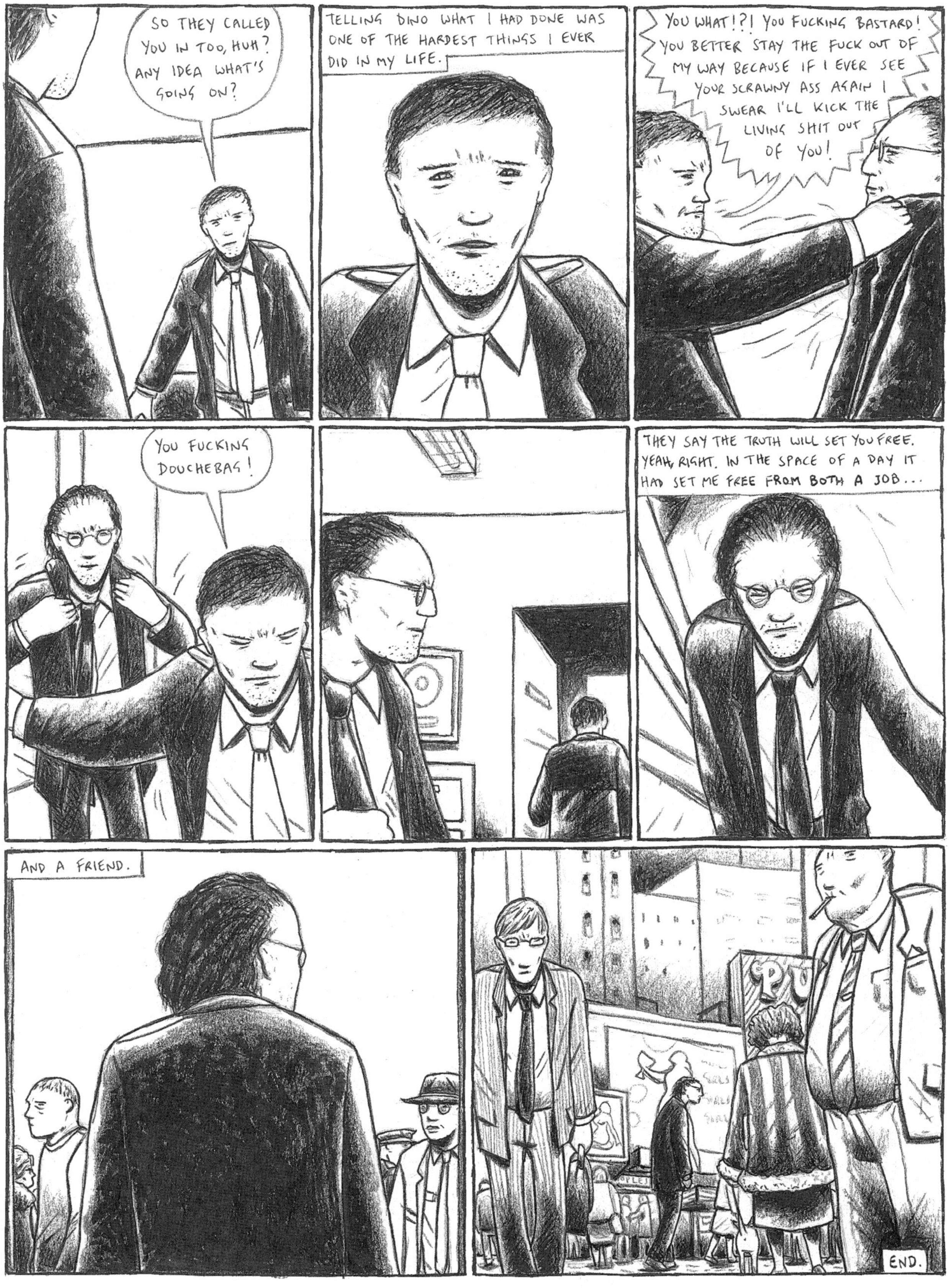
SO THEY CALLED YOU IN TOO, HUH? ANY IDEA WHAT'S GOING ON?
TELLING DINO WHAT I HAD DONE WAS ONE OF THE HARDEST THINGS I EVER DID IN MY LIFE.
YOU WHAT!?! YOU FUCKING BASTARD! YOU BETTER STAY THE FUCK OUT OF MY WAY BECAUSE IF I EVER SEE YOUR SCRAWNY ASS AGAIN I SWEAR I'LL KICK THE LIVING SHIT OUT OF YOU!
YOU FUCKING DOUCHEBAG!
THEY SAY THE TRUTH WILL SET YOU FREE. YEAH, RIGHT. IN THE SPACE OF A DAY IT HAD SET ME FREE FROM BOTH A JOB...
AND A FRIEND.
END.

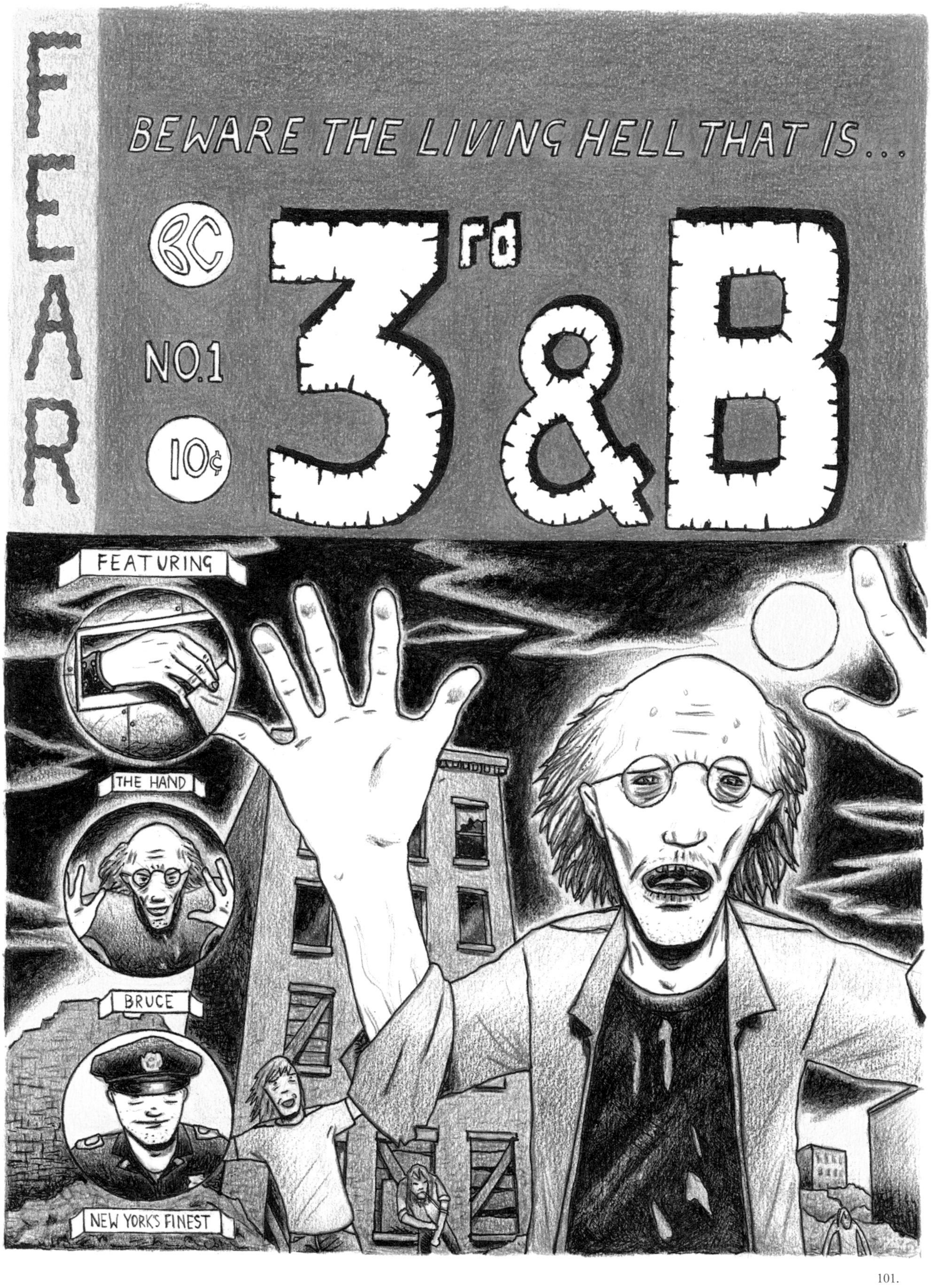
FEAR
BEWARE THE LIVING HELL THAT IS...
BC
NO.1
10¢
3rd & B
FEATURING
THE HAND
BRUCE
NEW YORK'S FINEST

3rd and B

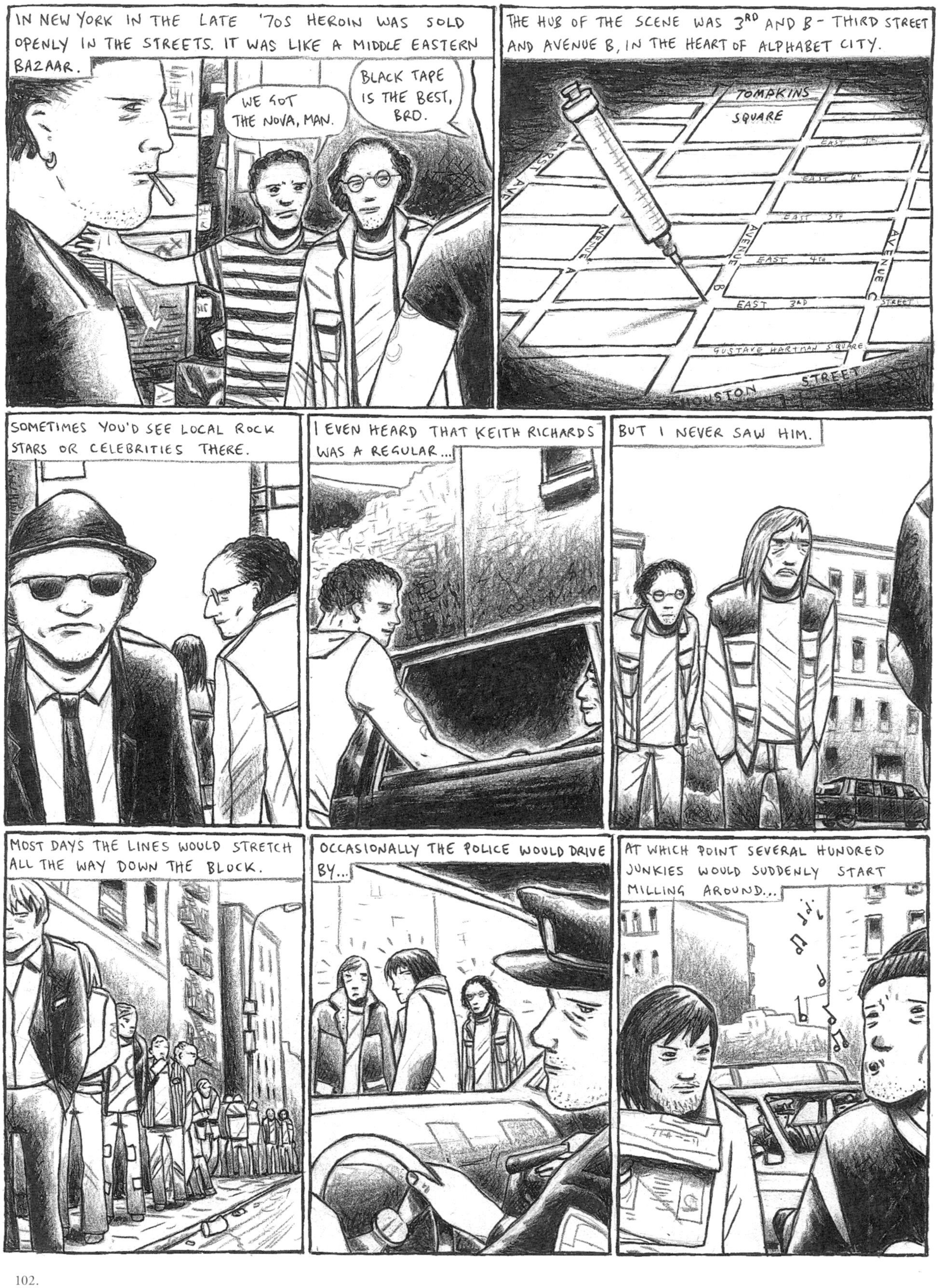

IN NEW YORK IN THE LATE '70S HEROIN WAS SOLD OPENLY IN THE STREETS. IT WAS LIKE A MIDDLE EASTERN BAZAAR.
WE GOT THE NOVA, MAN.
BLACK TAPE IS THE BEST, BRO.
THE HUB OF THE SCENE WAS 3RD AND B - THIRD STREET AND AVENUE B, IN THE HEART OF ALPHABET CITY.
TOMPKINS SQUARE
EAST 5TH
AVENUE A
AVENUE B
AVENUE C
EAST 4TH
EAST 3RD
STREET
GUSTAVE HARTMAN SQUARE
HOUSTON STREET
SOMETIMES YOU'D SEE LOCAL ROCK STARS OR CELEBRITIES THERE.
I EVEN HEARD THAT KEITH RICHARDS WAS A REGULAR...
BUT I NEVER SAW HIM.
MOST DAYS THE LINES WOULD STRETCH ALL THE WAY DOWN THE BLOCK.
OCCASIONALLY THE POLICE WOULD DRIVE BY...
AT WHICH POINT SEVERAL HUNDRED JUNKIES WOULD SUDDENLY START MILLING AROUND...

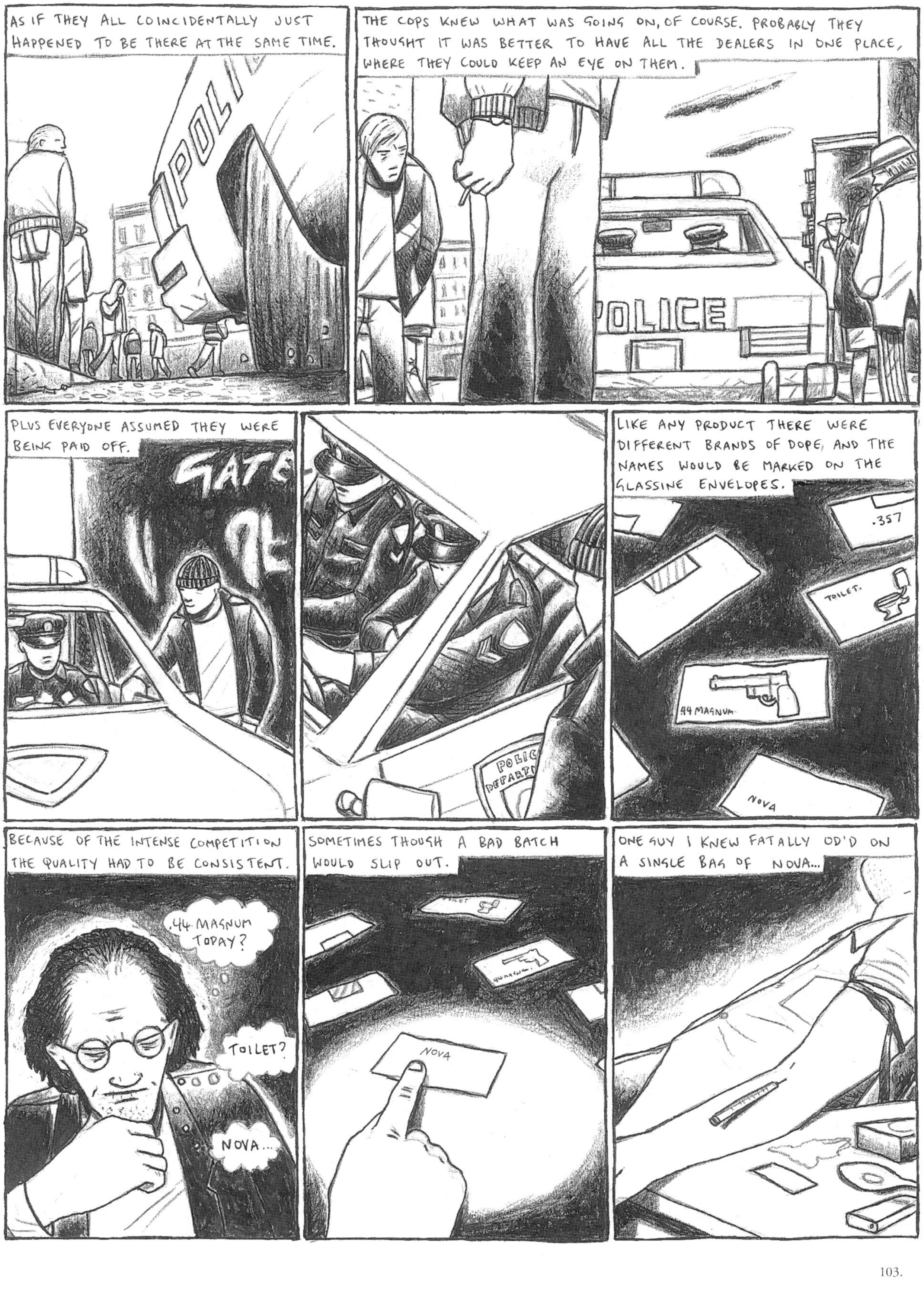
AS IF THEY ALL COINCIDENTALLY JUST HAPPENED TO BE THERE AT THE SAME TIME.
POLI
THE COPS KNEW WHAT WAS GOING ON, OF COURSE. PROBABLY THEY THOUGHT IT WAS BETTER TO HAVE ALL THE DEALERS IN ONE PLACE, WHERE THEY COULD KEEP AN EYE ON THEM.
POLICE
PLUS EVERYONE ASSUMED THEY WERE BEING PAID OFF.
GATE
POLICE DEPARTM
LIKE ANY PRODUCT THERE WERE DIFFERENT BRANDS OF DOPE, AND THE NAMES WOULD BE MARKED ON THE GLASSINE ENVELOPES.
.357
TOILET.
44 MAGNUM
NOVA
BECAUSE OF THE INTENSE COMPETITION THE QUALITY HAD TO BE CONSISTENT.
.44 MAGNUM TODAY?
TOILET?
NOVA...
SOMETIMES THOUGH A BAD BATCH WOULD SLIP OUT.
NOVA
ONE GUY I KNEW FATALLY OD'D ON A SINGLE BAG OF NOVA...

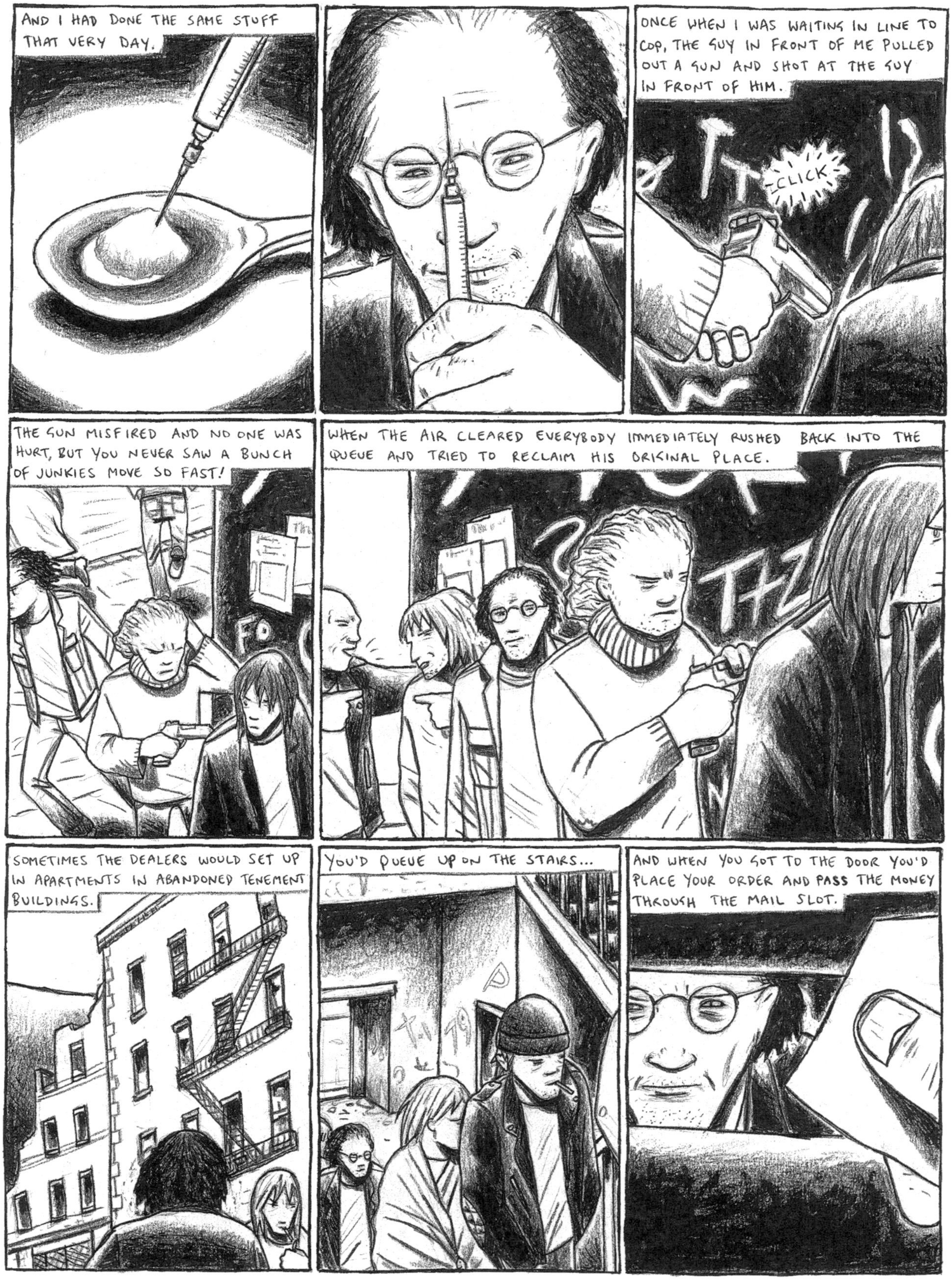
AND I HAD DONE THE SAME STUFF THAT VERY DAY.
ONCE WHEN I WAS WAITING IN LINE TO COP, THE GUY IN FRONT OF ME PULLED OUT A GUN AND SHOT AT THE GUY IN FRONT OF HIM.
CLICK
THE GUN MISFIRED AND NO ONE WAS HURT, BUT YOU NEVER SAW A BUNCH OF JUNKIES MOVE SO FAST!
WHEN THE AIR CLEARED EVERYBODY IMMEDIATELY RUSHED BACK INTO THE QUEUE AND TRIED TO RECLAIM HIS ORIGINAL PLACE.
SOMETIMES THE DEALERS WOULD SET UP IN APARTMENTS IN ABANDONED TENEMENT BUILDINGS.
YOU'D QUEUE UP ON THE STAIRS...
AND WHEN YOU GOT TO THE DOOR YOU'D PLACE YOUR ORDER AND PASS THE MONEY THROUGH THE MAIL SLOT.

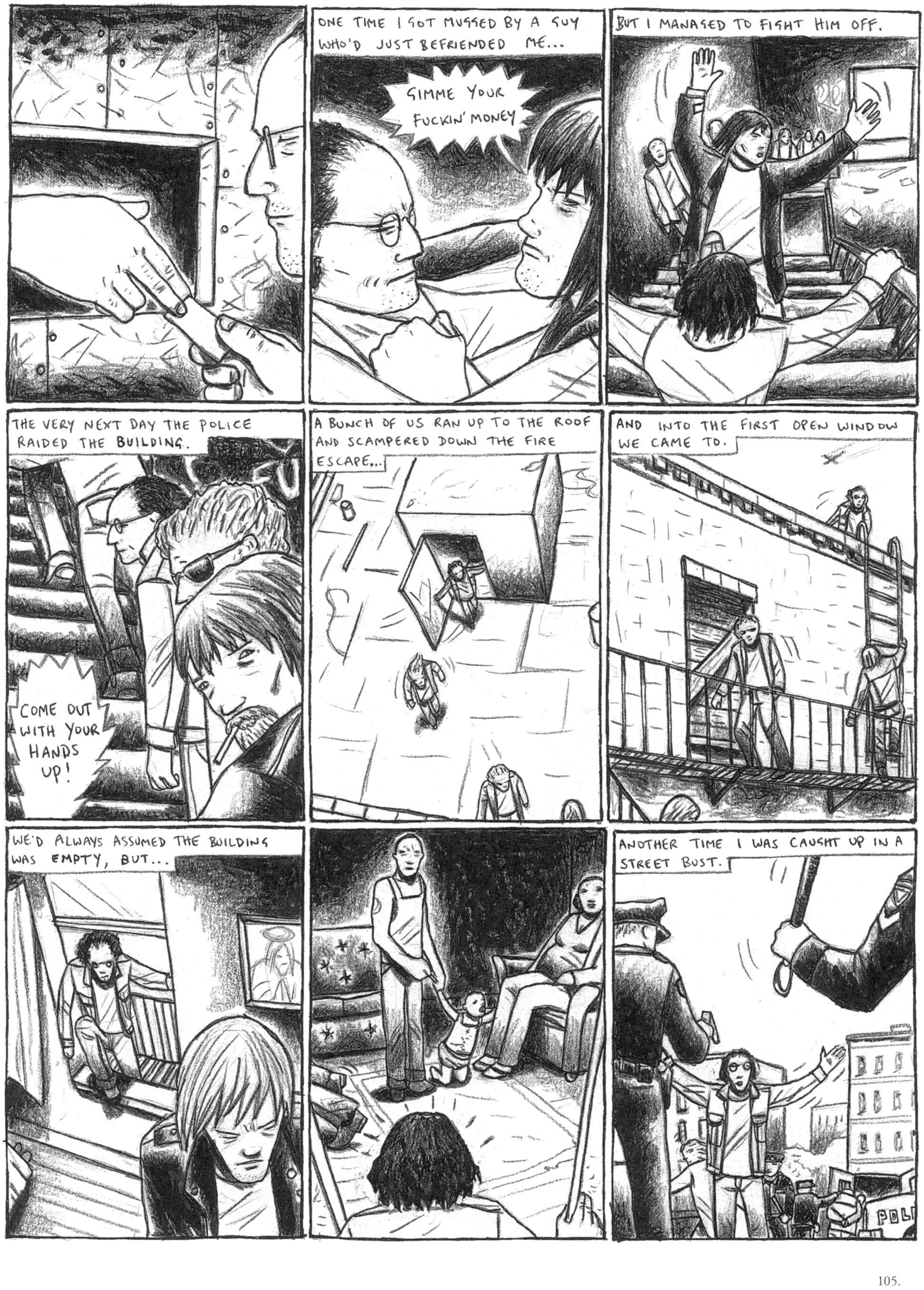
ONE TIME I GOT MUGGED BY A GUY WHO'D JUST BEFRIENDED ME...
GIMME YOUR FUCKIN' MONEY
BUT I MANAGED TO FIGHT HIM OFF.
THE VERY NEXT DAY THE POLICE RAIDED THE BUILDING.
COME OUT WITH YOUR HANDS UP!
A BUNCH OF US RAN UP TO THE ROOF AND SCAMPERED DOWN THE FIRE ESCAPE...
AND INTO THE FIRST OPEN WINDOW WE CAME TO.
WE'D ALWAYS ASSUMED THE BUILDING WAS EMPTY, BUT...
ANOTHER TIME I WAS CAUGHT UP IN A STREET BUST.
POLI

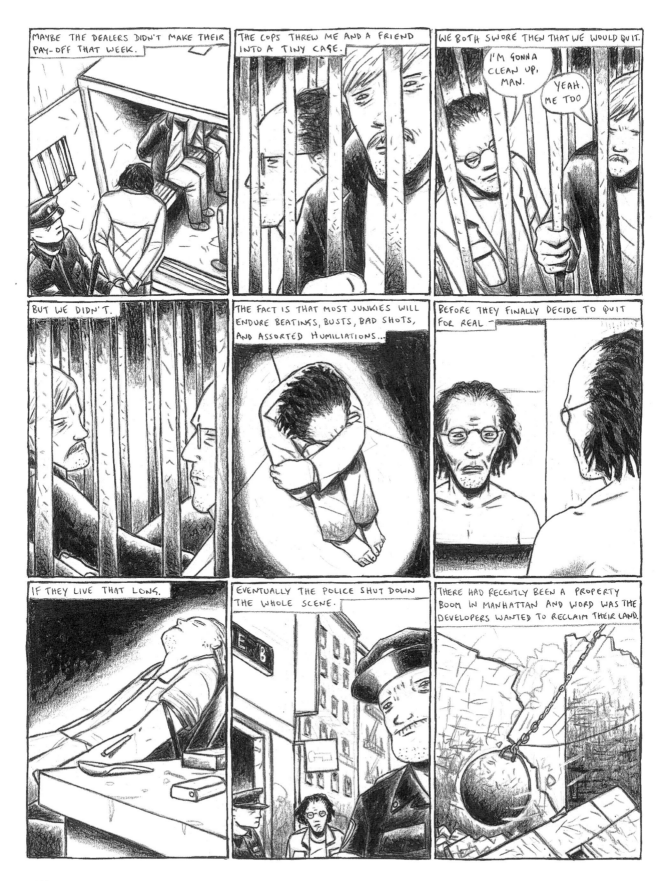

MAYBE THE DEALERS DIDN'T MAKE THEIR PAY-OFF THAT WEEK.

THE COPS THREW ME AND A FRIEND INTO A TINY CAGE.

WE BOTH SWORE THEN THAT WE WOULD QUIT.

I'M GONNA CLEAN UP, MAN.

YEAH, ME TOO

BUT WE DIDN'T.

THE FACT IS THAT MOST JUNKIES WILL ENDURE BEATINGS, BUSTS, BAD SHOTS, AND ASSORTED HUMILIATIONS...

BEFORE THEY FINALLY DECIDE TO QUIT FOR REAL —

IF THEY LIVE THAT LONG.

EVENTUALLY THE POLICE SHUT DOWN THE WHOLE SCENE.

THERE HAD RECENTLY BEEN A PROPERTY BOOM IN MANHATTAN AND WORD WAS THE DEVELOPERS WANTED TO RECLAIM THEIR LAND.

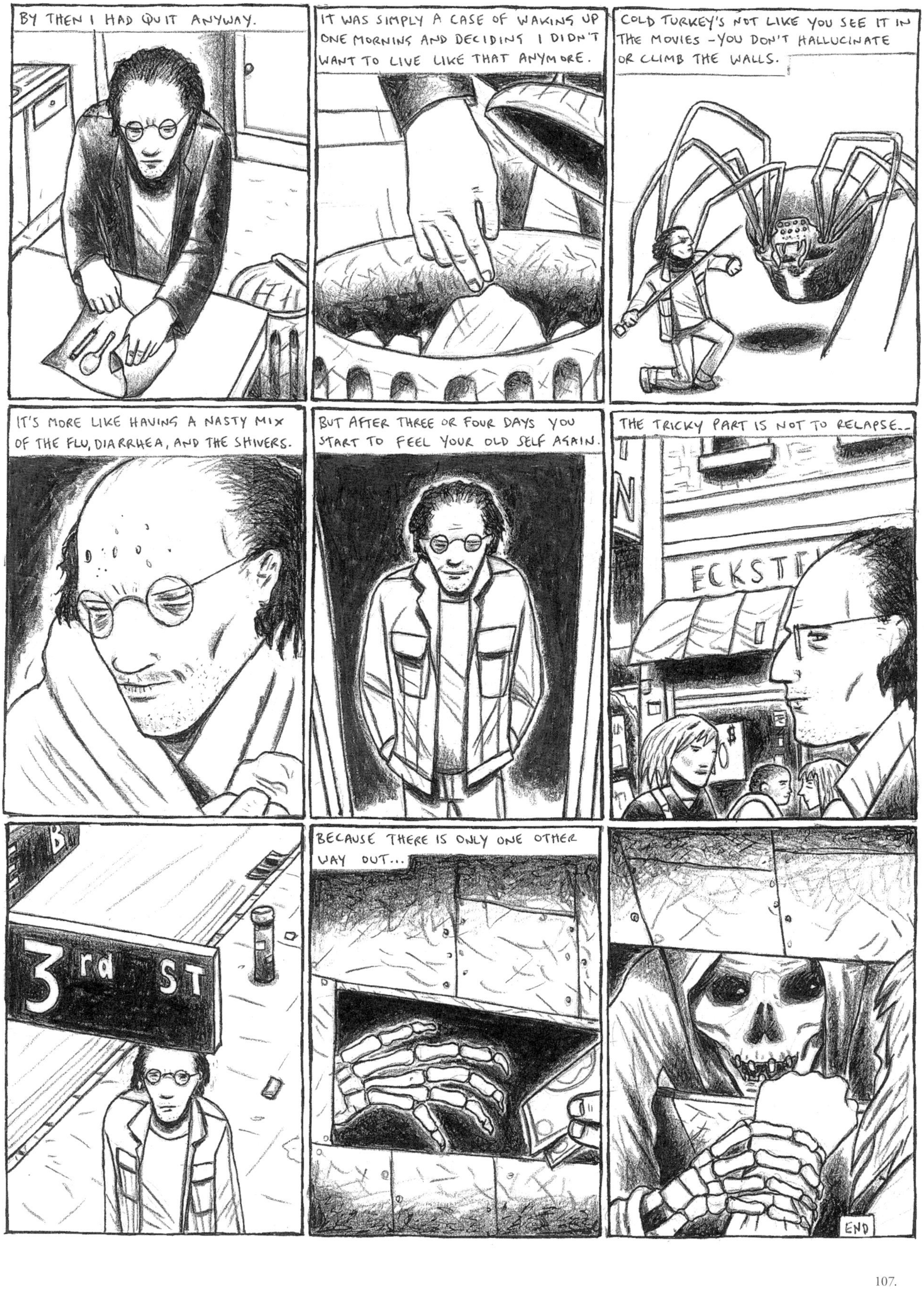

BY THEN I HAD QUIT ANYWAY.
IT WAS SIMPLY A CASE OF WAKING UP ONE MORNING AND DECIDING I DIDN'T WANT TO LIVE LIKE THAT ANYMORE.
COLD TURKEY'S NOT LIKE YOU SEE IT IN THE MOVIES - YOU DON'T HALLUCINATE OR CLIMB THE WALLS.
IT'S MORE LIKE HAVING A NASTY MIX OF THE FLU, DIARRHEA, AND THE SHIVERS.
BUT AFTER THREE OR FOUR DAYS YOU START TO FEEL YOUR OLD SELF AGAIN.
THE TRICKY PART IS NOT TO RELAPSE...
ECKST
3rd ST
BECAUSE THERE IS ONLY ONE OTHER WAY OUT...
END

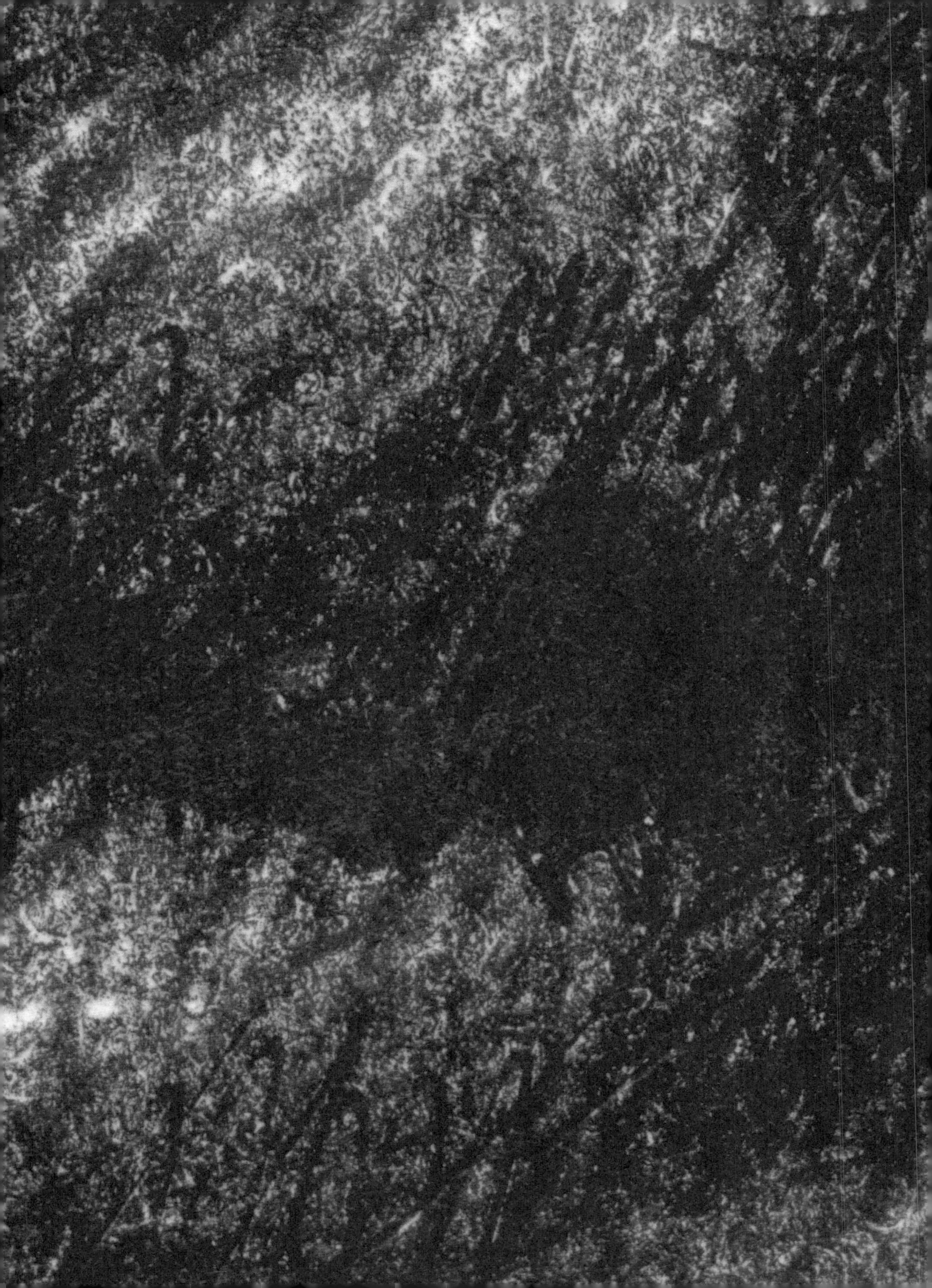

the tattoo artist, his wife, her girlfriend, and me.

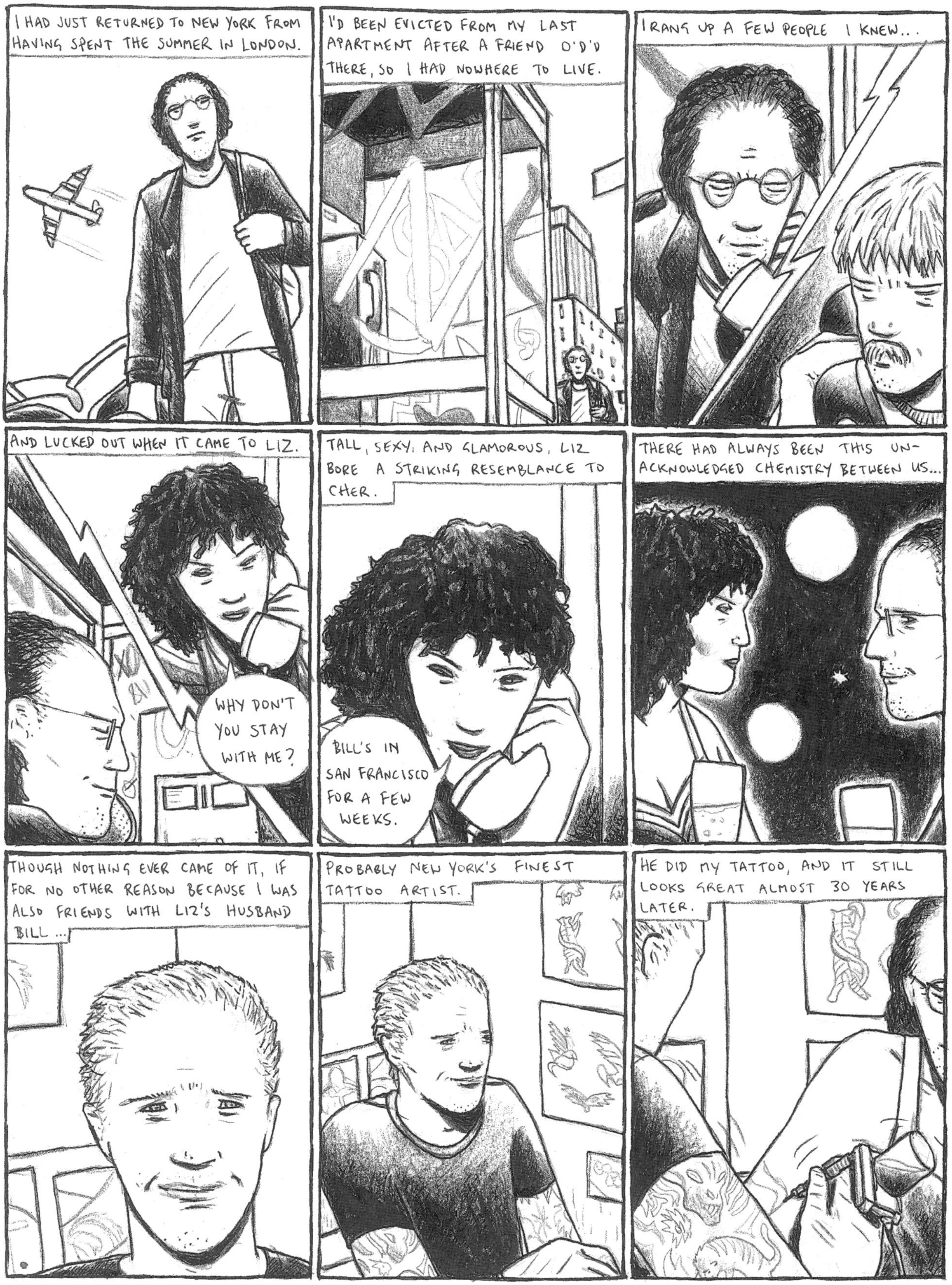
I HAD JUST RETURNED TO NEW YORK FROM HAVING SPENT THE SUMMER IN LONDON.
I'D BEEN EVICTED FROM MY LAST APARTMENT AFTER A FRIEND O'D'D THERE, SO I HAD NOWHERE TO LIVE.
I RANG UP A FEW PEOPLE I KNEW...
AND LUCKED OUT WHEN IT CAME TO LIZ.
WHY DON'T YOU STAY WITH ME?
TALL, SEXY, AND GLAMOROUS, LIZ BORE A STRIKING RESEMBLANCE TO CHER.
BILL'S IN SAN FRANCISCO FOR A FEW WEEKS.
THERE HAD ALWAYS BEEN THIS UN-ACKNOWLEDGED CHEMISTRY BETWEEN US...
THOUGH NOTHING EVER CAME OF IT, IF FOR NO OTHER REASON BECAUSE I WAS ALSO FRIENDS WITH LIZ'S HUSBAND BILL...
PROBABLY NEW YORK'S FINEST TATTOO ARTIST.
HE DID MY TATTOO, AND IT STILL LOOKS GREAT ALMOST 30 YEARS LATER.

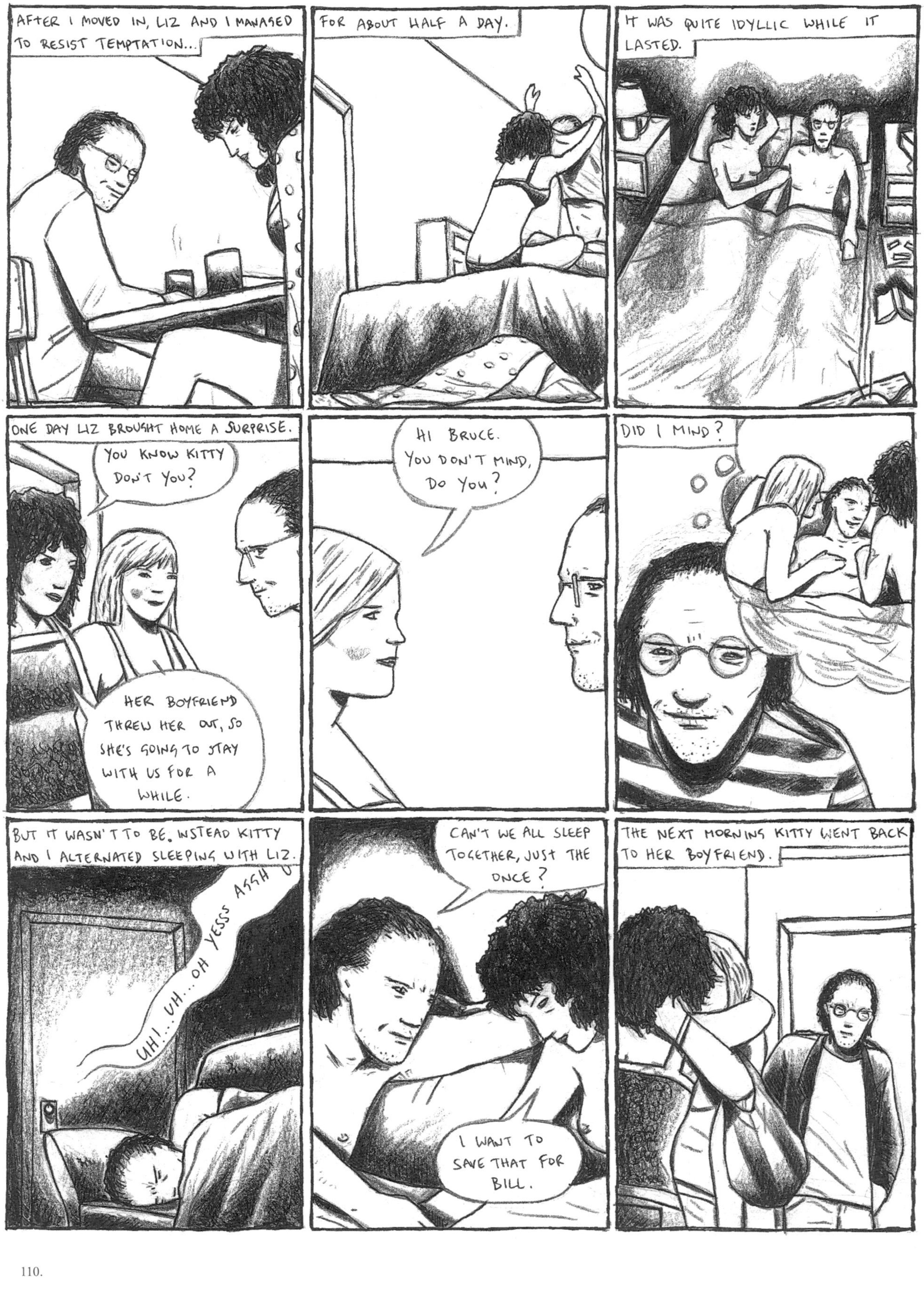

AFTER I MOVED IN, LIZ AND I MANAGED TO RESIST TEMPTATION...
FOR ABOUT HALF A DAY.
IT WAS QUITE IDYLLIC WHILE IT LASTED.
ONE DAY LIZ BROUGHT HOME A SURPRISE.
YOU KNOW KITTY DON'T YOU?
HER BOYFRIEND THREW HER OUT, SO SHE'S GOING TO STAY WITH US FOR A WHILE.
HI BRUCE. YOU DON'T MIND, DO YOU?
DID I MIND?
BUT IT WASN'T TO BE. INSTEAD KITTY AND I ALTERNATED SLEEPING WITH LIZ.
UH!...UH...OH YESSS AGGH
CAN'T WE ALL SLEEP TOGETHER, JUST THE ONCE?
I WANT TO SAVE THAT FOR BILL.
THE NEXT MORNING KITTY WENT BACK TO HER BOYFRIEND.

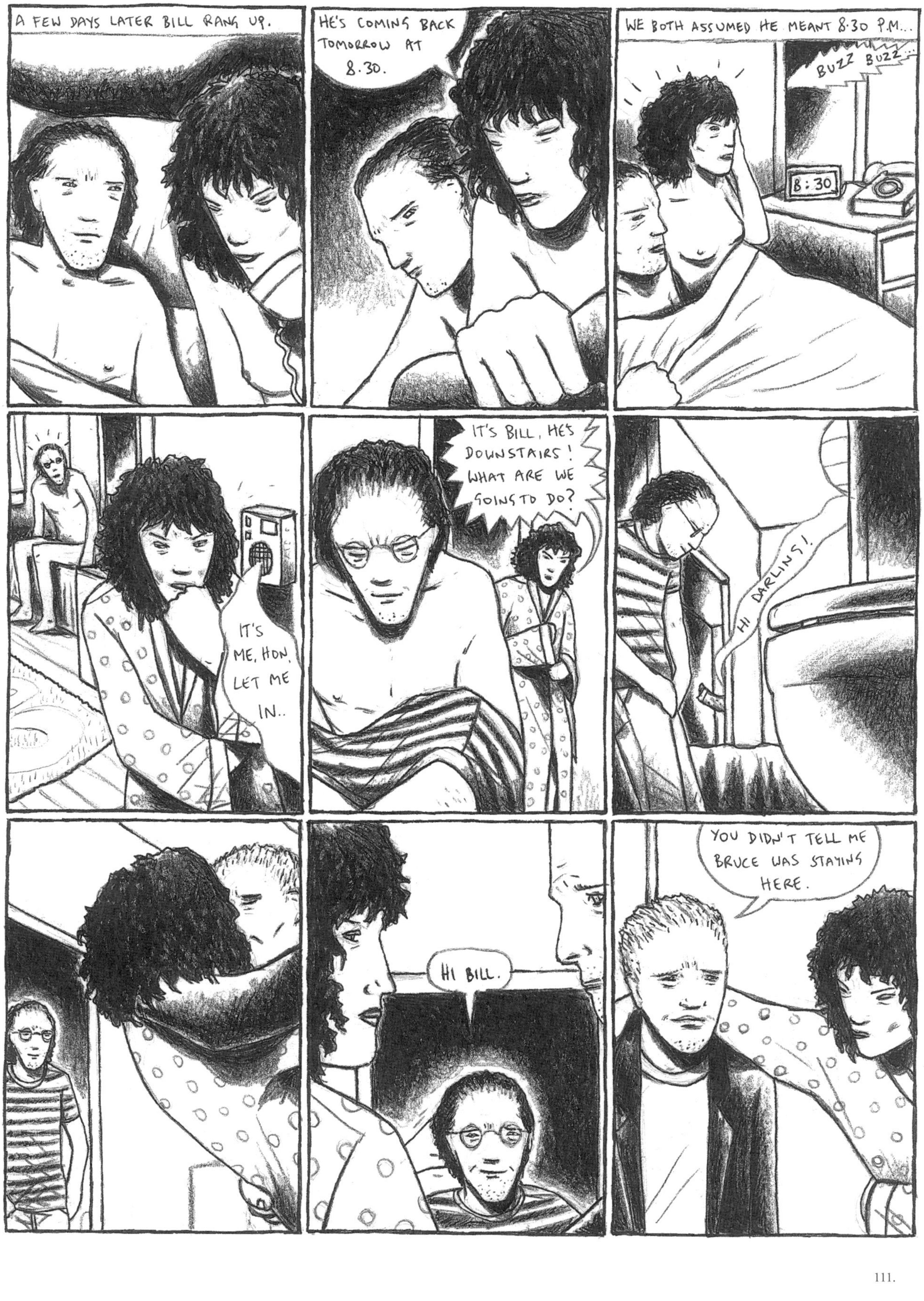
A FEW DAYS LATER BILL RANG UP.
HE'S COMING BACK TOMORROW AT 8.30.
WE BOTH ASSUMED HE MEANT 8.30 P.M...
BUZZ BUZZ...
8:30
IT'S ME, HON, LET ME IN..
IT'S BILL, HE'S DOWNSTAIRS! WHAT ARE WE GOING TO DO?
HI DARLINGS!
HI BILL.
YOU DIDN'T TELL ME BRUCE WAS STAYING HERE.

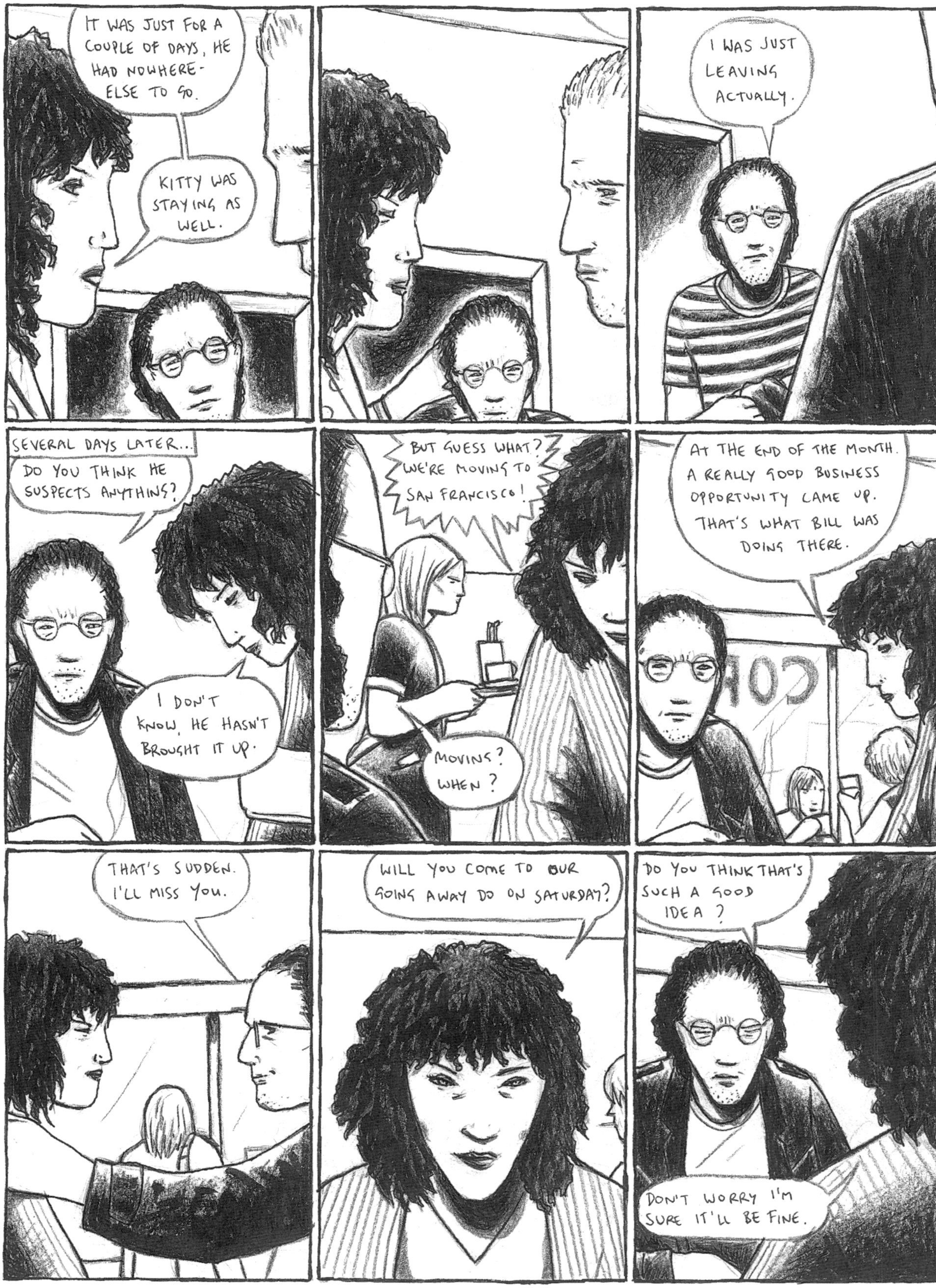
IT WAS JUST FOR A COUPLE OF DAYS, HE HAD NOWHERE ELSE TO GO.
KITTY WAS STAYING AS WELL.
I WAS JUST LEAVING ACTUALLY.
SEVERAL DAYS LATER...
DO YOU THINK HE SUSPECTS ANYTHING?
I DON'T KNOW, HE HASN'T BROUGHT IT UP.
BUT GUESS WHAT? WE'RE MOVING TO SAN FRANCISCO!
MOVING? WHEN?
AT THE END OF THE MONTH. A REALLY GOOD BUSINESS OPPORTUNITY CAME UP. THAT'S WHAT BILL WAS DOING THERE.
THAT'S SUDDEN. I'LL MISS YOU.
WILL YOU COME TO OUR GOING AWAY DO ON SATURDAY?
DO YOU THINK THAT'S SUCH A GOOD IDEA?
DON'T WORRY I'M SURE IT'LL BE FINE.

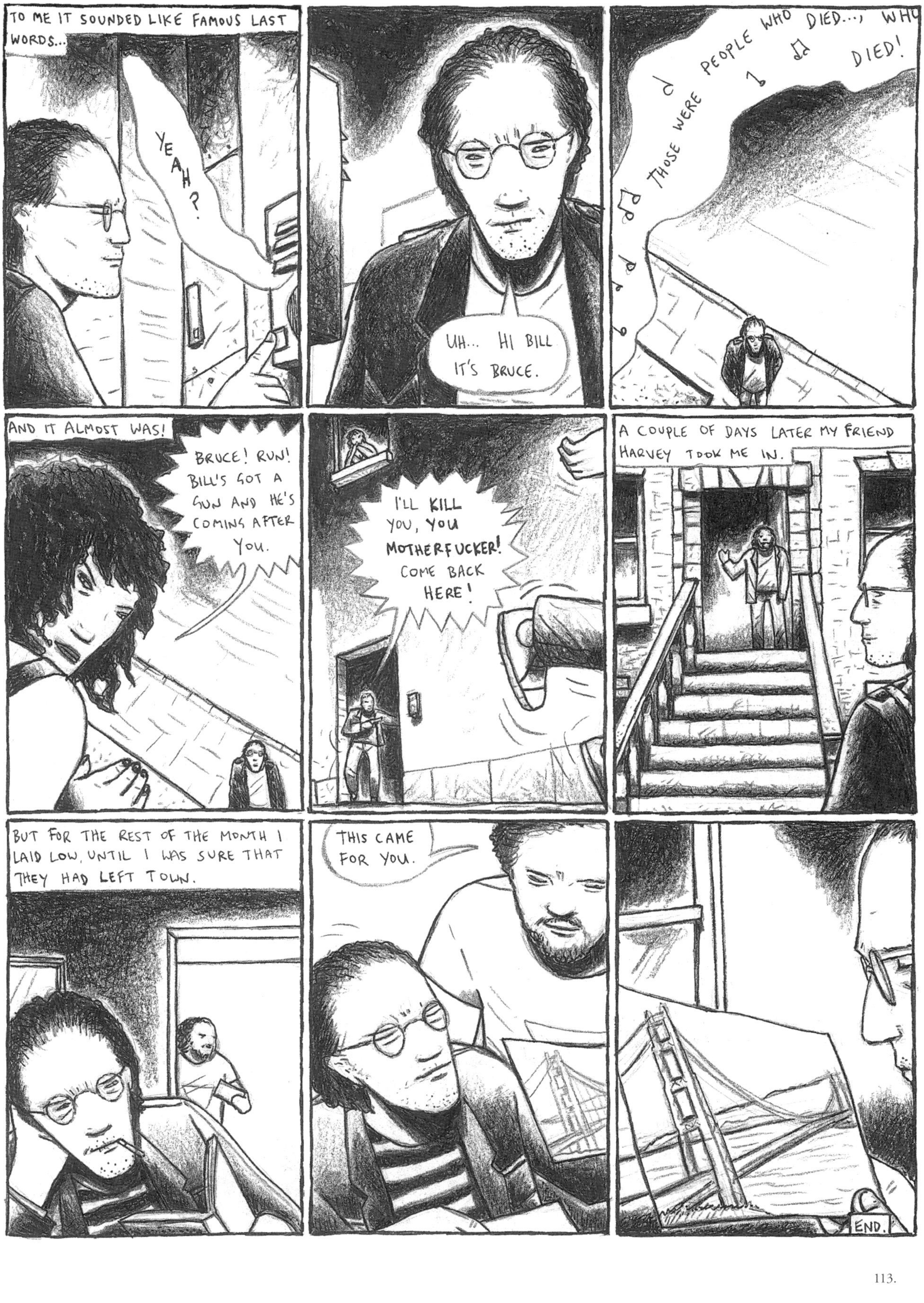

TO ME IT SOUNDED LIKE FAMOUS LAST WORDS...
YEAH?
UH... HI BILL IT'S BRUCE.
THOSE WERE PEOPLE WHO DIED..., WHO DIED!
AND IT ALMOST WAS!
BRUCE! RUN! BILL'S GOT A GUN AND HE'S COMING AFTER YOU.
I'LL KILL YOU, YOU MOTHERFUCKER! COME BACK HERE!
A COUPLE OF DAYS LATER MY FRIEND HARVEY TOOK ME IN.
BUT FOR THE REST OF THE MONTH I LAID LOW, UNTIL I WAS SURE THAT THEY HAD LEFT TOWN.
THIS CAME FOR YOU.
END.

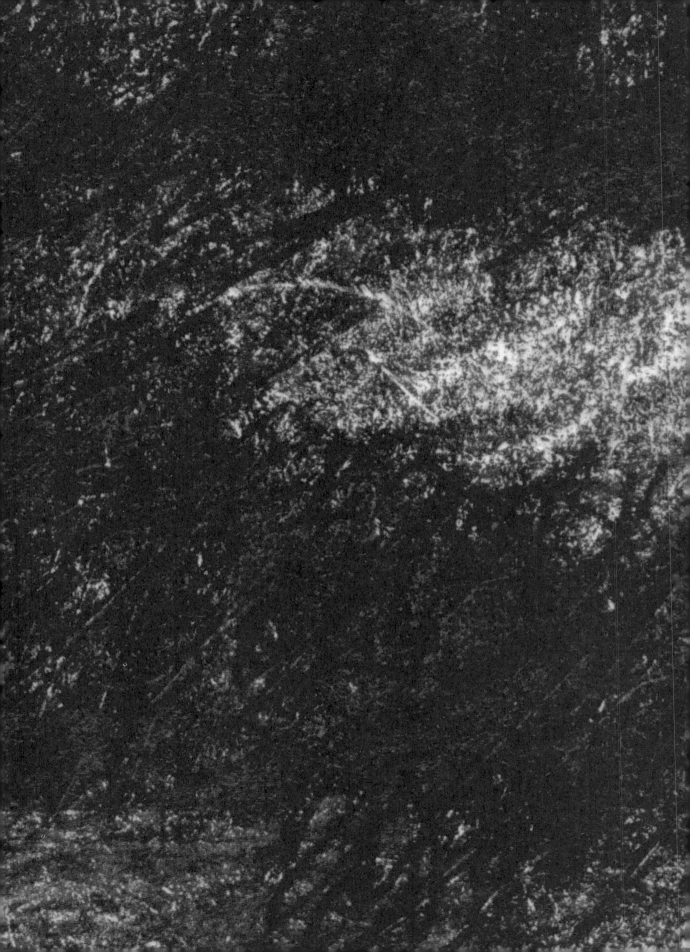

Johnny thunders

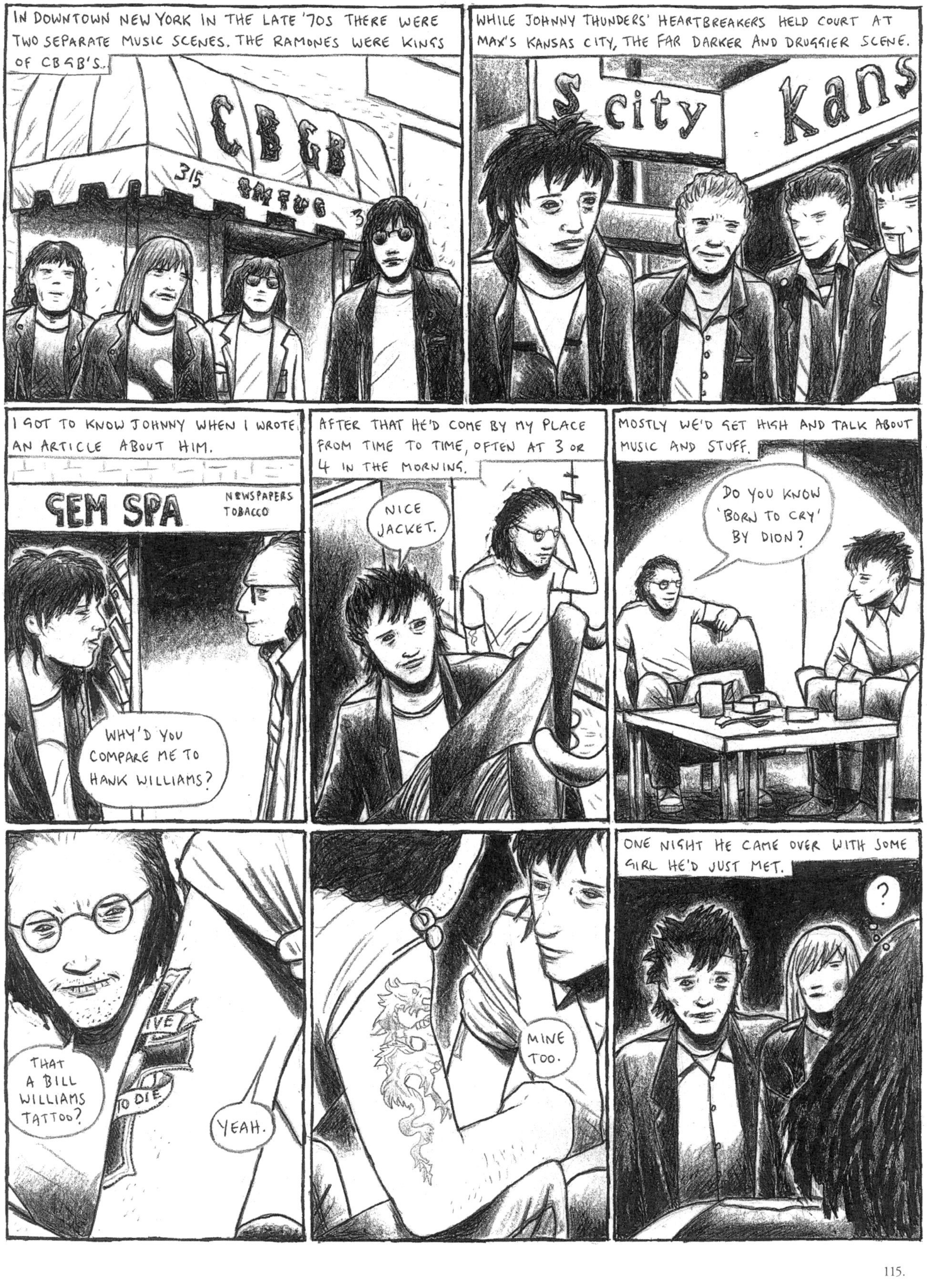

IN DOWNTOWN NEW YORK IN THE LATE '70S THERE WERE TWO SEPARATE MUSIC SCENES. THE RAMONES WERE KINGS OF CBGB'S..
CBGB
315
OMFUG
WHILE JOHNNY THUNDERS' HEARTBREAKERS HELD COURT AT MAX'S KANSAS CITY, THE FAR DARKER AND DRUGGIER SCENE.
S city
kans
I GOT TO KNOW JOHNNY WHEN I WROTE AN ARTICLE ABOUT HIM.
GEM SPA
NEWSPAPERS TOBACCO
WHY'D YOU COMPARE ME TO HANK WILLIAMS?
AFTER THAT HE'D COME BY MY PLACE FROM TIME TO TIME, OFTEN AT 3 OR 4 IN THE MORNING.
NICE JACKET.
MOSTLY WE'D GET HIGH AND TALK ABOUT MUSIC AND STUFF.
DO YOU KNOW 'BORN TO CRY' BY DION?
THAT A BILL WILLIAMS TATTOO?
IVE
TO DIE
YEAH.
MINE TOO.
ONE NIGHT HE CAME OVER WITH SOME GIRL HE'D JUST MET.
?

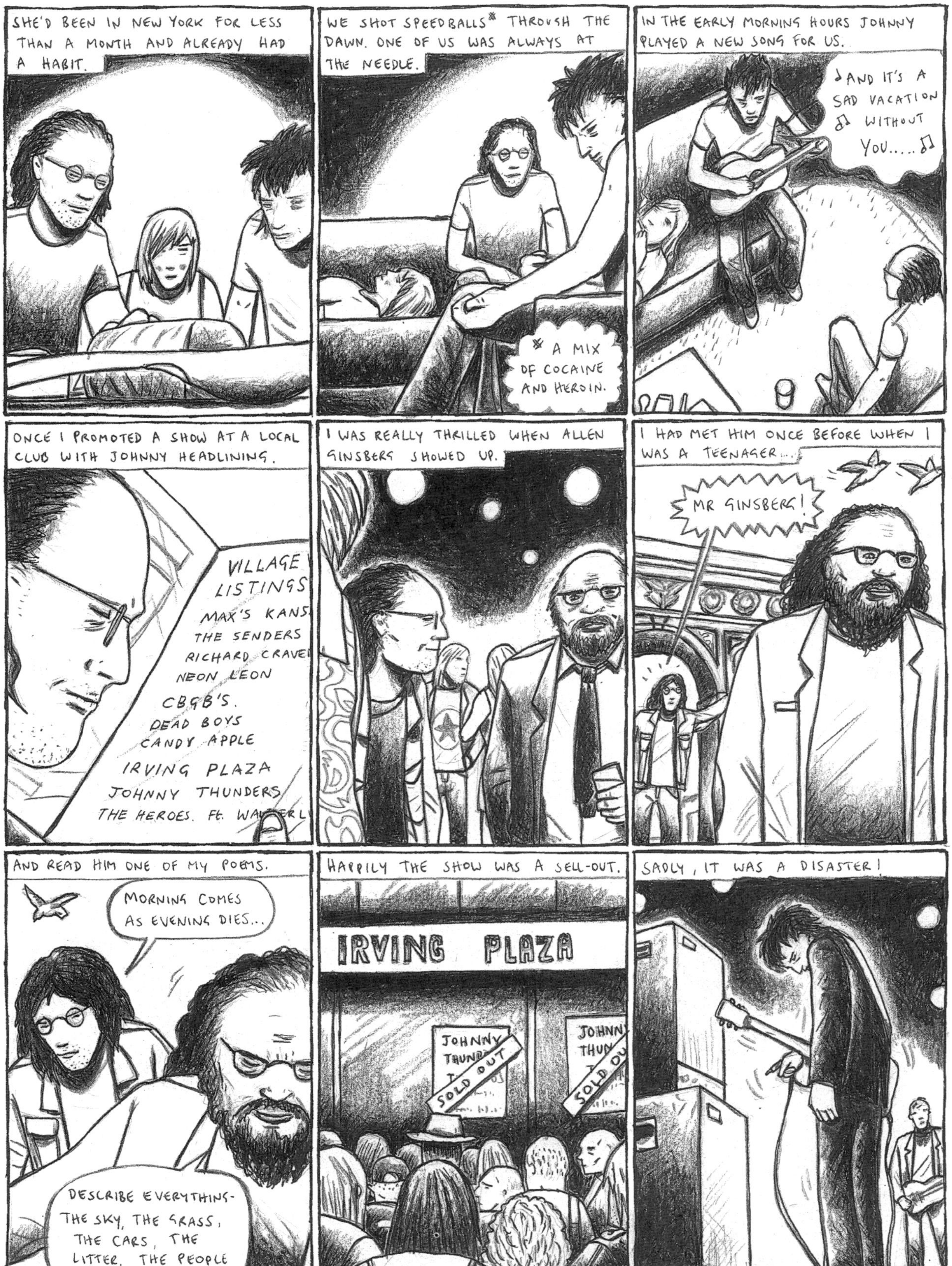
SHE'D BEEN IN NEW YORK FOR LESS THAN A MONTH AND ALREADY HAD A HABIT.
WE SHOT SPEEDBALLS* THROUGH THE DAWN. ONE OF US WAS ALWAYS AT THE NEEDLE.
* A MIX OF COCAINE AND HEROIN.
IN THE EARLY MORNING HOURS JOHNNY PLAYED A NEW SONG FOR US.
♪ AND IT'S A SAD VACATION ♫ WITHOUT YOU..... ♫
ONCE I PROMOTED A SHOW AT A LOCAL CLUB WITH JOHNNY HEADLINING.
VILLAGE LISTINGS
MAX'S KANS
THE SENDERS
RICHARD CRAVE
NEON LEON
CBGB'S.
DEAD BOYS
CANDY APPLE
IRVING PLAZA
JOHNNY THUNDERS
THE HEROES. FT. WA
I WAS REALLY THRILLED WHEN ALLEN GINSBERG SHOWED UP.
I HAD MET HIM ONCE BEFORE WHEN I WAS A TEENAGER....
MR GINSBERG!
AND READ HIM ONE OF MY POEMS.
MORNING COMES AS EVENING DIES...
DESCRIBE EVERYTHING - THE SKY, THE GRASS, THE CARS, THE LITTER, THE PEOPLE
HAPPILY THE SHOW WAS A SELL-OUT.
IRVING PLAZA
JOHNNY THUN
SOLD OUT
JOHNN THUN
SOLD OU
SADLY, IT WAS A DISASTER!

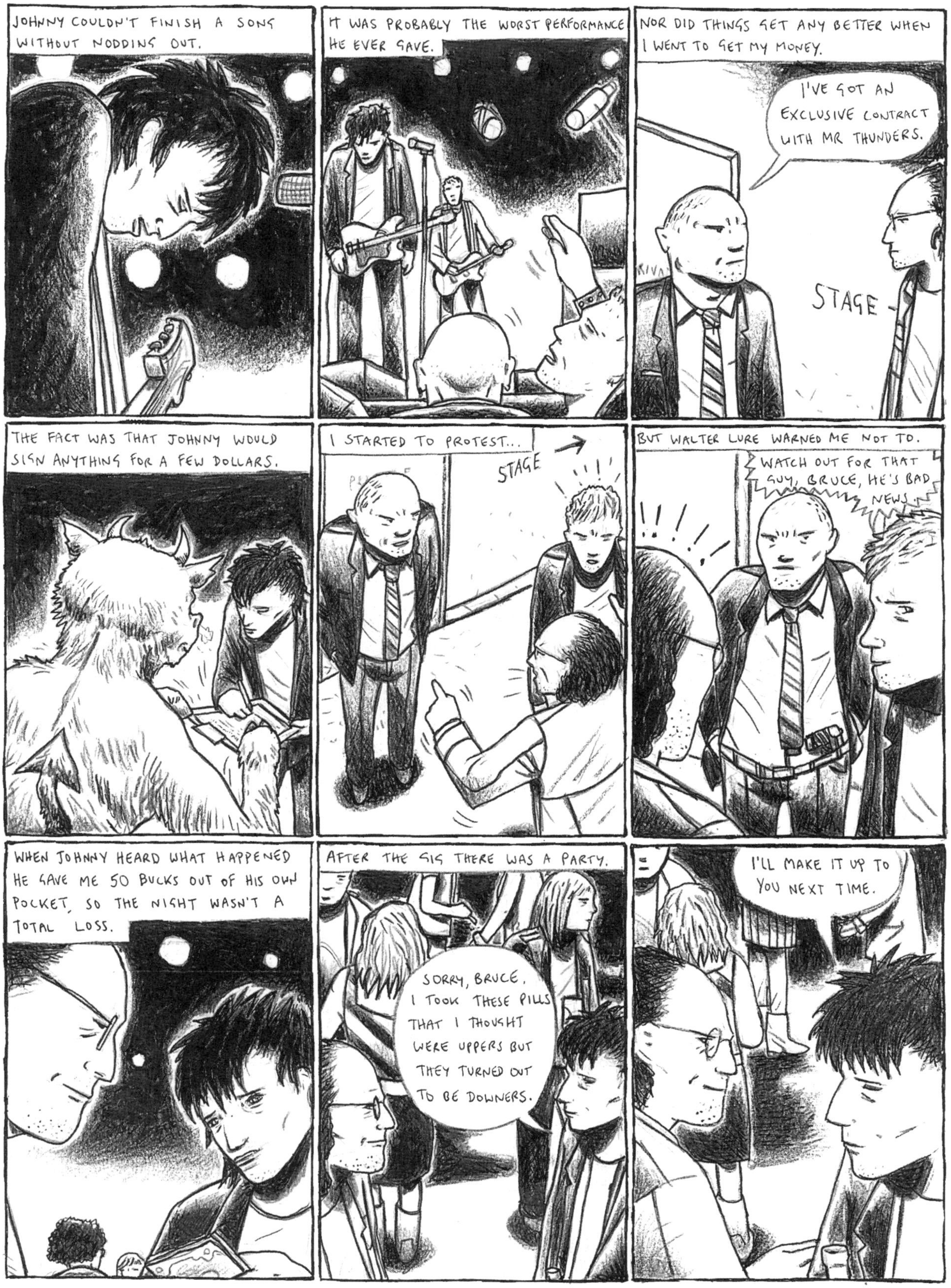

JOHNNY COULDN'T FINISH A SONG WITHOUT NODDING OUT.
IT WAS PROBABLY THE WORST PERFORMANCE HE EVER GAVE.
NOR DID THINGS GET ANY BETTER WHEN I WENT TO GET MY MONEY.
I'VE GOT AN EXCLUSIVE CONTRACT WITH MR THUNDERS.
STAGE
THE FACT WAS THAT JOHNNY WOULD SIGN ANYTHING FOR A FEW DOLLARS.
I STARTED TO PROTEST...
STAGE
BUT WALTER LURE WARNED ME NOT TO.
WATCH OUT FOR THAT GUY, BRUCE, HE'S BAD NEWS.
WHEN JOHNNY HEARD WHAT HAPPENED HE GAVE ME 50 BUCKS OUT OF HIS OWN POCKET, SO THE NIGHT WASN'T A TOTAL LOSS.
AFTER THE GIG THERE WAS A PARTY.
SORRY, BRUCE, I TOOK THESE PILLS THAT I THOUGHT WERE UPPERS BUT THEY TURNED OUT TO BE DOWNERS.
I'LL MAKE IT UP TO YOU NEXT TIME.

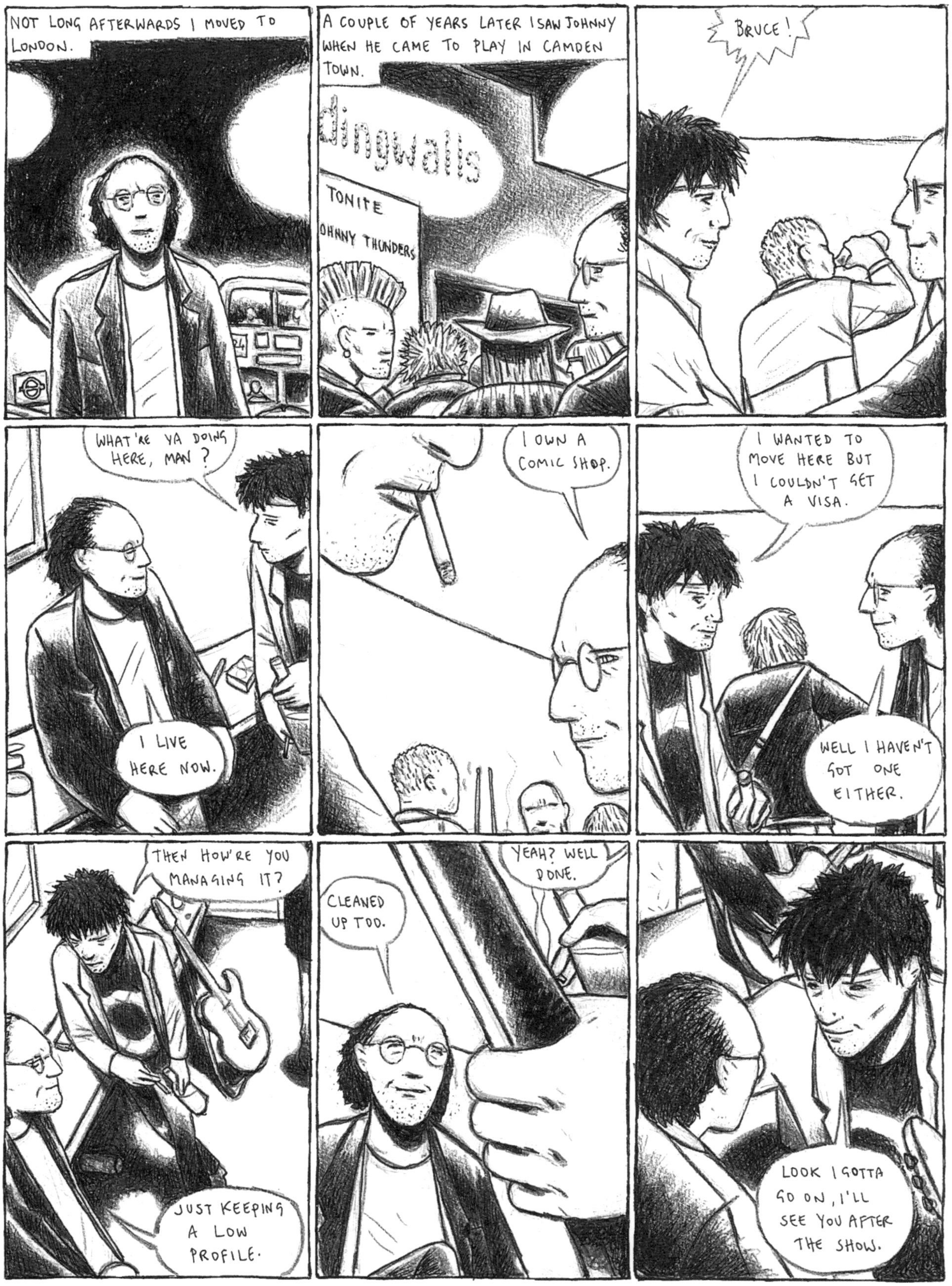
NOT LONG AFTERWARDS I MOVED TO LONDON.
A COUPLE OF YEARS LATER I SAW JOHNNY WHEN HE CAME TO PLAY IN CAMDEN TOWN.
dingwalls
TONITE
OHNNY THUNDERS
BRUCE!
WHAT'RE YA DOING HERE, MAN?
I LIVE HERE NOW.
I OWN A COMIC SHOP.
I WANTED TO MOVE HERE BUT I COULDN'T GET A VISA.
WELL I HAVEN'T GOT ONE EITHER.
THEN HOW'RE YOU MANAGING IT?
JUST KEEPING A LOW PROFILE.
CLEANED UP TOO.
YEAH? WELL DONE.
LOOK I GOTTA GO ON, I'LL SEE YOU AFTER THE SHOW.

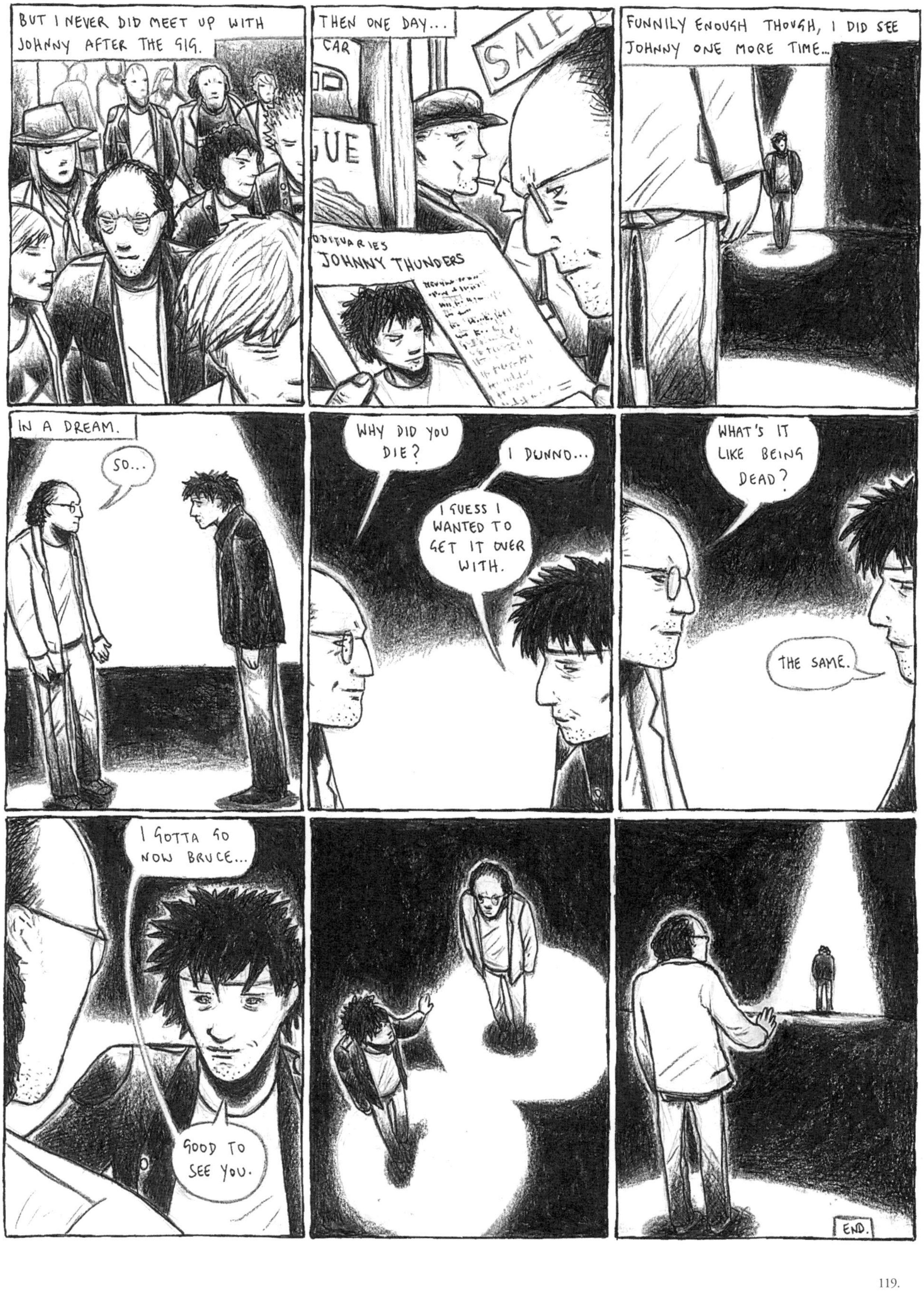
BUT I NEVER DID MEET UP WITH JOHNNY AFTER THE GIG.
THEN ONE DAY...
CAR
SALE
GUE
OBITUARIES
JOHNNY THUNDERS
FUNNILY ENOUGH THOUGH, I DID SEE JOHNNY ONE MORE TIME...
IN A DREAM.
SO...
WHY DID YOU DIE?
I DUNNO...
I GUESS I WANTED TO GET IT OVER WITH.
WHAT'S IT LIKE BEING DEAD?
THE SAME.
I GOTTA GO NOW BRUCE...
GOOD TO SEE YOU.
END.

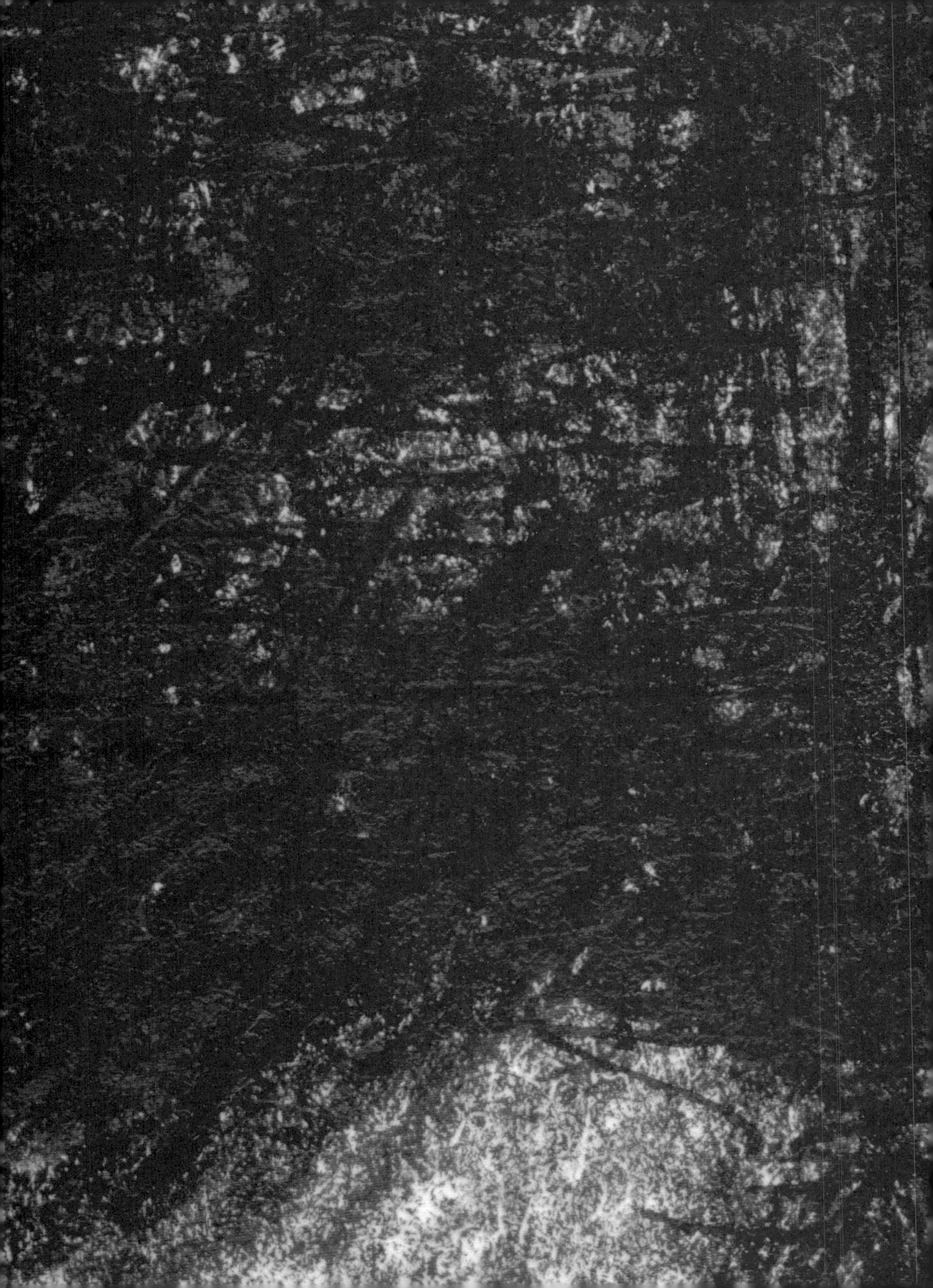

Needs must when the devil drives

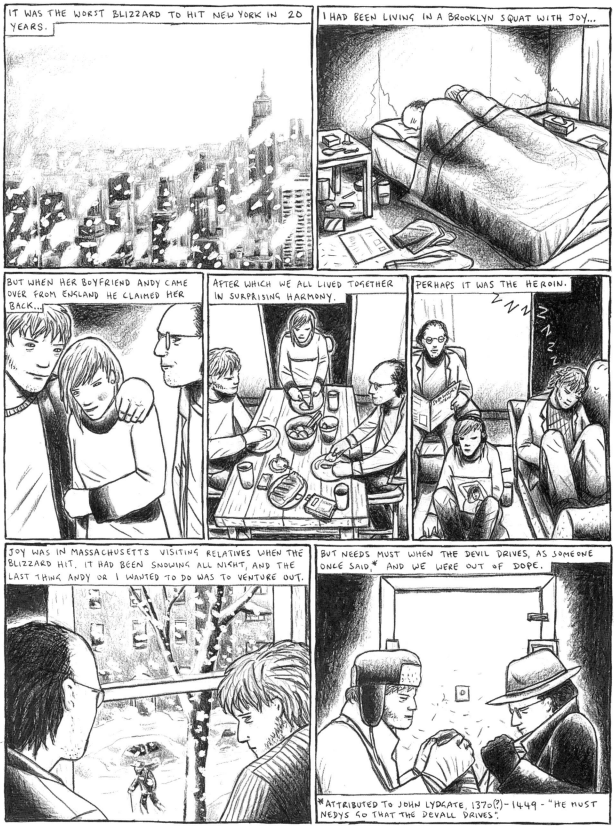

IT WAS THE WORST BLIZZARD TO HIT NEW YORK IN 20 YEARS.

I HAD BEEN LIVING IN A BROOKLYN SQUAT WITH JOY...

BUT WHEN HER BOYFRIEND ANDY CAME OVER FROM ENGLAND HE CLAIMED HER BACK...

AFTER WHICH WE ALL LIVED TOGETHER IN SURPRISING HARMONY.

PERHAPS IT WAS THE HEROIN.

JOY WAS IN MASSACHUSETTS VISITING RELATIVES WHEN THE BLIZZARD HIT. IT HAD BEEN SNOWING ALL NIGHT, AND THE LAST THING ANDY OR I WANTED TO DO WAS TO VENTURE OUT.

BUT NEEDS MUST WHEN THE DEVIL DRIVES, AS SOMEONE ONCE SAID,* AND WE WERE OUT OF DOPE.

*ATTRIBUTED TO JOHN LYDGATE, 1370(?)-1449 - "HE MUST NEDYS GO THAT THE DEVALL DRIVES".

121.

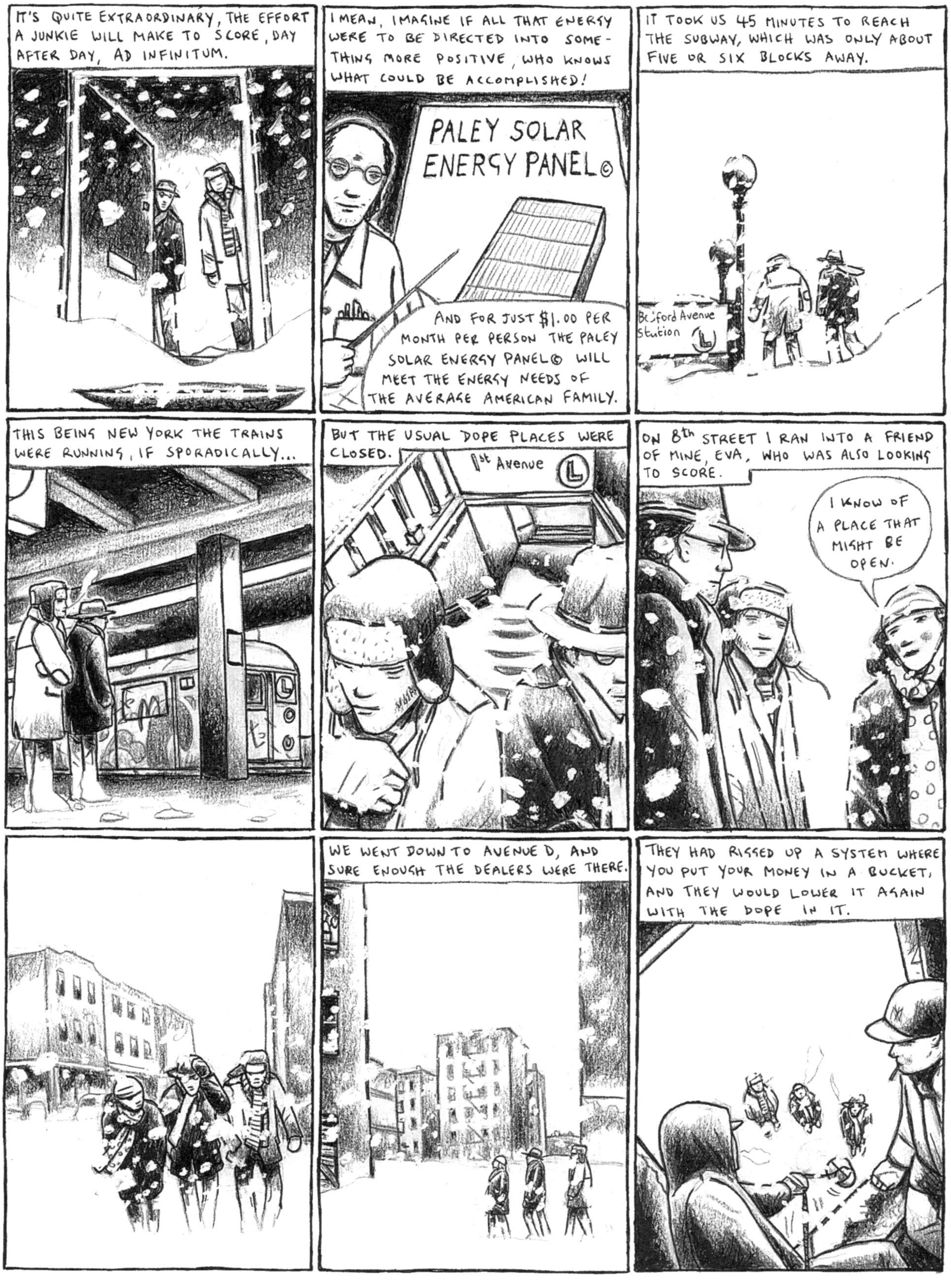
IT'S QUITE EXTRAORDINARY, THE EFFORT A JUNKIE WILL MAKE TO SCORE, DAY AFTER DAY, AD INFINITUM.
I MEAN, IMAGINE IF ALL THAT ENERGY WERE TO BE DIRECTED INTO SOMETHING MORE POSITIVE, WHO KNOWS WHAT COULD BE ACCOMPLISHED!
PALEY SOLAR ENERGY PANEL©
AND FOR JUST $1.00 PER MONTH PER PERSON THE PALEY SOLAR ENERGY PANEL© WILL MEET THE ENERGY NEEDS OF THE AVERAGE AMERICAN FAMILY.
IT TOOK US 45 MINUTES TO REACH THE SUBWAY, WHICH WAS ONLY ABOUT FIVE OR SIX BLOCKS AWAY.
Bedford Avenue Station
L
THIS BEING NEW YORK THE TRAINS WERE RUNNING, IF SPORADICALLY...
BUT THE USUAL DOPE PLACES WERE CLOSED.
1st Avenue
L
ON 8th STREET I RAN INTO A FRIEND OF MINE, EVA, WHO WAS ALSO LOOKING TO SCORE.
I KNOW OF A PLACE THAT MIGHT BE OPEN.
WE WENT DOWN TO AVENUE D, AND SURE ENOUGH THE DEALERS WERE THERE.
THEY HAD RIGGED UP A SYSTEM WHERE YOU PUT YOUR MONEY IN A BUCKET, AND THEY WOULD LOWER IT AGAIN WITH THE DOPE IN IT.

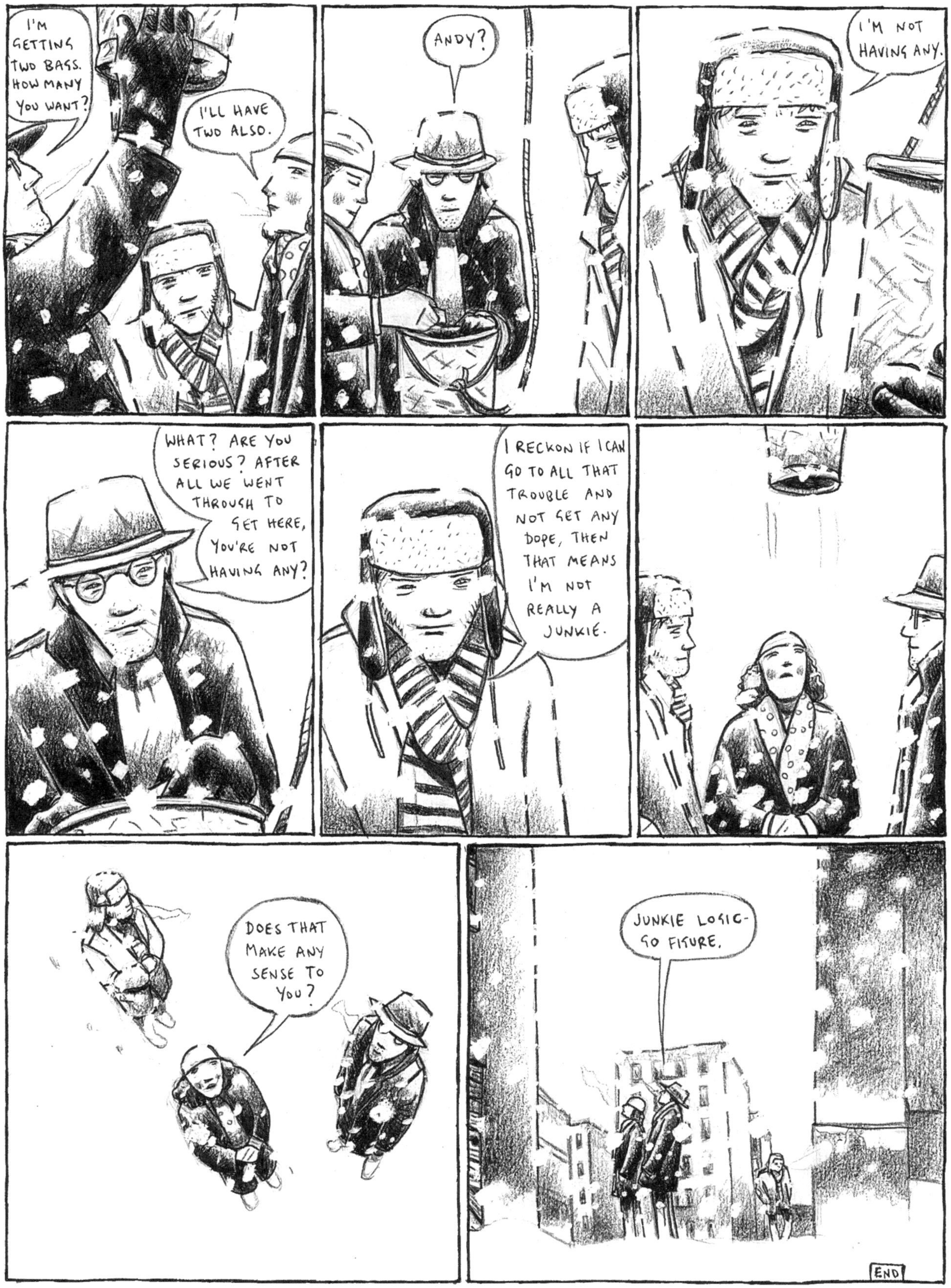
I'M GETTING TWO BAGS. HOW MANY YOU WANT?
I'LL HAVE TWO ALSO.
ANDY?
I'M NOT HAVING ANY.
WHAT? ARE YOU SERIOUS? AFTER ALL WE WENT THROUGH TO GET HERE, YOU'RE NOT HAVING ANY?
I RECKON IF I CAN GO TO ALL THAT TROUBLE AND NOT GET ANY DOPE, THEN THAT MEANS I'M NOT REALLY A JUNKIE.
DOES THAT MAKE ANY SENSE TO YOU?
JUNKIE LOGIC- GO FIGURE.
END

birthday blues

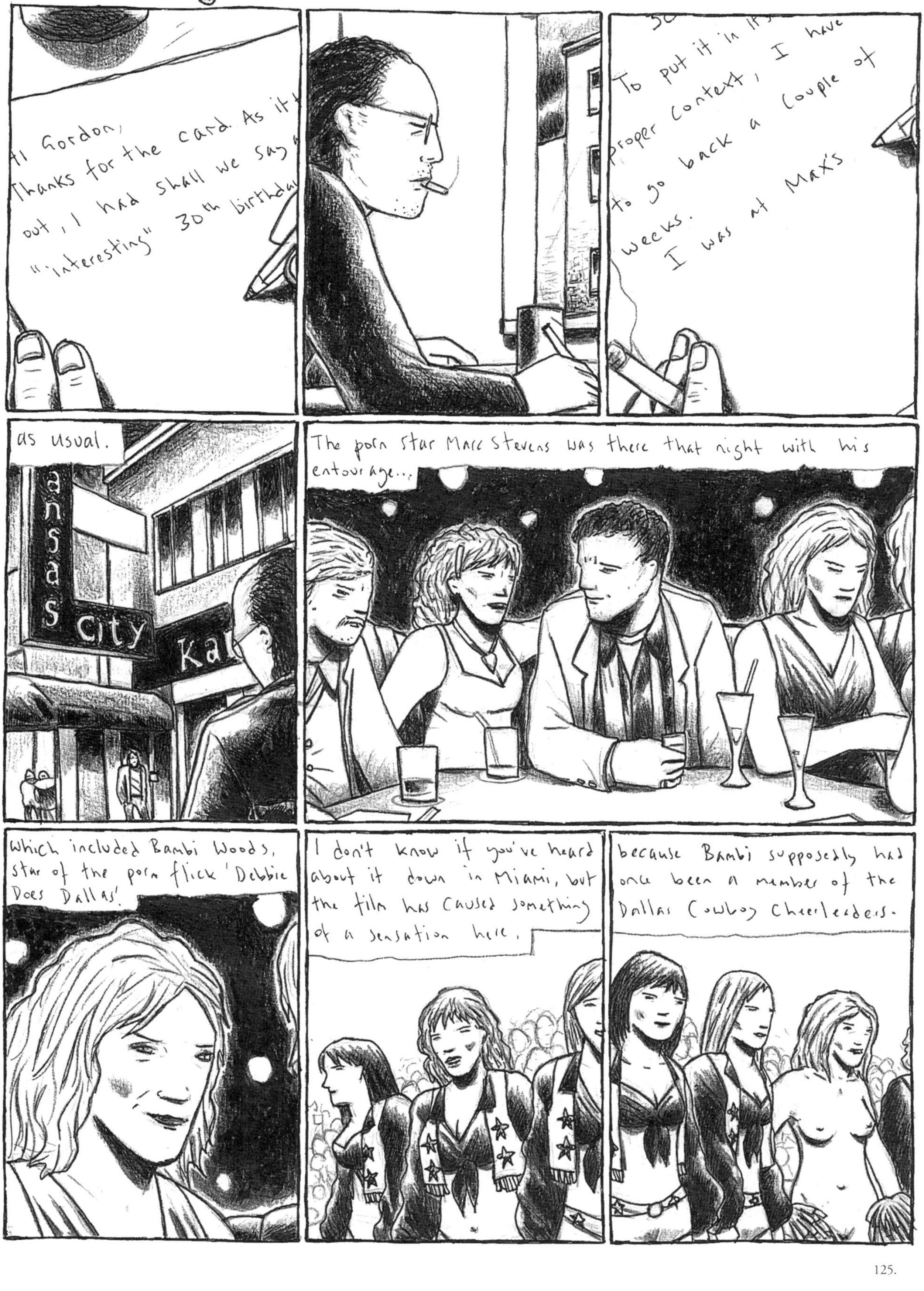

Al Gordon,
Thanks for the card. As it
out, I had shall we say
"interesting" 30th birthday
To put it in
proper context, I have
to go back a couple of
weeks. I was at Max's
as usual.
The porn star Marc Stevens was there that night with his entourage...
Which included Bambi Woods, star of the porn flick 'Debbie Does Dallas'.
I don't know if you've heard about it down in Miami, but the film has caused something of a sensation here,
because Bambi supposedly had once been a member of the Dallas Cowboy Cheerleaders.

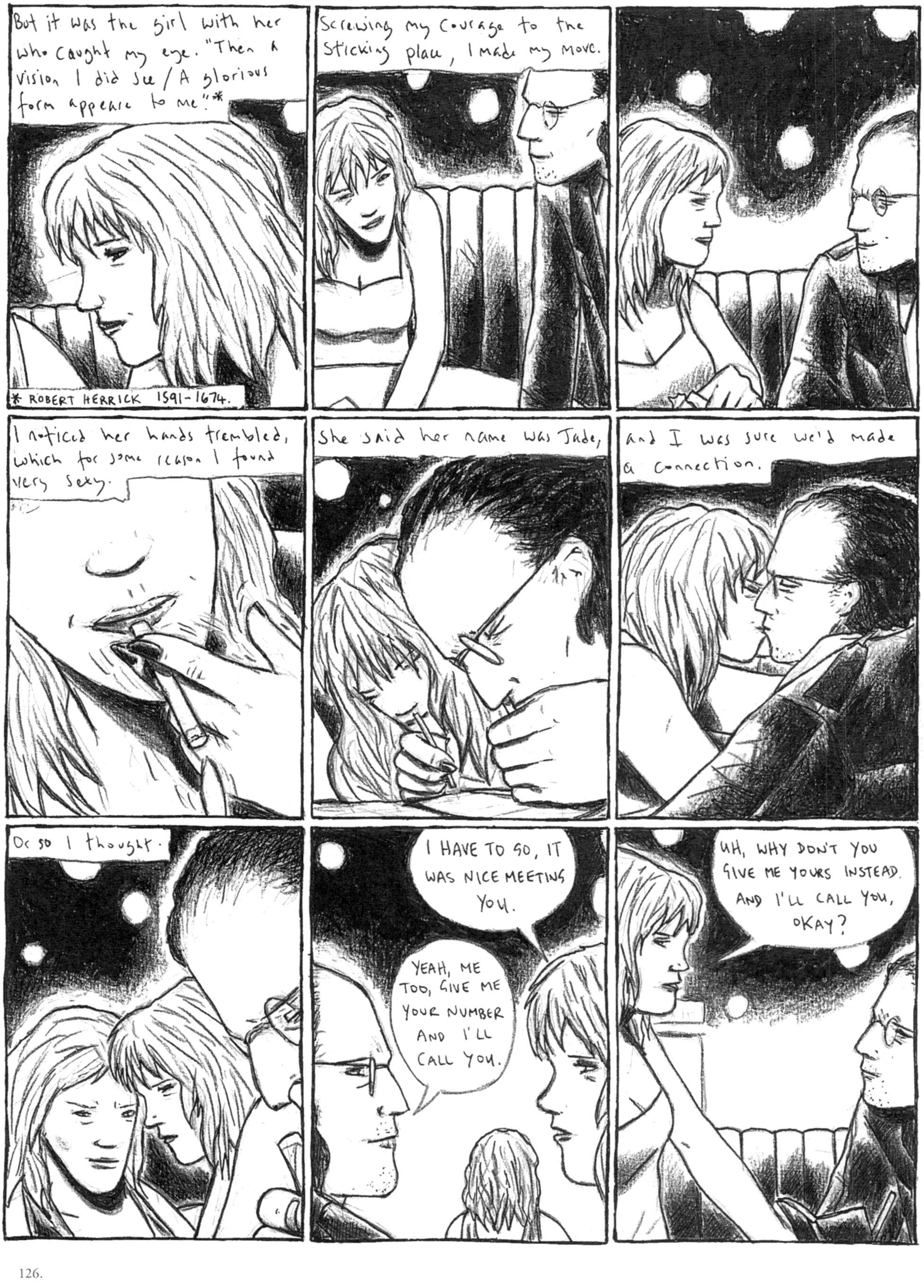
But it was the girl with her who caught my eye. "Then a vision I did see / A glorious form appeare to me."*
* ROBERT HERRICK 1591-1674.
Screwing my courage to the sticking place, I made my move.
I noticed her hands trembled, which for some reason I found very sexy.
She said her name was Jade,
and I was sure we'd made a connection.
Or so I thought.
I HAVE TO GO, IT WAS NICE MEETING YOU.
YEAH, ME TOO, GIVE ME YOUR NUMBER AND I'LL CALL YOU.
UH, WHY DON'T YOU GIVE ME YOURS INSTEAD. AND I'LL CALL YOU, OKAY?

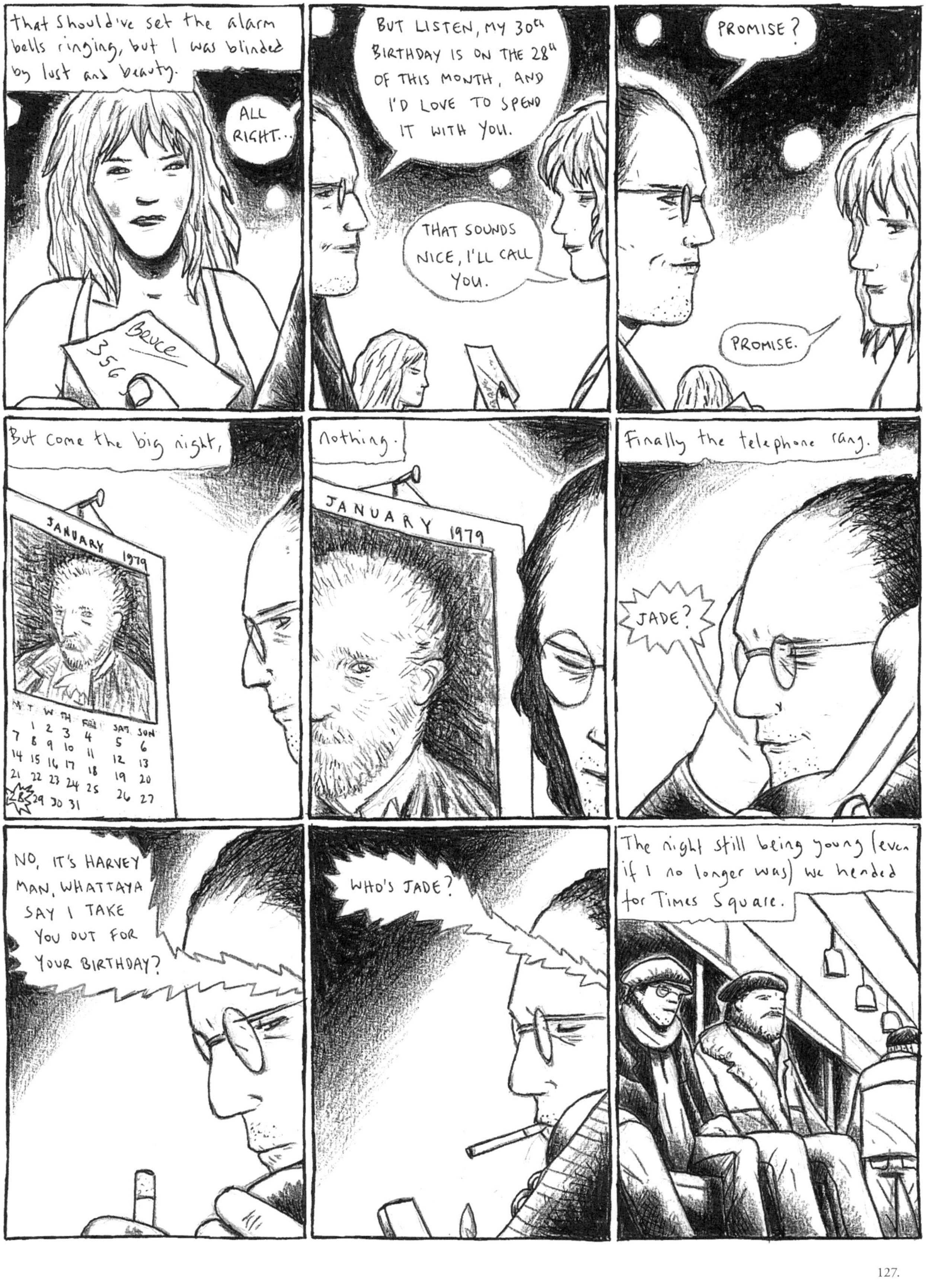
that should've set the alarm bells ringing, but I was blinded by lust and beauty.
ALL RIGHT...
Bruce
BUT LISTEN, MY 30th BIRTHDAY IS ON THE 28th OF THIS MONTH, AND I'D LOVE TO SPEND IT WITH YOU.
THAT SOUNDS NICE, I'LL CALL YOU.
PROMISE?
PROMISE.
But come the big night,
JANUARY 1979
Nothing.
JANUARY 1979
Finally the telephone rang.
JADE?
NO, IT'S HARVEY MAN, WHATTAYA SAY I TAKE YOU OUT FOR YOUR BIRTHDAY?
WHO'S JADE?
The night still being young (even if I no longer was) we headed for Times Square.

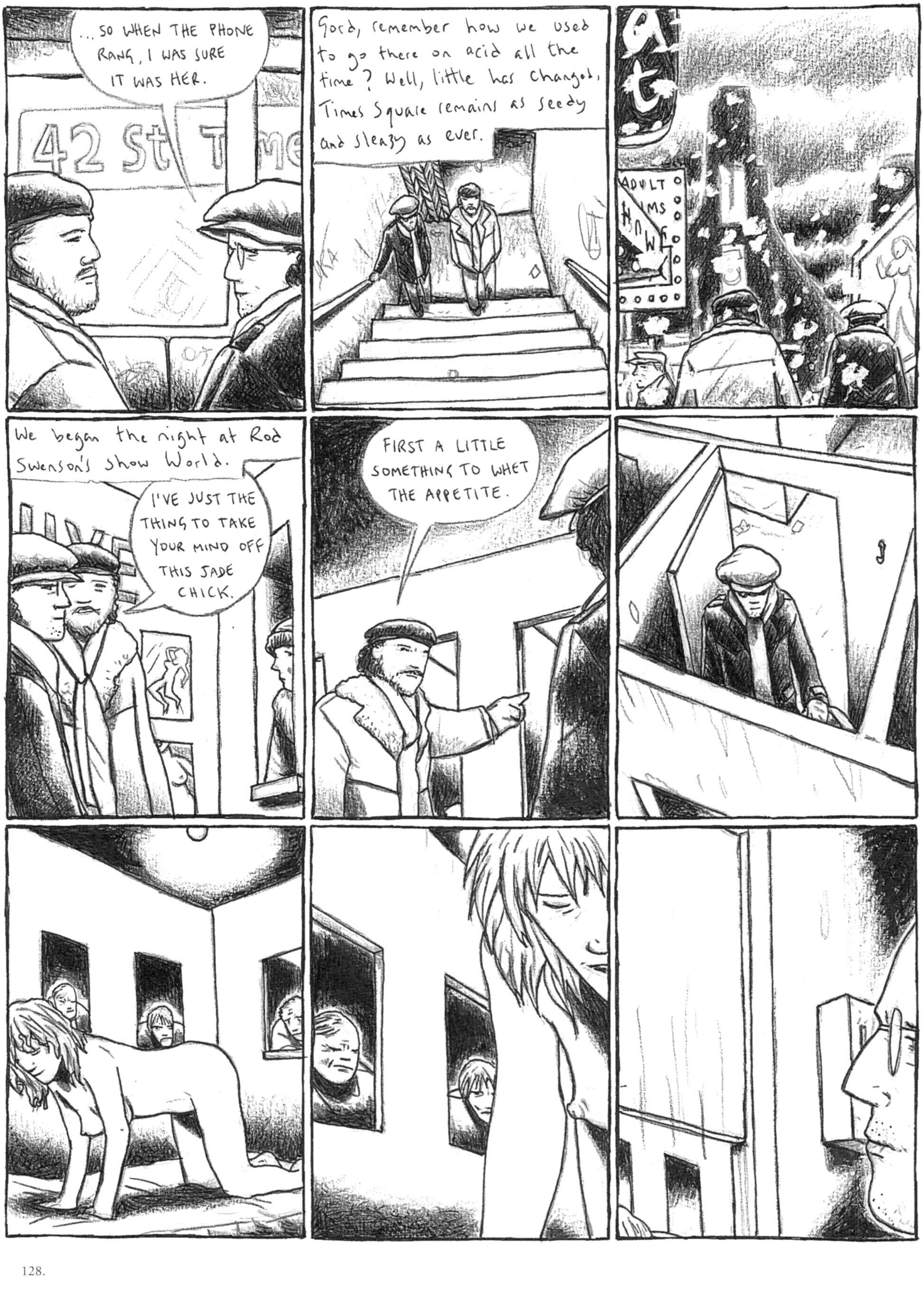
...SO WHEN THE PHONE RANG, I WAS SURE IT WAS HER.
42 St
Gord, remember how we used to go there on acid all the time? Well, little has changed, Times Square remains as seedy and sleazy as ever.
ADULT
We began the night at Rod Swenson's Show World.
I'VE JUST THE THING TO TAKE YOUR MIND OFF THIS JADE CHICK.
FIRST A LITTLE SOMETHING TO WHET THE APPETITE.

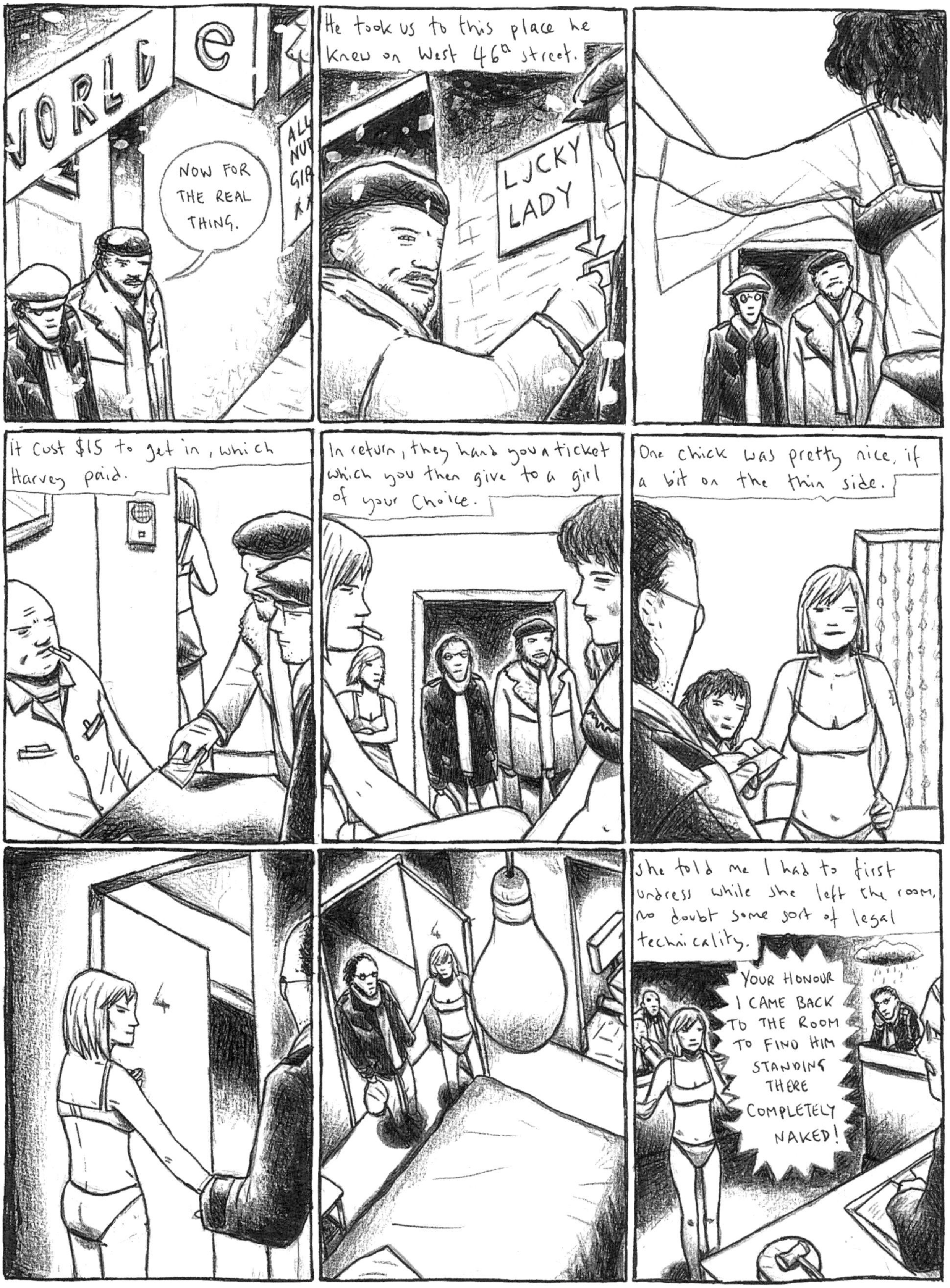
WORLD
ALL NU GIR
NOW FOR THE REAL THING.
He took us to this place he knew on West 46th street.
LUCKY LADY
It cost $15 to get in, which Harvey paid.
In return, they hand you a ticket which you then give to a girl of your choice.
One chick was pretty nice, if a bit on the thin side.
4
4
She told me I had to first undress while she left the room, no doubt some sort of legal technicality.
YOUR HONOUR I CAME BACK TO THE ROOM TO FIND HIM STANDING THERE COMPLETELY NAKED!

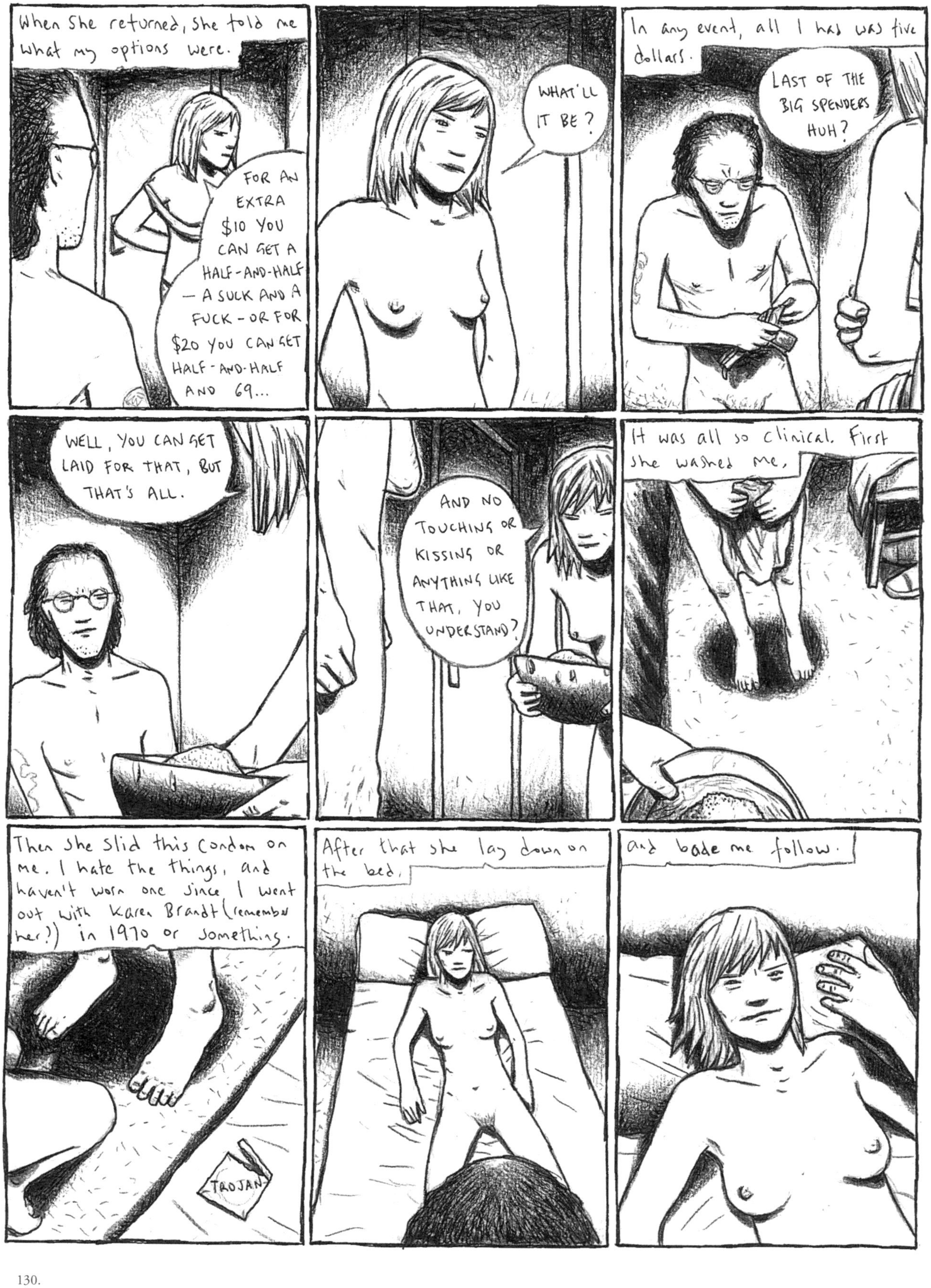
When she returned, she told me what my options were.
FOR AN EXTRA $10 YOU CAN GET A HALF-AND-HALF — A SUCK AND A FUCK — OR FOR $20 YOU CAN GET HALF-AND-HALF AND 69...
WHAT'LL IT BE?
In any event, all I had was five dollars.
LAST OF THE BIG SPENDERS HUH?
WELL, YOU CAN GET LAID FOR THAT, BUT THAT'S ALL.
AND NO TOUCHING OR KISSING OR ANYTHING LIKE THAT, YOU UNDERSTAND?
It was all so clinical. First she washed me,
Then she slid this condom on me. I hate the things, and haven't worn one since I went out with Karen Brandt (remember her?) in 1970 or something.
TROJAN
After that she lay down on the bed,
and bade me follow.

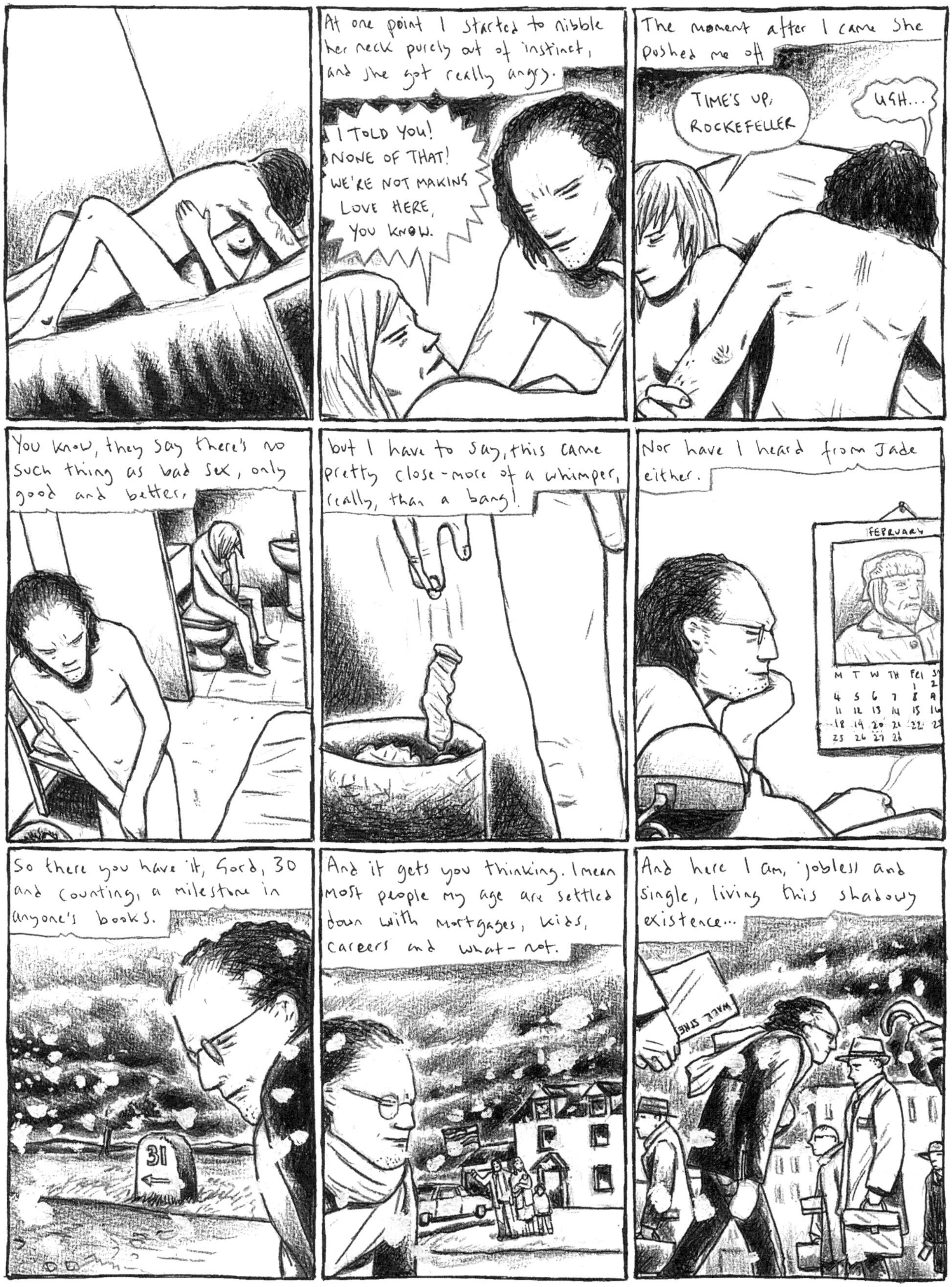
At one point I started to nibble her neck purely out of instinct, and she got really angry.
I TOLD YOU! NONE OF THAT! WE'RE NOT MAKING LOVE HERE, YOU KNOW.
The moment after I came she pushed me off
TIME'S UP, ROCKEFELLER
UGH...
You know, they say there's no such thing as bad sex, only good and better,
but I have to say, this came pretty close - more of a whimper, really, than a bang!
Nor have I heard from Jade either.
FEBRUARY
So there you have it, Gord, 30 and counting, a milestone in anyone's books.
31
And it gets you thinking. I mean most people my age are settled down with mortgages, kids, careers and what-not.
And here I am, jobless and single, living this shadowy existence...

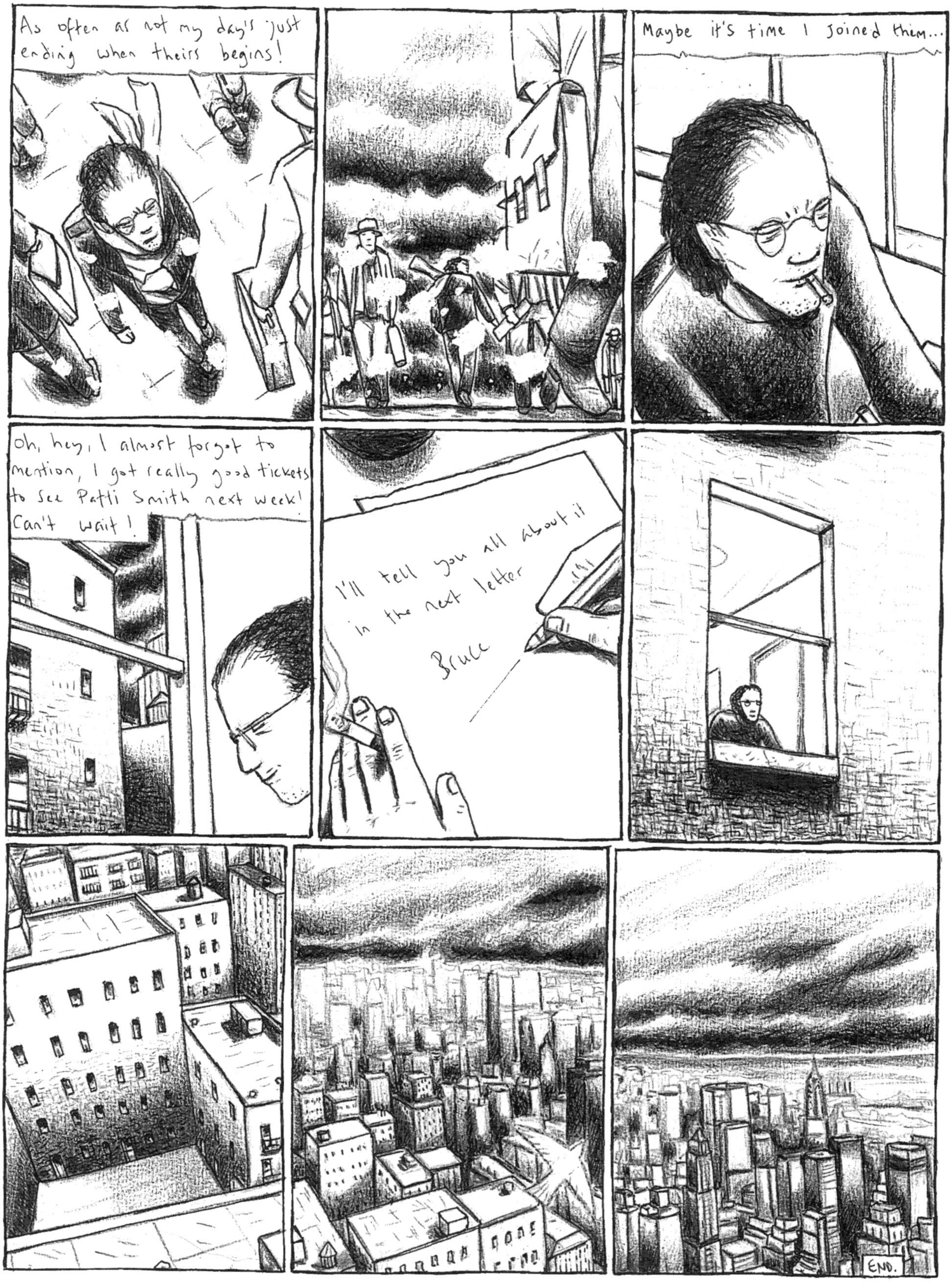
As often as not my day's just ending when theirs begins!
Maybe it's time I joined them...
Oh, hey, I almost forgot to mention, I got really good tickets to see Patti Smith next week! Can't wait!
I'll tell you all about it in the next letter
Bruce
END.